The National Interest

The National Interest

The Politics of Northern Development 1968-75

Edgar J. Dosman

Canada in Transition Series
McClelland and Stewart Limited

ISBN 0-7710-2851-2

The Canadian Publishers
McClelland and Stewart Limited
25 Hollinger Road, Toronto

Printed and bound in Canada

Contents

To Mieke

Foreword

The volumes in the series "Canada in Transition" attempt to place Canada's current dilemma in historical and comparative perspective. Each volume focuses on a particular crisis or turning point at which decisions (or non-decisions) have set a pattern for later developments. We find compelling the observation of Harold Innis that Canada has moved "from colony to nation to colony." The latter transition concerns us most, especially insofar as it conditions Canada's capacity to respond effectively to the difficulties that lie ahead. The series is designed to improve knowledge about our background and the way in which our political system has evolved, with a view to casting new light on the options and challenges of the future.

Edgar Dosman's volume on "The National Interest: The Politics of Northern Development" provides a particularly appropriate inauguration for the series. Not only is Professor Dosman a co-founding editor, but his book also opens up for the first time serious, informed debate on the pattern of development that has emerged with respect to the north. Emphasizing the period since 1968, Dosman traces the impact of technological and economic change on resource extraction in the Canadian Arctic, and carefully explains how these changes have created a crisis of national sovereignty unprecedented in the present century. He examines critically and with intimate knowledge the assumptions, policies, and political style of Ottawa decision-makers. He then explores the implications their decisions have for Canadian-American relations and the disparate aspirations of business interests, native peoples, and the Canadian public in general. These might be the ingredients of a best-selling Canadian novel: Dosman combines them to produce a penetrating scholarly analysis.

The timeliness of this volume should not obscure its enduring significance as a landmark study of policy-making at a critical stage in Canada's uncertain transition.

David V.J. Bell
Editor and Series Coordinator

Preface

Recent developments, particularly the discovery of oil and gas on the Alaskan North Slope in 1968, have opened a new era in the Canadian North. Potentially rich in natural resources, which have become increasingly available with advances in technology, the Arctic is becoming harnessed to the North American economy. The isolation of Canada North of 60 is over.

For Canada as a whole events in the enormous but thinly populated lands of the Yukon and Northwest Territories have created problems of national importance. Where there was once the romance of Robert W. Service, children's stories of Eskimo hunters, mystery and neglect, Ottawa is now confronted with hard decisions regarding sovereignty, pipelines and resources. The stakes have grown. Dangers as well as opportunities have appeared.

This book attempts to assess government and business relations in the North from 1968 to 1975. How has the North fared during this period? How have decisions been made? What are the prospects for the Indian and Inuit communities of the Arctic? Have the issues of sovereignty or pipeline planning placed Canada at a disadvantage in dealing with industry or Washington? These are among the questions posed in the following pages.

The focus of the book is on Ottawa, particularly on the inner decision-making elite that have established the chief contours of northern development. At the same time it is written for planners and the general public as well as colleagues and students. Although some harsh conclusions are reached, the attempt throughout has been to refrain from grinding axes for their own sake. There are few villains in Ottawa, but there are no heroes either.

I am indebted to many individuals in government, business and public interest groups as well as friends and colleagues in Canadian universities. David Hoffman, John Langford, F.F. Flynn, David V.J. Bell, Maureen Whitehead, H.T. Wilson, Francois Bregha, Grahame Beakhust and Susan Koch were particularly generous in their encouragement and assistance. Mrs. Florence Griffin and Mrs. Joanne Digabrielle were tireless in their preparation of the many drafts of the book. I am responsible for all errors.

Introduction:
The Northern Challenge

When, in January 1968, massive supplies of oil were discovered on the Alaskan North Slope, a new era opened for the Canadian Arctic as well. Official Ottawa was overjoyed. It shared, with business and the public, a belief that similar finds in the Mackenzie Delta and the Arctic islands of the Canadian North would soon be uncovered. Senior men in Indian Affairs and Northern Development felt certain that a secure base for northern economic development had at last been achieved. Diefenbaker's Northern Vision would be realized; the Arctic would be conquered and harnessed.

Before the year was out, however, the northern breakthrough had soured in Ottawa. It was far more complex and dangerous for Canada than officials had expected. Difficult decisions confronted the Government in domestic and external affairs as a direct result of the opening of the North, their difficulty compounded by unpreparedness.

Retrospectively the men at the top in Ottawa should have known that an economic breakthrough in the North might be sudden. They should have anticipated the accompanying political implications not merely within Canada, but in foreign relations as well — particularly with the United States. Both geographically and psychologically, the isolation of Canada's Arctic was progressively eroded after 1945. But neither the government in power, nor the senior officials managing the many bureaucracies active in the North by 1968 sensed danger. Without a crisis the

North was not a priority issue or area (except at election time). Attention lay elsewhere. Characteristically, the discovery of oil and gas reserves on the Alaskan North Slope found Canadian officials innocent of forward planning. The new North had arrived in a policy vacuum; the national interest was as yet undefined.

In 1968 the equally new Government of Prime Minister Pierre Elliot Trudeau was faced with the task of defining that interest, as the vast Canadian North became integrated into the economic and political framework of North America. What priorities would be chosen in the last great area of the country not yet possessed and exploited? Would Canada seize the opportunity now denied it in the South, to lessen Canadian dependence on the United States, to undertake a truly Canadian development of the North? Would Ottawa exercise leadership in the high Arctic to maintain national jurisdiction and to develop an internationally acceptable approach to activity in the polar area as a whole? Or would it follow the line of least resistance: foreign ownership of resources; exploitation with massive government subsidies paying only lip-service to environmental and native objections; transportation of raw materials to foreign markets; the abandonment of historic claims in the face of American diplomatic pressure? What was once the remote periphery was now central to the mainstream questions of Canadian development and Canadian-American relations.

After 1968, awareness of the North's importance gave birth to a new catch phrase, "the northern problem." The problem, however, was an extremely complex one, affecting more than the future of the native people north of 60° and the Arctic environment. It had major implications for Canada as a whole. According to an eminent Canadian Scholar and an authority on the North:

> Apart from the general question of Canada-United States economic and cultural relations and their meaning for the future of Canadian decision-making autonomy and identity, perhaps no other subject has so polarized the idea of the national interest as the continuing debate over Canada's Arctic claims and plans for its future.[1]

Choosing a pattern of economic and political development for the North involved three levels of issues. First, there was the more specific regional component, affecting the type and pace of economic activity in the Arctic. Geophysically, the northern mainland and islands, as well as the waters between the islands of the Arctic Archipelago were very favourable for further development of fossil fuels and already well-known as the largest unexplored region in the western hemisphere. Similarly, although prospecting for hard rock mineral deposits had turned up few commercially feasible finds, geologists were confident about enormous mineral wealth in the North. If indeed a "treasure-house" existed, and if there was now the technological capability of exploiting it commercially, how and for whose benefit should the wealth be extracted? Should the native people get a share? Should the resources be safeguarded for future Canadian needs or should they supply foreign markets regardless of these considerations? The answers would depend heavily on the degree of foreign ownership and Ottawa's relationship with the business community. If the past in the Arctic was any guide, Ottawa would opt for stripping it as rapidly as possible.

How would the native people and the northern environment fare? A decade earlier, these considerations would have been considered of minimal importance to policy makers. The growth of native consciousness even in southern Canada was slow; not until the mid-1960s could one discern a coherent Indian voice in the country. While the development of native organizations proceeded rapidly after this time, it had not yet penetrated the Arctic. But the existence of obvious grievances and unsettled land claims promised the emergence of northern native groups. Moreover, Alaskan native people were well in advance of their Canadian neighbours in articulating grievances and demanding a voice in resource development. Ottawa would maintain its tradition of ignoring native demands in the North, but here too the end of an era was approaching.

Second, there was an international dimension, centring on Canadian jurisdiction in the Arctic Archipelago and Canada's willingness and ability to lead a responsible development effort in the Arctic basin. The massive Alaskan discoveries of oil and natural gas confronted Ottawa with defining its position in the North. Canadian jurisdiction over the Arctic islands and water among the islands; the management of Arctic resources and resource extraction and transportation; and new scientific challenges concerning the protection of the northern environment — these issues (and others) demanded immediate attention if Canada were not to lose its position in the North. To what extent, or did it matter, would the "international" community agree with Canadian initiatives?

In effect, the opening of the Arctic produced a third Canadian coastline. With advances in marine technology, it was feasible to send out resources through the Northwest Passage, with all the environmental and navigational hazards such commercial shipping entailed. Did Canada have the means to develop and regulate northern transportation, given its many existing responsibilities on the Pacific and Atlantic coasts? From this point of view, events in the Arctic reinforced Canadian security fears stemming from developments quite distinct from those associated with the Cold War and peace-keeping. As one observer has pointed out:

> In 1968 there was a growing awareness that Canada — the country with the longest coastline, the largest Continental Shelf, frozen terrain, highly vulnerable to oil spills, threatened fishing stocks in adjacent waters, resources in increasingly short supply and subject to growing pressure from the South — would be faced with international developments that could have an overwhelming relevance for its future well-being, its sovereignty and survival.[2]

Finally the emergence of the North affected bilateral relations with the United States. Developments initiated by the two countries in the region inevitably elevated this dimension of "the northern problem" to a commanding significance relative to the local and international factors. In most well-established countries, the development of a peripheral region would be largely a domestic issue. In Canada, however, the development of the North was inextricably linked to the issue of the Canadian relationship with a foreign power, the United States. Whatever *model* of development was chosen in Canada to guide northern economic development, it would depend heavily on decisions made in Washington as well as Ottawa. Some implications of this factor are worth noting carefully at the outset, so that we may appreciate their catalytic effect on Canada's position within the American orbit.

First, northern development after 1968 affected Canadian trade relations with the United States, particularly oil and natural gas exports. The Alaskan oil and gas discoveries were perceived in Ottawa as a grave threat to the Canadian oil industry, which was heavily dependent on United States markets. It was feared that the United States might no longer buy Canadian oil when it had full access to Alaskan supplies. How could the Canadian Government prevent the closure of American markets? What concessions were permissible to protect the West and the Canadian oil industry?

To Ottawa decision-makers, a Mackenzie pipeline linking Alaska and United States markets via Canada offered the best way to protect Canadian oil exports, at least during the years of construction. But such a pipeline would drastically increase the United States' economic and security stake in Canada. The shipment of vital resources across Canadian territory would inevitably involve measures to ensure non-interruption of supplies; the direct involvement of Washington in Canadian politics would be sure to grow. Not only that, but the very vastness of the project, the largest civil engineering project in history, would strain and possibly distort the Canadian economy. Traditionally docile and accepting, the Canadian people might well want to know who was benefiting from their sacrifice.

Similarly, rapid economic development in the Arctic might be most easily achieved in the short run by giving free rein to foreign interests. But to do this would exacerbate the already explosive issue of American corporate domination of the Canadian economy. Public fears of foreign control would intensify if American multinationals dominated the North as well as the South.

Third there was the issue of northern sovereignty. The United States was bound to test a Canadian claim of sovereignty over the entire high Arctic. Washington would not likely acquiesce in any Canadian jurisdictional claims in the waters of the Arctic Archipelago and the straits of the Northwest Passage. Yet Canadian public opinion would not tolerate the concept of a "North American" as opposed to a "Canadian" Arctic. Canadians had come to think of the Arctic as their own — the icy frontier of the Dominion of the North. The North was now an indispensible part of the Canadian self-image, a land of darkness and mystery, remote and secure by virtue of its apparent impenetrability. Its immense emptiness, accounting for 40 per cent of Canada's land mass but less than 0.25 per cent of its population, and its exclusion from the economy of the more habitable regions South of 60 , magnified the public romance. Canadians, troubled by cultural self-doubts, were coloured by the Arctic with an irrefutable uniqueness. They were true Northerners. Few issues were as volatile as northern sovereignty, or as dangerous to a Government in power. But among the Great Powers, only the United States, our closest friend and ally, would seriously challenge Canadian jurisdiction in the North.

These questions, trade relations, resource policy, and northern sovereignty touched on the most sensitive issues in Canadian-American relations. Northern development after 1968 therefore could only contribute to a gathering crisis in Canadian-American relations. No solution to the issues discussed above could simultaneously serve all aspects of the Canadian national interest, and deepen its relationship with the United States as well.

The problem, however, was not merely one of choosing between Canadian and United States interests, but also one of clearly defining the Canadian interest itself. Canadian political and economic, foreign and domestic, short and long-range goals, all indicated different solutions; priorities would have to be established among them.

After 1968, a new and uncertain period of northern development began with substantial potential for unsettling Canadian foreign and domestic policy. Canada's political geography was now permanently altered.

Part I of the book traces Ottawa's initial reaction to the Alaskan North Slope discoveries in 1968 against a backdrop of its ill-preparedness for such an eventuality. After a period of confusion and crisis and as soon as the American challenge to Canadian sovereignty was dealt with, a consensus was achieved by senior officials in Ottawa in 1970 on the *future pattern* of northern economic and political development. It was carefully meshed with legislation in April 1970 outlining the new Canadian position on Arctic sovereignty and pollution and it reflected the evolution of American trade and energy relations in the wake of the Alaskan discoveries. The centre of attention was the promotion of a Mackenzie pipeline system linking Alaskan (and presumably Canadian) energy supplies with American markets in the South.

Particular emphasis will be given to the assumptions of the

framework of northern development selected, which clashed with the *stated* objectives and priorities of the Trudeau Government.

The chief focus is not on the development of local government in the Yukon and Northwest Territories, important and interesting as that topic might prove. Rather, and necessarily, it centres on Ottawa and relations with Washington and business at the highest levels that determined the framework of northern development after 1968. Decision-making in this area was largely *in camera*; rarely was Parliament or the public consulted or involved in the central decisions. Even during the sovereignty crisis of 1968-70, the most significant confrontation with the United States since the Diefenbaker period, the Trudeau Government consciously and wilfully misled Parliament into a sense of false security. Central control over information and a careful management of public opinion in all areas of northern development after 1968 produced a policy environment which maximized the discretion of the inner circle in Ottawa. The key therefore to understanding northern policy lies in these secret internal disucssions within the elite and between it and the business community.

Caught unprepared, ill-coordinated, frightened of the challenge, secure only in the secrecy of its apparatus, the Government chose to conceal its actions in the North from Parliament and the public. Relations with business, particularly the multinational corporations, and Washington, rather than public debate or consultation with Northerners, set the pattern of development that is now being pursued in the North. Major commitments were made to pipeline and resource developers (the decision to proceed with a Mackenzie Valley Gas Pipeline prior to a land settlement with the native people of the North was made five years ago). The National Energy Board remains heavily compromised.

Part II, in turn, demonstrates the remarkable developments that undermined the validity of Ottawa's preferred model of northern development even before the proposed Mackenzie Valley Gas Pipeline could be initiated. Politically, the project developed intense and effective opposition within Canada. World energy shortages conspired further against selling out in the North. Brought up short by its near defeat in October 1972, Trudeau's Government had no choice but to move slowly. Two years later, in a great electoral victory, he won a second chance. Northerners hoped, against odds, that their fortunes would be as well served.

Before further corners are turned, it is important to clarify how their hopes and how the requirements of the country as a whole have been satisfied in the Arctic since 1968.

NOTES

1. Maxwell Cohen, "The Arctic and the National Interest," *International Journal* XXVI, No. 1, 1970-71.
2. A.F. Gotlieb and C. Dalfen, "National Jurisdiction and International Responsibility: New Canadian Approaches to International Law," *A.J.I.L.*, Vol. 67, 1973, p. 15.

Part I

CHAPTER ONE
The Anatomy of Failure

The failure to foresee massive changes in the North before 1968 may appear surprising at first glance. Britain had transferred its northern claims to Canada almost a century before; many brave statements had been made in Ottawa regarding the wealth and promise of the Arctic. Indeed, Diefenbaker's "Northern Vision," trumpeted throughout the entire country, appeared to summon the Arctic from its millenia of frozen silence. On the defence side, the construction of the DEW line, and in particular the heavy involvement of Americans in its construction and operation, had focussed official attention on the North. The notion of the Arctic as Canada's chief line of defence became as firmly established during the Cold War as the inevitability of American participation in defence efforts North of 60 .[1]

Moreover, Government programmes and activities expanded in the North after 1945, following decades of relative neglect. Commercial aircraft development, both long and short range, gave Ottawa an incentive and a tool to supply outlying communities and mining operations. By 1968 air transportation services in the North were being managed efficiently and with relative safety. Arctic resupply also had been greatly improved. The purchase in 1965 of Yellowknife Transport Company and Arctic Shipping Limited by Northern Transportation Company Limited, a federal Crown Corporation, yielded a powerful policy instrument in the North. That year, for the first time in northern history, no freight was left undelivered.

But in other areas as well — telecommunications, economic

incentives, and welfare and resource projects — government expenditures increased. The number of civilian employees almost tripled between 1954-55 and 1965-66. Federal spending reached $99,548,000 by 1964, from outlays of $22,500,000 ten years earlier. Economic development, in particular, yielded visible programmes and slogans — Diefenbaker's "Roads to Resources"; prospectors' incentive grants; the Remote Resource Airports Programme, for example — which were allocated substantial sums during the 1960s.[2] Of even greater importance was the Diefenbaker Government's decision to release Arctic lands for oil and gas leasing under the Canada Oil and Gas Land Regulations of 1961. The terms set out were extremely generous, designed to draw industry into the North.[3]

Nor could it be said that Ottawa lacked structures in the North. A Department of Northern Affairs and National Resources had been created in 1953 to recommend and implement federal policies and to ensure the orderly development of the area. Some men of quality had been attracted to the Department, and several members of the Ottawa inner circle had side-interests in the North. Indeed, Ottawa's most powerful civil servant in 1968, Gordon Robertson, Clerk of the Privy Council and Secretary to the Cabinet, had formerly been with the Department of Northern Affairs and National Resources as Deputy-Minister, and had inspired the formation of a Royal Commission on the Development of Government in the Northwest Territories in June 1965.[4]

In the Advisory Committe on Northern Development the federal Government seemed to possess machinery for drawing together the diverse levels of policy-making in the North. The Advisory Committee was established in January 1948 to coordinate matters relating to northern development, for advice to Cabinet. Chaired by the Deputy Minister in charge of Northern Affairs and including the Deputy Ministers of all the concerned Departments, it appeared to be an adequate instrument for necessary information exchanges and interest aggregation. Someone ought to have been able to warn the Government.

Nevertheless, the Alaskan discoveries did catch Ottawa by surprise, and it took the government almost a year to realize their implications for the country.

1. THE PROBLEM OF COORDINATION

The first level of failure in the North, although not the most decisive, lay in the Department of Indian Affairs and Northern Development's inability to lead and to coordinate policy.

Both in the Northwest Territories and the Yukon, this Department exercised provincial-type jurisdiction from Ottawa, but some sixty federal departments and agencies operated alongside each other without central direction and often at cross purposes. The Department itself was a conglomerate of many diverse and squabbling agencies (see following Organization Charts for 1970 and 1973) whose lack of coordination provided a familiar topic within the Advisory Committee.

At the February 1967 meeting of the Advisory Committee on Northern Development, Commissioner James Smith of the Yukon presented the issue in stark terms. Agencies were working at cross-purposes in the absence of clear leadership from Indian Affairs and Northern Development. Decisions were fragmented among a host of jurisdictions and were made on an *ad hoc* basis, responding to the broad range of issues affecting the individual Departments, and at different times. No overall objectives and priorities were established; there was no explicit framework of development in the North. A myriad of federal activities and services had grown, but no underlying rationale had ever been thought out.

Different agencies and departments used different administrative regions for their northern activities and operated often under conflicting legislation. At least twenty federal agencies performed transport related activities North of 60. Even greater confusion resulted from the Department of Indian Affairs and Northern Development's failure to recommend the adoption of coherent expenditure categories for northern affairs. In their absence, federal outlays relating to northern development could not be systematically examined, and adequate programme forecasts without a coherent regional statistical set were impossible. The various departments and agencies had different definitions of costs, direct, indirect, etc., and there was no way that they could be easily identified for purposes of northern planning.

Commissioner Smith complained bitterly about Ottawa's apparent disinterest in the North during quiet periods and, conversely, the sudden and ill-considered bursts of activity when

Department of Indian Affairs and Northern Development

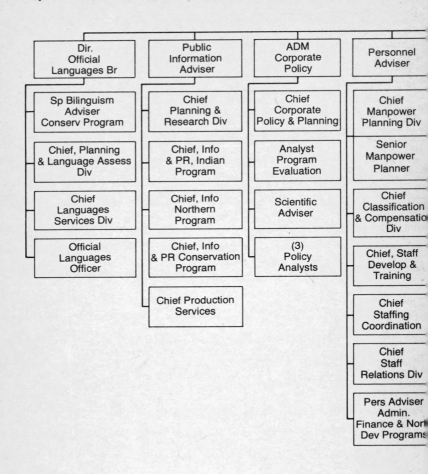

Source: *Organization of the Government of Canada*, 1973 (Ottawa; Information Canada, 1974).

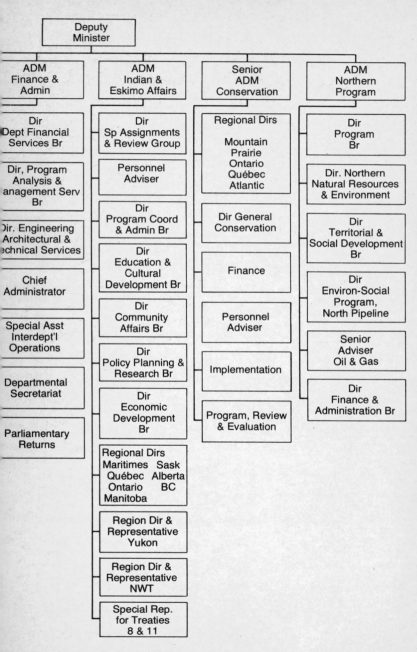

Deputy Minister

ADM Finance & Admin
- Dir Dept Financial Services Br
- Dir, Program Analysis & Management Serv Br
- Dir. Engineering Architectural & Technical Services
- Chief Administrator
- Special Asst Interdept'l Operations
- Departmental Secretariat
- Parliamentary Returns

ADM Indian & Eskimo Affairs
- Dir Sp Assignments & Review Group
- Personnel Adviser
- Dir Program Coord & Admin Br
- Dir Education & Cultural Development Br
- Dir Community Affairs Br
- Dir Policy Planning & Research Br
- Dir Economic Development Br
- Regional Dirs Maritimes Sask Québec Alberta Ontario BC Manitoba
- Region Dir & Representative Yukon
- Region Dir & Representative NWT
- Special Rep. for Treaties 8 & 11

Senior ADM Conservation
- Regional Dirs Mountain Prairie Ontario Québec Atlantic
- Dir General Conservation
- Finance
- Personnel Adviser
- Implementation
- Program, Review & Evaluation

ADM Northern Program
- Dir Program Br
- Dir. Northern Natural Resources & Environment
- Dir Territorial & Social Development Br
- Dir Environ-Social Program, North Pipeline
- Senior Adviser Oil & Gas
- Dir Finance & Administration Br

Department of Indian Affairs and Northern Development

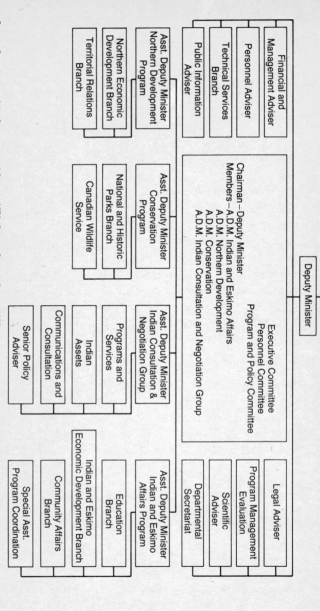

Source: *Organization of the Government of Canada, 1970* (Ottawa: Queen's Printer, 1970)

6

major resources were uncovered. Much harm had been done by such federal responses to the boom and bust cycle that had afflicted the North in the past decades.

What was required was a careful, consistent planning process which could anticipate rather than merely react to change. It was not good enough that the Advisory Committee on Northern Development agreed to carry out a major social, economic, and political review within the next ten years. Something had to be done immediately to limit the damage and to maximize the benefits from increased federal expenditures. He warned the Advisory Committee members that Imperial Oil and Shell were drilling in the Mackenzie Delta and that events might not await the ponderous Ottawa bureaucracy.

The Advisory Committee on Northern Development: For its part, the Advisory Committee on Northern Development never managed to fulfil its initial mandate of coordinating the operations of all the Departments and agencies involved in the North. Still less did it establish a coherent northern policy, based on a careful definition of the role of the North in overall Canadian development. During the 1950s, in the first years after its formation, the Advisory Committee had been tolerably effective as an advisory body to Cabinet on security matters, but it fell into obscurity during the 1960s. The main factor contributing to its decline was the waning of the Soviet manned bomber threat in the 1960s. This development took the attention of more powerful departments such as the Department of External Affairs and the Department of National Defence away from the North. Ottawa had been concerned about the implications for Canadian sovereignty of the American military presence in the North during the mid-1950s and had remained vigilant.[5] A decade later these earlier fears dissipated and Ottawa relaxed. Now even the Americans might leave the North. After 1965 it remained only to negotiate the Canadian takeover of DEW sites by National Defence.[°]

° Even this process got off to a bad start. For example, at the very time that dramatic oil discoveries were being made on the North Slope in Alaska, in the summer of 1968, the Canada Transport Commission (CTC) met in Yellowknife and Frobisher Bay to consider applications from commercial carriers for licences. On October 10, 1968, it went on to approve new scheduled air services, or extensions, to five DEW Line sites (Hall Beach, Tuktoyaktuk, Lady Franklin Point, Broughton Island, and Cape Dyer). Unfortunately, according to

In these circumstances, the Department of Indian Affairs and Northern Development alone did not have the visibility to maintain the prestige of the Advisory Committee on Northern Development at Cabinet level in the absence of a crisis. The evidence of this is manifold. The meetings of the ACND during the 1960s were poorly attended. There were no staff to provide continuity or to take up initiatives suggested during the meetings. Between 1964 and 1969, only five meetings were called by its Chairman. In some cases, minutes were not circulated for months. The Transportation Sub-committee fell into abeyance altogether and no longer attracted real attention from powerful senior officials in Ottawa. By 1968, northern administration had become over-bureaucratized and resistant to change, a lush garden of competing and overlapping jurisdictions even in the bitter cold and permafrost.

2. PRIORITIES

The corollary of administrative confusion was fragmented decision-making in an extreme form. Without clear leadership from any agency, policy direction dwindled. The initiative passed to the private sector which at least had a clear-cut objective: profit.

Traditionally, budgetary requests from the Department of Indian Affairs and Northern Development had stressed four reasons for special assistance to the North. First, increased activities would strengthen Canada's claims to Arctic sovereignty by establishing a permanent presence in the North. Second, the federal Government had a special statutory obligation derived

---

the Exchange of Notes of May 5, 1955, which set down the terms of the agreement between the two countries, the CTC could not assure extensive commercial traffic without prior clearance with the United States Air Force, and that would have to be channelled through the Department of National Defence. For although the United States Air Force (USAF) used the sites solely for the support of the DEW system, and although it was available for the Royal Canadian Air Force (RCAF) as well as Canadian civil air carriers when such traffic did not impede military usage, the USAF was not responsible for providing accommodation, fuel, servicing or related facilities. It goes without saying that the Department of National Defence was confused by the CTC awards. It is also clear that coming when it did, the CTC decision could only embarrass the Canadian government now involved with delicate questions of sovereignty in the North.

from the British North America Act to assist the scattered indigenous populations in the Territories. Third, in view of its delicate ecological balance, the northern environment deserved special protection. Finally, the federal Government encouraged the economic development of the most underdeveloped regions of Canada by assisting interested companies.

There is no question that, prior to 1968, the promotion of mining and petroleum activity was Ottawa's first priority in the North. The bulk of public expenditures was devoted to attracting and subsidizing business operations in the North. Speaking in New York in 1967, the Minister of Indian Affairs and Northern Development urged investors to come to northern Canada. He explained:

> What is lacking perhaps is an awareness by the potential investor of both prizes to be won in the North and the willingness of the Canadian Government to assume a reasonable part of the risk. The traditional roles between the private and public sectors of the country are maintained in the North with the government recovering its share of the risk where success is achieved through the normal processes of royalty and taxation.[6]

Ottawa was content to leave the initiative in the North to the private sector, and investment decisions were facilitated and rewarded by promises of support in the transportation and communication fields and by taxation privileges.[7] Economic development, the Department of Indian Affairs and Northern Development believed, would yield employment opportunities for the northern people, as well as eventual monies for the federal treasury. It was not Ottawa's job to define the direction of economic development — that was the role of the private sector. If businessmen chose to exploit non-renewable resources at the expense of the northern environment, their reasoning must be sound. Ottawa's duty was to assist and encourage rather than criticize.

Instead of planning, therefore, the Department chose private sector collaboration on the assumption of harmony between the profit motive and the national interest. In practice this gave private sector clients a great deal of leverage over the policy process. The crucial factors here were industry's access to confidential data and information in government files denied to other groups (including Parliament) and the collaboration of government officials at all levels who approved and assisted projects.

The lack of leadership within the Department itself further facilitated intimate relations between business and administrators at all levels. The Northern Economic Development Branch emerged as the central decision-making centre in the North. But it had no alternative to collaboration, since it lacked the requisites of planning. It depended on information from the private sector as much as the private sector depended on it for federal largesse.

It is worth stressing, however, that the pre-1968 government-business relationship in the North reflected governmental preferences throughout Canada. Canada had no overall investment policy, nor was its capital market conducive to formulating one. It lacked a national industrial strategy, and its wartime experience in planning had been long forgotten. Not only had Ottawa failed to define the national interest in the North; it had also neglected to define it for the country as a whole.

In southern Canada, however, large political constituencies existed to guard the public interest. In contrast, the North in 1968 was still in a colonial relationship with Ottawa. The native people in the area were as yet unorganized and politically apathetic; an environmental lobby simply did not exist. The only real constituency was business.

For its part the media displayed little interest in the North and its people during the mid-1960s. Even in the area of Indian Affairs, the politicization of southern Canadian natives had shifted the attention of the Indian Affairs Branch and the media to the South. Not until September 1967 did a Commissioner establish residence in the new Northwest Territories capital of Yellowknife, and his responsibilities were not extensive.[8]

Finally, the Department's low profile in the Ottawa community ensured the recruitment of mediocre staff at all levels. It had few top-flight personnel capable of controlling and forecasting northern development. The nearly imperceptible but nevertheless momentous gathering of change in the Arctic therefore went unnoticed. By the later 1960s the great resource-extracting corporations commanded the technology and markets to exploit northern resources, particularly oil and gas. Senior officials, oblivious to these technological developments in the resource field that were rapidly undermining their traditional, comfortable view of the North, were equally blind to the erosion of federal power that resulted from their neglect.

3. THE EROSION OF FEDERAL POWER IN THE NORTH

The Department of Indian Affairs and Northern Development had failed to lead and the Advisory Committee on Northern Development was in disarray. Some reasons for this serious situation — personnel; the role of business; and the low visibility of northern affairs prior to 1968 — can be readily identified. Nevertheless these contributing factors are intelligible only within the framework of decision-making in Ottawa as a whole. Beyond the issue of the Department's failure lurks the question of ultimate governmental power and control. Who in Ottawa set priorities? Who permitted business control over the policy process? Who were the senior officials of rank that recommended major policy direction; how did the network operate?

In the strict sense of the term, there was no "northern problem" at all. Rather, before and after 1968, it was a matter of choosing alternative policies that affected all of Canada. Ultimately the entire Government, not merely the Department of Indian Affairs and Northern Development, was involved in setting the broad guidelines for Northern development. Senior officials across the Departments in Ottawa concurred in the priorities set for the North during the 1960s and none advocated their alteration. Official Ottawa agreed that the chief challenge facing the North was the attraction of business, "opening up the North."

The key domestic policy areas in the 1960s such as Quebec's role in Confederation, pension and welfare planning, and government reorganization, left little room for thinking about the North within the top elite before 1968. Inaction, however, is also policy. Options close and dangers arise when decisions are not taken. By 1968, the failure to demarcate the broad contours of the national interest in the North had seriously impaired the Canadian position. It was policy-making by default. In effect, Ottawa's inability to provide central coordination to offset disintegrative patterns in northern development, permitted a dangerous vacuum of power to develop. New contenders would not hesitate to fill the gap.

11

First, large-scale resource activity and the transportation of resources out of the North would directly involve multinational corporations and their governments in northern policy-making. Their power would introduce an entirely new and unpredictable factor in northern politics. Moreover, the magnitude of required investments would produce industrial groupings rather than an economic environment of competing firms. Nobody of importance in the Capital had planned for this development either. Pipeline and resource consortia, supported directly or indirectly by the relevant foreign governments and presenting a united front to senior officials in Ottawa, would change the political rules of the game in matters affecting the North. New stakes and stakeholders were about to emerge.

Provincial interest in the North had also grown during the 1960s. Perched between Alaska and the American west coast, vulnerable to oil spills and water pollution, British Columbia would have a direct interest in any major hydrocarbon developments in Alaska that involved tanker movements down the Pacific along its coastline.[9] Alberta, on the other hand, looked upon the Mackenzie Valley as its gateway to the North. The transportation system as it had emerged piecemeal in the 1960s supported this claim. But important questions relating to it had not been asked in Ottawa. What role would northern energy discoveries play in Canadian oil planning? As the core of that industry, Alberta would want answers. How would Alaskan discoveries affect Alberta? One thing was certain: the Alberta and British Columbia Governments would descend on Ottawa in consternation should a breakthrough occur.

NOTES

1. See for example Robert Sutherland, "The Strategic Significance of the Canadian Arctic," in R. St. John Macdonald, ed., *The Arctic Frontier* (Toronto, 1966).

2. *Government of Canada,* Advisory Committee on Northern Development, *Government Activities in the North,* (Annual Reports).

3. Peter H. Pearse, ed. *The Mackenzie Pipeline: Arctic Gas*

and Canadian Energy Policy (Toronto, 1973). Many other standard accounts describing the decision are available.

4. *The Advisory Commission on the Development of Government in the North West Territories*, known as the Carrothers Commission, after its Chairman, Dean A.W.R. Carrothers, Faculty of Law, University of Western Ontario — included (with the Chairman) John H. Parker, Mayor of Yellowknife and Mr. Jean Beetz, Professor of Law, University of Montreal.

5. "Agreement between Canada and the United States to Govern the Establishment of DEW System on Canadian Territory," *Canadian Treaties Series*, 1955, No. 8.

6. *Government of Canada*, Advisory Committee on Northern Development, *Government Activities in the North* (Annual Reports). The Minister was speaking to the New York Society of Security Analysts, April 26, 1967.

7. T.N. Brewis, *Regional Economic Policies in Canada* (Toronto, 1969), pp. 237 ff.

8. D.H. Searle, "The Carrothers Commission Report," *Alberta Law Review* Vol. 5, 1966-67, *Canadian Annual Review*, 1967, pp. 173-75.

9. Hedlin-Menzies, *Canadian Northwest Transportation Study*, November, 1970.

CHAPTER TWO
Crisis

Not until late in 1968 did Ottawa awake to the challenges facing Canada as a result of the opening of the North. Indeed a fascinating insight into the state of mind among senior officials during the summer of that year is provided by the tone of a June 1968 meeting of the Advisory Committee on Northern Development. Called to assess the significance of the Alaskan discoveries earlier that year for the Canadian North, it concluded with the least appropriate recommendation to Cabinet in recent history: "That this Committee sees no advantage in permitting Russian icebreakers to move through Canadian Arctic territorial waters to Coronation Gulf."[1]

The Alaskan find was considered good news; the Department of Indian Affairs and Northern Development was particularly enthusiastic. Nobody foresaw a direct American challenge to Canadian sovereignty in the North or a threat to Canadian trade. Approvingly, the Committee noted the interest of the Arctic Institute of North America in a comprehensive study of northern transportation as well as an indication of interest by the United States Coast Guard in such research. Concern, such as there was, was centred on the Russian icebreaker fleet.

1. THE SOVEREIGNTY CHALLENGE

By October 1968, however, External Affairs and the ACND realized that Washington rather than Moscow was determined to test Canadian jurisdictional claims in the High Arctic. Official Ottawa was astonished. It was bad enough that Atlantic Richfield,

British Petroleum, and Humble Oil were demanding scientific information on northern ice conditions in the Northwest Passage that Ottawa simply did not possess. Canadian officials had to admit among themselves that they had little worthwhile information of any kind on ice and marine questions to offer the companies. The situation was awkward.

The Department of External Affairs had no contingency plans for an American threat to Arctic sovereignty. The tranquil years of the 1960s had not been used to clarify and nail down Canada's jurisdictional claims and the Department of National Defence had no policy at all. The other Departments, such as Transport, Indian Affairs and Northern Development, and Energy, Mines and Resources, charged with responsibilities for surveillance and control, were similarly thrown into confusion in late 1968. Collectively Government Departments had neglected basic research and development responsibilities in the Arctic. The crisis painfully revealed that the Canadian Government had not done its homework in ensuring that communication and transportation facilities, as well as the ownership of resources in the North, were sufficiently developed according to national priorities to meet a direct American challenge to Canadian sovereignty without excessive tradeoffs, much less to direct with confidence the course of Arctic political and economic development.

Senior oil executives indicated that the oil companies might seek their own answers if Canada would not or could not provide them. The United States Coast Guard similarly volunteered to assist Canada. Ottawa officials sensed an impending demand from Washington for a joint Canadian-American development agency in the North. Moreover, to complicate matters still further, the Prudhoe Bay discoveries now rendered a tanker route through the Northwest Passage to the American east coast a serious enough possibility to warrant a trial with a reinforced supertanker. Humble Oil's decision to refit the S.S. *Manhattan* to try the Northwest Passage was announced in October, 1968.

Politically, the knowledge that the State Department in Washington was refusing to acknowledge Canadian jurisdiction in Arctic waters was much more alarming. Although the Government was not yet convinced that the United States Navy was funding the S.S. *Manhattan* trials, set for the summer of 1969, there were unmistakable signs that all was wrong. At the seventy-third meeting of the Advisory Committee on Northern Development in early December, 1968, this time well-attended, senior officials of all Departments articulated their sense of urgency in the light of the S.S. *Manhattan* trials. The United States Coast Guard had already indicated its intention of sending a vessel to accompany the S.S. *Manhattan*, but Washington had failed to request permission for this mission in northern waters from the Canadian government. It was this development that sparked an awareness in the Department of External Affairs that a crisis situation had emerged.

Ottawa immediately suggested informally to the State Department that the United States apply for permission for the sending of a Coast Guard escort. But Washington's silence was eloquent. From its point of view any such application for permission from Canada would be taken as a recognition of Canadian sovereignty beyond the three mile limit in Arctic waters.

2. ALBERTA ALARMED

A major confrontation with the United States had now emerged. The smell of cooperation between the multinationals (the S.S. *Manhattan* was being refitted in Sunoco's Sun Shipyard and Drydock Company) and the State Department was overpowering. And if this were not enough, Alberta, also in October 1968, argued in Ottawa that the western Canadian economy was threatened with ruin unless access to American markets for Canadian crude oil was somehow maintained.

Apparently more expensive than Middle East or Venezuelan oil, Alberta crude could not be sold ouside North America and therefore had only one export market, the United States. Until the Alaskan strike, the crucial impediment to further export expansion was an American oil import quota, limiting imports to 21 per cent of total domestic consumption. During the 1960s Canada as well as American consumer groups tried to undermine the U.S. oil quota system which protected oil producers in the United States against foreign competition at a cost, estimated in Ottawa, of $4 billion annually. Alberta during the 1960s lived in the shadow of quota politics. Ottawa's oil "policy" was an all-out attempt to gain free entry for western crude oil.

These positions were not changed as a result of the Alaskan North Slope discoveries: the objective of free entry to American markets remained. What did change however, was the assumption of provincial and federal policy-makers that Canadian oil enjoyed a secure future market in the United States. Alberta officials now foresaw an altered supply and demand situation in North America after Alaskan supplies came on-stream, in which Alaskan oil would permit the United States to achieve total or near self-sufficiency independent of Canadian producers. Industry was already talking of delivery to mainland markets by 1972 via a trans-Alaskan pipeline system. The crisis, it was argued, could be delayed until then, but Ottawa had better start some hard bargaining with Washington to protect the western encomy.

The Government was nettled by this development. It turned to the Interdepartmental Committee on Oil for advice. Chaired by the Chairman of the National Energy Board, and including the Secretary of State for External Affairs, the Deputy Minister of Energy, Mines and Resources, as well as representation from central agencies such as the Privy Council Office, the Interdepartmental Committee advised Cabinet on all matters relating to national oil policy. The participation of the Secretary of State underlined the importance of exports to the United States and the role of Canadian foreign policy in promoting trade in this area. For his part, the Chairman of the National Energy Board must have reflected at times on his activity in the Committee. The most important policy-making instrument in Canadian energy matters, the Committee had the advantage of obtaining the "impartial" views of the Energy Board. Later we shall see a third role assumed by its Chairman — the promoter of a Mackenzie Valley pipeline.

The Interdepartmental Committee on Oil was quickly persuaded that an emergency indeed existed. The Alaskan discoveries represented a further blow to the so-called "National Policy" adopted by the Diefenbaker Government in 1961. That policy decision split Canada into two markets along the Ottawa Valley: Quebec and the Atlantic Provinces would consume imported crude oil; Ontario and the West would use Alberta (and to a lesser extent Saskatchewan) supplies.

The basic premise of the National Oil Policy was that reserves of crude oil in Alberta were in excellent condition. Industry, the Government of Alberta, and the Interdepartmental Committee on

Oil were therefore in agreement that the western oil industry should expand its capacity, which implied a Continental market.

The decision to expand the western oil industry through exports to the United States rather than sales to eastern Canada led in turn to a pipeline grid directed to the South and even over United States territory between Alberta and Toronto. Since the success of the National Oil Policy depended on United States cooperation, the National Energy Board strove continually to convince the United States of its permanent good will. It emphasized that it fully supported the construction of Canadian-owned pipeline facilities in the United States, and the carriage of Canadian oil in bond through United States territory, as well as dependence on United States markets. The deeper in, the better.[2]

The dependence on the United States was therefore extreme: Alaskan oil augured badly for the future. Two other developments, however, increased the apparent danger. First, given the absence of deep-water ports on the Atlantic coast of the United States, as well as the "vagueness," as one official put it, of Canadian energy policy, industry had decided to construct satellite refineries in the Atlantic provinces, geared to processing off-shore crude for re-export to this market. Here was another Canadian energy sector geared entirely to American import policy.

Second, if the American quota system were decisively relaxed, North American oil prices might fall low enough for Middle East and Venezualan crude to displace Alberta oil in some areas, not least in Ontario. Officials on the Inter-Departmental Committee on oil chafed at the pro-rationing policy followed by the Alberta Oil and Gas Conservation Board. Even if American import policies were changed, it was not at all clear that the Board would allow high volume, low unit-cost fields to compete more freely. If the "Sam Rayburn practice" of permitting the most inefficient drillers and fields to produce and sell as much as more efficient operators continued when high quality Alaskan crude hit the market, Alberta oil might be displaced from the United States market. As for Ontario, outside what was then termed "the favoured zone," low price off-shore supplies in a buyers market produced complaints about subsidizing the western oil industry. Alaska might drive this awkward situation to the breaking point.

It all added up to big trouble for Canada. A very difficult period lay ahead in which Canada must be fully prepared for all contingencies. The whole North American supply and demand structure appeared to be radically altered by events in the Arctic. Trade relations centring on American oil import policy, and difficult at the best of times, now were in a state of crisis. What leverage did Canada have in these negotiations? Were there new policy instruments that could assist Ottawa in protecting the Canadian oil industry and preserving American markets?

3. THE TASK FORCE ON NORTHERN OIL DEVELOPMENT

Existing machinery was immediately perceived as inadequate. The economic and political ramifications of the discoveries for Canada, which made a more coherent northern strategy essential, were far too important to leave to the Advisory Committee on Northern Development or the Department of Indian Affairs and Northern Development. The attention of Ottawa's inner elite was now focussed on the North — a new, small, and more efficient structure was therefore required for rapid action. Cabinet recommendations had to be speeded up; the old, time-consuming routines and conventions in the preparation of Cabinet Memoranda must be side-stepped, at least during the crisis.

The new structure for achieving rapid action at the highest level was the Task Force on Northern Oil Development, formed in December 1968 to assess the national implication of the new situation in the North for recommendations to Cabinet. The Advisory Committee on Northern Development was by-passed.

The Task Force's terms of reference as announced by the Acting Minister of Energy, Mines, and Resources, Jean-Luc Pepin, on December 20, 1968 in the House of Commons covered four areas of study:

1. It would assess the technical and economic feasibility of an oil pipeline from Prudhoe Bay to United States markets through Canada. This study would be led by the Energy Board Chairman, assisted by the Department of Energy, Mines, and Resources and Indian Affairs and Northern Development and the National Research Council.

2. Another Committee would assess the economic feasibility of the transportation of crude oil through the Northwest Passage. The Ministry of Transport conducted the inquiry, with the assistance of Energy, Mines and Resources, Indian

LAND PERMITTED FOR OIL AND GAS EXPLORATION, BY AREAS BY CONTROLLING COUNTRY
(50% resident membership of common shares issued and outstanding)

Controlling Country°	Assumption 1		Assumption 2	
	Acres	%	Acres	%
Canada				
Mainland	22.3	15.5	22.3	15.5
Arctic Islands	96.9	41.7	67.5	29.1
Marine	4.5	18.4	4.5	18.4
Total	123.7	30.9	94.3	23.5
United States				
	93.4	64.9	93.4	64.9
Arctic Islands	98.4	42.4	111.7	48.1
Marine	11.1	45.5	11.1	45.5
Total	202.9	50.7	216.2	54.0
United Kingdom				
Mainland	8.9	6.2	8.9	6.2
Arctic Islands	9.8	4.2	21.7	9.3
Marine	0.5	2.1	0.5	2.1
Total	19.2	4.8	31.1	7.8
France				
Mainland	7.6	5.3	7.6	5.3
Arctic Islands	20.9	9.0	23.5	10.1
Marine	0.3	1.2	0.3	1.2
Total	28.8	7.2	31.4	7.8

°Others   25.8   in acres

6.4%

27.4

Source: CALURA 1969   6.8%

Affairs and Northern Development, the National Energy Board, and the Northern Transportation Company, Ltd.

3. The National Energy Board would conduct a study of the effect of North Slope oil on North American supply and

Task Force on Northern Oil Development

```
                    ┌──────────────────────────┐
                    │         Chairman          │
                    │ Energy, Mines and Resources│
                    └──────────────────────────┘
           ┌──────────────┬──────────┴──────────┬──────────────┐
    ┌──────┴──────┐ ┌──────┴──────┐ ┌──────┴──────┐ ┌──────┴──────┐
    │  Pipeline   │ │  Economic   │ │  Transport  │ │  Marketing  │
    │  Committee  │ │   Impact    │ │  Committee  │ │  Committee  │
    │  National   │ │  Committee  │ │  Transport  │ │  National   │
    │Energy Board │ │   Finance   │ │             │ │Energy Board │
    └─────────────┘ └─────────────┘ └─────────────┘ └─────────────┘
```

demand and in turn on the Canadian oil industry. Energy, Mines and Resources and Indian Affairs and Northern Development would assist the Board in this study.

4. The Department of Finance would assess the costs and benefits to the Canadian economy of the different policy alternatives. Energy, Mines and Resources, the National Energy Board, and the Departments of External Affairs, Industry, Trade, and Commerce, and Indian Affairs and Northern Development would all participate in this study.[3]

Pepin stressed the broad issues involved in the northern discoveries: resource administration and development; Canadian sovereignty in northern waters; and negotiations concerning possible pipeline facilities from Alaska to the American midwest through Canadian territory. Given the national and international ramifications of the Alaska discoveries, a task force approach would best facilitate the extensive inter-agency contacts required to recommend policy.

> The purpose will be to bring together all information on the existing oil situation in the north, on transportation routes that might be used, and to coordinate all available information, from all federal agencies and departments, and then to report and make proposals to the government.[4]

For the next four years the Task Force on Northern Oil Development became the central body for determining northern resource policy. The importance of the issues involved meant that the attention of the Ottawa elite was focussed on the North and the Task Force on Northern Development. Its members, the Deputy Ministers of Energy, Mines and Resources, Transport, and Indian Affairs and Northern Development, along with the Chairman of the National Energy Board, had the ear of their most senior colleagues in Privy Council, Finance, and Treasury Board. In moments of crisis, the Task Force members could call this group together for consultation and advice, to decide what to recommend to their Ministers; at the time this advantage was shared by few other committees in the capital, and explains the Task Force's effectiveness after it was set up.

Business also quickly realized that the Task Force rather than the Advisory Committee on Northern Development would be developing guidelines (for submission to Cabinet of course) for the integration of the North into the North American economy. In short, the Task Force became a transmission belt for industry initiatives requiring speedy approval by Cabinet. Its deliberations were highly classified. The net effect of this arrangement was to give a very few individuals, including the Chairman of the National Board and the Deputy Minister of Energy, Mines and Resources, enormous influence over northern affairs that affected all Canadians.

The Task Force's chief purpose from the first was the successful promotion of a Mackenzie pipeline corridor rather than the two most probable transportation alternatives for Alaskan oil and gas: tanker transportation via the Northwest Passage; or a trans-Alaska pipeline to the port of Valdez with tanker shipments to the Cherry Point refineries in the State of Washington, near the British Columbia border. If Prudhoe Bay oil were transported across Canada, linking up with Alberta's existing pipeline system, Canada's bargaining position would be improved. It would provide an argument for freer entry for Alberta crude at least during the pipeline construction period. More important, once in existence, such a pipeline would make it much more difficult for Washington to turn off the tap when Alaskan oil began to flow in quantity. The United States would, of course, demand political concessions but they could scarcely be higher than the alternative: a *de facto* United States embargo on Alberta crude.

In the sovereignty issue as well, the Task Force emerged as a central policy forum.

The Advisory Committee on Northern Development had recommended the creation of a special task force of the Interdepartmental Committee on Territorial Waters to programme in detail a Canadian position in Arctic waters. But its proposed interdepartmental group never met. Instead, its planned functions were taken over by the Task Force. This decision to extend the advisory role of the Task Force on Northern Development brought everything under one roof — jurisdictional issues, economic and trade considerations, and northern oil and gas exploration activity. It also greatly augmented the Task Force's position within the bureaucracy. Most important, the linking of trade and jurisdictional matters both illustrated and contributed to Ottawa's increasing willingness to protect Canadian trade by adopting a northern strategy that would accommodate corporate and American interests. It foreshadowed, in effect, the decisions of 1970.

Interesting as the formation of powerful new committees may be to observers of Government, the native people had every cause for alarm at the creation of the Task Force on Northern Oil Development. Their interests were not represented in the Committee. No channels existed for the articulation of their concerns. They had no way of knowing what was going on, or what decisions had already been taken. Yet pipeline and resource decisions would change and probably destroy their traditions and way-of-life.

In theory at least, the Advisory Committee on Northern Development had a broad mandate and representation to address the broad multidimensional character of development in the North. In practice, the Advisory Committee was ineffective. But at the same time it was too clumsy and exposed to serve as an adequate tool for pipeline decision-making. Something brand new, *ad hoc*, without commitments to existing jurisdictions — a secret forum and transmission belt where senior officials could meet in confidence with business executives — this was required. Above all, it could not be bureaucratized, or it would lose its effectiveness. Like the Interdepartmental Committee on Oil it had to hang free, below the firing-line, without exposure to the press or Parliament.

Unfortunately for the native people, these conditions meant their exclusion from the policy process both directly and indirectly — indirectly because apart from business no one else knew what was happening either. Allies in the House of Commons, Yellowknife, and Whitehorse, or among public interest groups could by definition not be mobilized. Native people sensed but could not prove that absolutely crucial decisions were being made behind their backs.

The Task Force itself was purely and entirely development-oriented. Indeed the new group gave the most development-minded officials in Indian Affairs and Northern Development unfettered opportunity to "open the North." Both the National

Energy Board, chairing the Task Force on Northern Oil Development Pipeline Committee, and Energy, Mines and Resources had their gaze fixed on resource development. Nevertheless, the decision to establish the Task Force on Northern Oil Development in December 1968 generated a powerful instrument for resolving the new dangers unleashed by events in Alaska. It set about immediately to convince the oil industry of the merits of a Mackenzie pipeline system.

NOTES

1. Advisory Committee on Northern Development, 72nd Meeting, Ottawa, June 15, 1968.
2. Shaffer, E.H., "Canada's Energy Policy," in E.H. Shaffer, ed., *Industrial Organization in Canada* (2nd ed.) (New York, 1971); also Shaffer, *The Oil Import Programme of the United States* (New York, 1968).
3. McDougall, I. "The Canadian National Energy Board; Economic 'Jurisprudence' in the National Interest or Symbolic Reassurance," *Alberta Law Review*, Vol. 11, 1973; R. J. Gibbs et al. "A Review of the National Energy Board Policies and Practices and Recent Hearings," *Alberta Law Review*, Vol. 9, 1971.
4. *Government of Canada*, House of Commons, *Debates*, December 20, 1968, pp. 4221 ff.

CHAPTER THREE
Pipeline Planning 1968-70

High hopes and some disappointments marked the first phase of pipeline planning in the North — disappointment that Atlantic Richfield, British Petroleum, and Humble announced their support for a trans-Alaskan pipeline as early as February 1969; high hopes given the political uproar that confronted such a pipeline in the United States, and industry's apparent increasing interest during the period in a Mackenzie oil or natural gas pipeline system linking Alaska and United States mainland markets. It was a difficult period for pipeline planners within the Federal agencies most involved: until the sovereignty threat was stabilized, northern resource development would not be given top priority by Government. But impressive progress nevertheless was made in attracting and focusing industry attention on a Mackenzie pipeline.

1. THE FORMATION OF MACKENZIE VALLEY PIPELINE RESEARCH LIMITED

The National Energy Board initiated contacts with industry at the close of 1968 to sound out interest in a Canadian alternative to a trans-Alaskan pipeline system in the Mackenzie Valley. Although the National Energy Boards' activities in this area preceded the formation of the Task Force they were heartily endorsed by the group.

In the first *Progress Report* to Cabinet in March 1969, for example, the Task Force Pipeline Committee sought authority to encourage industry to undertake a programme of practical on-site tests of pipeline construction and operations in the Canadian North. It saw industry implementing such testing but suggested the possibility of Government financial assistance, and recommended close cooperation between industry and the National Energy Board, the Departments of Energy, Mines, and Resources and Indian Affairs and Northern Development, and the National Research Council Sub-committee on Pipeline Technology in Northern Areas.

As the months passed, the Energy Board was encouraged by several developments, including the rapid increase in permit-taking in the Canadian North. First, Northern Natural Gas Company approached the Canadian Embassy in Washington to discuss its interest in participating in northern natural gas development. External Affairs reported that far-reaching possibilities were mentioned: the acquisition of a special company, or at least financial participation in some gas producing companies; an exploration and development programme in the Arctic; and "hopefully" the development of extensive natural gas pipelines tapping both Alberta and the Northwest Territories. Briefings with Northern Natural Gas were also scheduled in Ottawa, Alberta, and with "other Canadian entities."

The impression was left that:

Northern is serious and has made a basic decision to constructively participate in Western and Northern Canadian gas and oil plans. . . . One result of Northern's determination to go where the action is may well be applications before Canadian regulatory bodies for export and the Federal Power Commission for import (permits).

The Task Force was buoyed up by the knowledge that Northern Natural Gas was discussing plans for increasing its participation in Canadian northern oil and gas exploration. In Ottawa this was taken as a sign of confidence that Canadian oil and gas prospects in the North were widely respected in industry.

Second, and more specifically, the National Energy Board and the Task Force discovered some interest in a Mackenzie Valley oil pipeline consortium. By May 1969, the Task Force could report success in the formation by industry of the Mackenzie Valley Pipeline Research Co. Limited. Initiated originally by Trans Mountain Pipe Line Company and Interprovincial Pipe Line Co.

it provided for entry by other companies as appropriate; through financial participation in this organization they gained the right to copies of research studies undertaken by the consortium as well as an option to buy equity should a line be constructed. The concept was successful in attracting an impressive array of participating companies.[1]

E.C. Hurd, President of Trans Mountain, envisioned a Mackenzie oil pipeline linking up with the already established rights-of-way of the Rainbow Pipeline Company in Alberta. Both Trans Mountain and Rainbow were closely linked to the integrated firms. Imperial Oil, for example, owned 8.6 per cent and 33 per cent respectively of the two companies; Shell owned 8.6 per cent of Trans Mountain Pipe Line Co.[2]

Momentum was quickly established: a technical committee of the Mackenzie Valley Pipeline Research Co. set out immediately to investigate the feasibility of the Mackenzie route for the transportation of Alaskan oil. A station set up in Inuvik in September 1969 with a 2,000-foot test pipe received wide publicity in the Canadian press. The National Energy Board was delighted by this interest and noted that the Task Force on Northern Oil Development might want to follow up discussions with Hurd to clarify outstanding points. For example, it was rumoured that certain American integrated oil companies had voiced concern about the standards which Canada might impose on pipeline construction in northern Canada. The Task Force should be in a position to reassure industry at such critical moments in pipeline discussions.

2. THE ROLE OF NORTHERN TRANSPORTATION COMPANY LIMITED

Pipeline regulation in the Arctic would not necessarily involve the close attention of the Ministry of Transport. However, although this Ministry was originally invited to join the Task Force on Northern Oil Development to investigate marine traffic feasibility in Arctic waters rather than pipeline matters, many important planning and operational responsibilities associated with northern pipeline construction would concern transport: calculating the efficiency of pipeline transport compared to other modes; adequate barge and road capacity expansion; coping with increased air traffic associated with northern oil and gas development and pipeline construction, including the massive expansion of privately-owned facilities and aircraft after 1968; the access of British Columbia and Alberta to a Mackenzie pipeline route; and the role of the CNR both in terms of its role in the surface transportation system supporting the pipeline and the possibility of its purchasing equity in a northern pipeline. Whatever the jurisdictional problems, the Mackenzie pipeline was a key transportation facility and part of a larger investment process that necessarily involved the Ministry of Transport.

The new Deputy Minister was determined that the Ministry perform this role efficiently and organized a special agency, the Arctic Transportation Agency, for this purpose.

A rather different problem involving transportation centred on an important Crown Corporation, the Northern Transportation Company Limited. A common carrier on the Mackenzie and heavily involved in Arctic resupply, it had rapidly expanded its northern transportation services especially after 1958. In 1968 it initiated a major expansion programme and had found it possible to reduce rates significantly in response to increased traffic. In all, during the 1960s, an average decrease of 25 per cent in rates occurred. Above all, Northern Transportation remained financially sound. As a Class C Crown Corporation it was expected to pay its own way and it did. In short, it was a rare animal, a self-supporting Government agency, which dominated traffic on the river.

The possibility of a Mackenzie pipeline altered NTCL's potential growth. Pipeline construction would require vastly increased transportation facilities. In other words, the current prospects offered a golden opportunity for the continuing expansion of Northern Transportation. The President of the Company, under these circumstances, championed the concept. Impatient of Government delays and red tape, he became an instant lobbyist for the pipeline. That he headed a Crown Corporation was irrelevant.

Convinced that an oil and/or gas pipeline was "virtually certain," the President of Northern Transportation proceeded in fall, 1969 to negotiate with the Mackenzie Valley Pipeline Research Company Ltd. for shipping contracts. By November 1969 he was able to obtain a "firm" commitment from Bechtel

Corporation for the entire project. The pipeline consortium would underwrite the $46 million required for capital expenditure; Northern Transportation would return $20 million of this amount but retain the equipment. At the same time the transportation of pipeline materials, estimated at 76,045 tons, would produce revenues of an estimated $40 million. Securing the entire contract would benefit both the North and Northern Transportation. But he felt there was little time for procrastination. The Task Force should formulate a pipeline policy as soon as possible.

There was, of course, a rider: a major dredging programme on the river. Northern Transportation argued that dredging and the expansion of its fleet were urgently required to enable the Company to provide the required support services for pipeline construction.

Northern Transportation then became a major pipeline promoter within the Government. Indirectly, aside from its President's personal connections with Task Force members, Northern Transportation also tied into the Task Force. Since it reported through Indian Affairs and Northern Development, and after June 1970 the Ministry of Transport, it had a mechanism for influencing the ongoing Northern pipeline debate. It wanted action.

3. STALLING THE TRANS—ALASKAN PIPELINE SYSTEM

In its first Cabinet *Memo* of March 1969, the Task Force indicated four prospects for pipeline construction resulting from the Alaskan finds:

1. a trans-Alaskan pipeline system with Pacific tankers
2. a Seattle to Chicago line complementing this route
3. a Canadian alternative down the Mackenzie to American mid-west markets, and
4. an extension of the Interprovincial pipeline system east of the Ottawa valley.

The last alternative was rejected from the first and was not taken up in further deliberations. It was not considered feasible or worthy of extensive discussion.

The Alaskan route had been approved by industry a month earlier. Atlantic Richfield, Humble, and British Petroleum (which in February 1969 had also reported extensive finds) had committed themselves to the rapid construction of the system at a projected cost of $900 million with deliveries to begin in 1972. The Pipeline Consortium formed for the construction of the trans-Alaskan system promptly placed orders in Japan for the 48-inch pipe. The project, however, had not been approved by the relevant American authorities and native-environmentalist opposition to the pipeline was rapidly crystallizing. But few people believed that the project would be stalled for five years.

The approval by industry was received with dismay in Ottawa. Energy Board officials believed that Canadian oil export growth would be set back from five to ten years. Nonetheless the Task Force Pipeline Committee decided to prepare for Cabinet a study indicating the comparative position of Alaskan oil transported by the Canadian route relative to other routes and methods being considered by industry. Particular attention was to be given to route selection, methods of construction, design, power require-ments, construction costs, methods of financing, and rates of return. The hope was that the rationale for the Canadian alternative would show important financial and marketing advantages over the Alaskan route, and impel industry to abandon it in favour of a Mackenzie pipeline.

There was one serious obstacle to the preparation of a Canadian position, however. The President's Task Force on Oil, established in February 1969, had not yet reported, and without knowing the American position, Canadian officials were operating in a vacuum.[3] Until they could predict the likely direction of American import policy, the crucial determinant of Canadian oil policy, they could not proceed; the whole issue of Canadian-American oil relations hung fire with Ottawa waiting for something to react to.

But officials feared that Washington would be very tough. As one commented in January, 1970, "the U.S. has controls ready if suasion isn't enough."

Other factors rendered the situation even more complex. First, National Energy Board estimates of oil reserves at Prudhoe Bay in Alaska were now growing rapidly; by mid-1969 Task Force officials thought they might be as high as 40 billion barrels. Such enormous supplies might justify two pipeline systems, both a trans-Alaskan system and the Mackenzie route. Second, oil and gas exploration in Arctic Canada, both in the Mackenzie Delta and

Arctic islands, had bounded forward following the discoveries in Alaska. Between July 1968 and October 1969 the area under permit in the Canadian North increased from 189.9 to 437.6 million acres. Imperial had struck oil at Atkinson Point in January 1970 although the extent of the find was far from certain; and Panarctic Oils was predicting success in the Sverdup Basin of the Arctic islands. These finds could not in themselves justify pipeline planning from Canadian sources but they indicated great promise. Third, land claims and environmentalist injunctions were seriously bogging down the promoters of the Alaska route. The consortium found itself involved in a maze of native land claims and environmentalist legal barriers; it was far from certain that construction would proceed to meet a delivery date of 1972. Fourth, Ottawa could only guess what the oil companies were thinking about the Mackenzie route. Without sufficient data for purposes of analysis, National Energy Board and Energy, Mines and Resources officials waited for communications from industry, but industry was not easily drawn out. In December 1969, the Chairman of the Energy Board noted that estimates of comparative costs for the four main transportation alternatives changed daily. The trend, he felt, was toward equal costs "with the ultimate choice depending upon geo-political considerations which vary from company to company."

Throughout the summer and fall of 1969, however, the Task Force became increasingly divided concerning the most advisable strategy to adopt in relations with business on the Mackenzie Valley pipeline issue. Both within the Government and from industry, pressures were developing for a decision by Cabinet endorsing in principle northern pipeline construction. The importance of such a decision was evident to all members of the Task Force. While it would not be a "final" decision — this would only come after hearings before the NEB — acceptance in principle of this point would represent a decision by the Government of Canada and would be extremely difficult to reverse. It would initiate joint collaboration between National Energy Board, Energy, Mines and Resources, and industry on the premise that the pipeline would go forward.

A Task Force recommendation to approve-in-principle one of the largest capital projects in the history of international business called for a careful weighing of the evidence regarding costs and benefits. But Ottawa had little information on which to base a decision of this kind; and the National Energy Board possessed little data-gathering capability. The Board and Energy, Mines and Resources relied on confidential information supplied by industry and had traditionally accepted without question the validity of this data. The whole Canadian regulatory structure in energy and transportation depended upon a collaborative strategy premised on a notion of "partnership."

But reliance on the private sector for research and dependence on the willingness of the oil companies to share information with the federal government, found the Task Force on Northern Oil Development without an adequate basis for decision-making on pipeline policy in the North in the autumn/winter of 1969-70. The Mackenzie Valley Pipeline Research group promised to produce an interim report for Ottawa by January 1970 and the Task Force set great importance on this document. However the consortium then decided that the report was to be considered an internal paper to be released only on June 30, 1970. Energy, Mines and Resources and the National Energy Board but particularly the Ministry of Transport and Indian Affairs and Northern Development were acutely worried, the latter agencies because of their responsibilities for transporting pipeline materials and establishing a logistics support system along the Mackenzie River in the event of pipeline construction. The National Energy Board, with its close personal ties to the industry, felt that the integrated oil companies were as perplexed by the choice of alternatives as the Canadian Government, and were not as inclined to be suspicious about the silence from industry.

An attempt to determine industry's plans as a guide for action, however, failed. Commencing in early November 1969, the Ministry of Transport and the Department of Indian Affairs and Northern Development officials initiated a joint investigation into the ramifications of a Mackenzie pipeline. It got nowhere. Task Force officials, particularly in the National Energy Board, could supply the team with little new information because the Mackenzie Valley Pipeline Research group had decided to delay its report until June 1970. Moreover, contacts with industry proved fruitless in determining their plans for pipelines in the North.

Opinion in Ottawa was divided on what this meant. The

National Energy Board felt that industry didn't have much new information and that the decision would rest purely on reserves and market demand considerations. These forecasts were only now being firmed up. Northern Transportation Company Ltd., claiming an association with Bechtel Corporation no less intimate than Energy Board links to the Canadian oil and gas sector, thought that a precise timetable regarding pipeline construction up the Mackenzie could be available as early as June 1970. If this were indeed the case then prompt action certainly was necessary. Other officials thought that the pipeline consortium was deliberately withholding information from Ottawa pending approval-in-principle by the Government.

Academic and professional opinion sought out by Ottawa officials in particular in the spring of 1970 seemed divided as well on the relative merits of the Alaska route as opposed to the Canadian alternative. According to their reports, T. R. Stauffer, a member of the United States Task Force on Oil, which had reported to President Nixon in February 1970, privately indicated his confidence in Canada's oil potential. The Mackenzie Valley in his opinion was perhaps the only way to ensure secure and economic supplies to the American east coast; and the Athabaska tar sands represented "the ultimate petroleum insurance policy for North America." But he added that the failure to arrive at a continental oil policy with Canada would inevitably lead to American import restrictions on Canadian oil.

The Executive Vice-President of W. J. Levy, Consultants, Milton Lipton, apparently also linked the choice of delivery systems to Canadian-American economic relations in general. The whole American energy policy was premised on the assumption that Canada would be "reasonable." Canada, in his opinion, had great bargaining power since the United States needed Alaskan and northern Canadian natural gas via a Mackenzie pipeline in the energy hungry midwest states. However, he felt that industry officials believed that there would be even more environmentalist opposition to the Mackenzie Valley pipeline than that confronting the one in Alaska and that Canada had to clarify this eventuality with company officials. If Canada could assure early approval of a Mackenzie Valley oil pipeline it would probably win out over a trans-Alaskan route since it held a competitive advantage in the midwest market. If the Alaskan system went forward, however,

Lipton felt that the next logical pipeline would be built from Seattle to Chicago and not along the Mackenzie. Again, in his view, pipeline policy represented the outcome of continental energy negotiations.

Officials maintained that John Giese, Manager, Economic and Planning Department of Bechtel Corporation, admitted he had done a great deal of work on the engineering and feasibility study of the Mackenzie Valley Pipeline Research group and that the consortium now had a complete report before it. He did not see any significance in the June 30, 1970 reporting deadline to the Canadian Government and was unwilling to go into the report's findings, indicating that detailed comments would have to come from consortium members. But he felt that it would be either a Mackenzie Valley oil pipeline or the Alaskan system, and that Canada would face the kind of environmental and social problems that were now confronting the Alaskan route. He did however underline that a great deal of research activity was going on with respect to a possible Mackenzie oil pipeline.

James Cross of Sunoco apparently felt that the Alaska pipeline would go first with a Mackenzie oil line as a second priority. Supertankers, he felt, were increasingly unlikely given the absence of deep-water harbours on the North Slope of Alaska. However, in his opinion, the Mackenzie route was the best and would certainly be the choice of the oil companies if Canada and the United States were one country. It was best for American national security; it was all-weather; cheaper; and had access to crude supplies along the route in northern Canada. Any construction of a Mackenzie oil pipeline, however, would have to involve a clear division between product sources in Canada and the United States before investment would be attracted. A concerted Canadian drive might very well influence industry one way or the other and he gave it as his opinion that the fate of the Mackenzie route rested in the lap of the Canadian Government. He estimated Prudhoe Bay reserves at 20 billion barrels.

On the one hand, then, there was evidence to suggest that a determined initiative by Ottawa could push the Canadian alternative over the top. On the other hand, federal officials were aware that the consortium urging the Alaskan route was determined to press forward, and that business circles shared the opinion that the huge financing required for even one pipeline would not permit the construction of two oil pipeline systems from Alaska in the 1970s whatever the magnitude of North Slope reserves. The oil companies appeared confident that the Department of the Interior would approve the line, and that the environmentalist and Alaskan native opposition would ultimately be overcome. They were correct in this belief.

4. THE APRIL 1970 POSTURE: PASSIVE PROMOTION

Natural Gas Pipeline Prospects: An equally significant development in the Task Force Pipeline Committee's deliberations during 1969 was the recognition of the excellent prospects of a natural gas pipeline from Prudhoe Bay up the Mackenzie to serve American and Canadian markets with or without an accompanying oil line. Proven reserves of natural gas in the Alaskan North Slope oil fields had increased immensely, and were beyond the threshold level of 15 trillion cubic feet considered commercially necessary for northern pipeline construction. According to the Committee, such a pipeline would be attractive to industry given the increasing recognition of natural gas as a fuel in the American midwest markets and the high cost of alternative delivery systems from the North Slope that would involve liquifaction. Moreover a gas line would provide a ready source of fuel for pumping stations and the electric generators required for an oil pipeline system.

Apparently serious industry submissions regarding a natural gas pipeline along the Mackenzie were presented to the Task Force. In effect, the Mackenzie gas pipeline research groups, two of which were to merge into the Canadian Gas Arctic consortium in the summer of 1972, were in a process of formation. In June 1969, Northern Natural Gas; TransCanada (with Peoples' Gas Company and American Natural Gas); and the Mountain Pacific system (West Coast Transmission, Canadian Bechtel, El Paso Natural Gas, Southern California Edison, and Pacific Lighting Gas) respectively had announced plans for Arctic pipelines.

The National Energy Board and Energy, Mines and Resources were pleased, for a natural gas pipeline would be as useful in Canadian-American relations as the northern oil pipeline project. Already, in January 1970, National Energy Board officials in the Task Force expressed their opinion that a gas pipeline was an earlier prospect than an oil delivery system.

But by autumn 1969 nothing was certain; indeed the scarcity of information was appalling. Both, or either, oil and natural gas pipelines were possible. Industry-Government discussions were proceeding on the assumption that the decision could go either way.

The April 1970 Memo to Cabinet: When the Task Force, after much reworking and hesitation, finally sent its second *Progress Report* to Cabinet in April 1970, the Pipeline Committee was still not in a position to offer more than generalities. It repeated its opinion that Canada should encourage the Mackenzie alternative as one way of preventing the Alaskan route, but it could not clarify its competitive position versus the trans-Alaskan pipeline for central United States markets. The cost of such a pipeline system (with a connecting pipeline from Seattle to Chicago) was felt to be roughly equal to a Prudhoe Bay-Mackenzie-Chicago system utilizing existing links from Alberta to American points.

Inevitably the question of the Canadian Government's posture toward the oil and pipeline industry formed a controversial part of the Cabinet *Memorandum* After much debate prior to its submission, a consensus had been achieved among Task Force members that a strategy of "passive promotion" represented the safest policy position for the time being. By this they meant that industry proposals should be treated cautiously to avoid commitments pending a Government decision regarding guidelines for northern pipelines. A stepped-up research and development programme on the Mackenzie route should be initiated immediately to enable the Government to move forward quickly should oil and gas actually be discovered in large quantities.

But it was undesirable, according to the Task Force, for the federal Government to become wedded to any one proposal until all briefs had been properly considered and the respective national and international benefits evaluated. The Task Force was plainly worried about the inherent difficulties in giving commitments to industry in an area of great importance in Canadian affairs and Canadian-American relations. Government-industry relationships centred on mutual trust; it was better not to make a commitment at the outset rather than to make an overly hasty decision and regret it later.

Indeed the Task Force members agreed to follow a common

strategy in dealing with industry representatives: all proposals should be received by the respective department and industry spokesmen presenting them might do so in person before the senior officials. But, it was agreed, Ministers should not comment, or meet with lobbyists until the Cabinet had accepted northern pipeline construction in principle and had approved guidelines. This in turn had to await a satisfactory resolution of the northern sovereignty crisis. Between November 1968 and April 1970, this issue pushed other bilateral matters into the background.

NOTES

1. AMOCO Canada Petroleum Limited
   Ashland Oil Canada Ltd.
   Atlantic Richfield Canada Ltd.
   BP Oil Ltd.
   Cities Service Company
   Elf Oil Exploration and Production Canada Ltd.
   Gulf Oil Canada Ltd.
   Hudson's Bay Oil and Gas Company Ltd.
   Imperial Oil Limited
   Interprovincial Pipeline Ltd.
   Mobil Oil Canada Limited
   Shell Canada Limited
   Standard Oil Company and British Columbia Limited
   Texaco Inc.
   Trans Mountain Oil Pipe Line Company
   TransCanada Pipelines Ltd.

2. Imperial Oil, *Annual Report*, 1973, *Financial Post*, "Survey of Oils," 1974.

3. President Nixon's *Task Force on Oil* reported in February, 1970.

CHAPTER FOUR
Northern Sovereignty

Northern sovereignty provoked the most serious confrontation between Ottawa and Washington since the nuclear arms issue of the Diefenbaker years. It was very sharp; it got the relationship between Trudeau and Nixon off to a bad start. Finally it became acrimonious. The American challenge to Canadian sovereignty in the North, 1968-70, precipitated an increased awareness in Ottawa of the extent of Canadian dependence on the United States, as well as Washington's use of that dependence as a weapon in relations with Canada.

The Canadian Government had encountered previous threats in the North, primarily from the United States. But the multidimensional character of the 1968-70 challenge gave it a unique flavour. Never before had the interrelationships between jurisdictional questions and economic relations been as complex. Previous challenges. had occurred before Canada had been as fully integrated into the American economy. Now, however, the sovereignty debate carried on within the federal Government in 1968 and 1970 could not be confined to questions of jurisdiction. Rather, the intense internal discussions culminating in the decision to retain control of Panarctic Oils, the enactment by Parliament of the Arctic Waters Pollution Prevention Act, and the extension of the territorial sea to twelve miles, revealed the intimate association of the sovereignty, economic, trade, and energy aspects of Canadian-United States relations.

1. ECONOMIC SOVEREIGNTY — PANARCTIC OILS

It can be safely argued that the Northern Economic Development Branch of Indian Affairs and Northern Development has never been distinguished by excessive nationalism. In the promotion of economic activity in the North to 1968, foreign capital had been eagerly sought out and welcomed. Nevertheless, as concern about the S.S. *Manhattan* and its implications for Canadian sovereignty mounted, senior officials increasingly worried about the foreign ownership on the northern mainland and Arctic islands that threatened to overwhelm a significant Canadian presence in the Arctic. Following the Alaska strike, oil and gas land permit-taking spread like wildfire on the Canadian side. By August 1969, 400.4 million acres had been obtained by 276 companies and individuals, over 75 per cent of all sedimentary areas in the North. A year earlier only 189.9 million acres had been under permit.

Using a criterion of 50 per cent ownership of common shares, the Northern Economic Development Branch of Indian Affairs and Northern Development estimated that Canadians controlled 15.5 per cent of lands leased on the mainland and 30.9 per cent of total land areas. In contrast, American companies and individuals had obtained leases on 50.7 per cent of total potential oil and gas producing areas. No less than 64.9 per cent of the mainland, particularly the Mackenzie Delta, and 45.5 per cent of all marine area leases were American controlled. Officials of the Task Force on Northern Oil Development were alarmed and concluded that the relatively slight Canadian presence in this sensitive resource bearing area was dangerous. A *de facto* loss of sovereignty was a possibility that had to be faced.

Finally, and perhaps of greatest importance, the Task Force debated the question of foreign ownership itself. Should further land alienation be temporarily halted in light of Ottawa's concern over foreign activity? Should Ottawa demand 51 per cent Canadian ownership of northern permit-holding companies and individuals? The last question was raised in the Task Force, only to be dismissed as unrealistic and impractical. Most of the integrated oil companies were large permit-holders. The former possibility, however, was considered seriously during the land boom 1968-69, but it was rejected until 1970 when the most promising areas were already gone. Ottawa did not want to discourage exploration itself in the North. It did not want to appear anti-business, and discourage risk capital. The difficulty, given this preference, was doing anything substantive to ease the problem which "excessive" foreign ownership created.

Fortunately, the Task Force did have one lever for the assertion of Canadian control, without discriminating between Canadian-owned and foreign companies. This was Panarctic Oils of Calgary, in which the federal Government had purchased a 45 per cent equity participation in 1966. With a controlling interest, Ottawa had a ready-made policy instrument to offset somewhat the foreign control of oil and gas lands in the North.

The federal involvement in Panarctic Oils originally had nothing to do with this objective. Rather, it was a rescue operation for private developers on the edge of collapse in their northern operations during the lean years of the early and mid-1960s. In this period, business did not enter the North as rapidly as Diefenbaker had anticipated. By the mid-1960s, oil and gas exploration in the Arctic remained in the doldrums, despite the Canada Oil and Gas Land Regulations. Acreage under permit to 1968 included less than a quarter of the geo-physically attractive land and offshore areas. Not until 1964 did serious work begin in the Mackenzie Delta, where Imperial Oil, Shell Oil, and British-American Oil placed a first well on Richards Island by 1966.

Four years earlier, Canadian Superior and Texaco initiated activity some 100 miles northeast of the Delta at Liverpool Bay. Seismic work aside, only two wells were drilled in Canada's entire northern coastal plain prior to 1968.[1]

The situation was even worse in the Arctic islands. After an initial rush to pick up Arctic oil rights with the release of land in 1959, exploration activity in the islands by 1964 was in deep trouble. There appeared to be a real possibility of its closing down altogether. A Calgary geologist and promoter, Dr. J. C. Sproule, whose extensive experience in the Arctic convinced him of the potential of the area, set about to attract government support to rescue existing permit-holders. Many were small Canadian companies with limited financial reserves; Sproule argued that to survive they should pool their acreage and launch an ambitious exploration program. To the Government he stressed the need for assistance in raising money.

On the first score he was successful in forming Panarctic Oils

Ltd. of Calgary, which acquired 44,137,577 acres of oil and gas permits in the Arctic islands from 75 companies and individuals. He also won a new incentive scheme in Ottawa, the Northern Mineral Exploration Programme, whereby the Government would lend to Canadians unable to write-off exploration expenditures for tax purposes, up to 40 per cent of approved exploration costs in the North, repayable after commercial production began.

Three wells were drilled, at Winter Harbour, Bathurst Island, and Cornwallis Island at a cost of $ 10.5 million. The new group was then, however, at the end of its funds, despite the new 1966 grant programme to qualified Canadian corporations and individuals. "Lest this unique exploratory assault for oil in the Arctic Islands should founder because of insufficient interest and financial support from oil and gas and mining companies," Indian Affairs and Northern Development under the leadership of Arthur Laing, persuaded the Cabinet in 1966 to buy into the project with $ 9 million for a 45 per cent interest and keep it afloat. Twenty private companies put up $ 11 million for the remaining 55 per cent. It was the humble birth of Ottawa's controlling interest in Panarctic Oils Ltd., a reflection of the consensus among senior officials that an economic breakthrough in the North was still far away.

Now that the Arctic appeared promising all that changed. With between 60 and 80 million acres under permit, a large Canadian-controlled operation was actually in place in the Arctic Islands. Senior officials argued that the public interest demanded that the federal Government maintain its 45 per cent equity in the operation to retain control and prevent its falling into foreign hands.

Panarctic represents a positive approach to ensure a high Canadian content . . . .(it serves) to demonstrate an effective occupation of Canada's frontier and affords further protection of Canada's sovereignty of the land area, and indirectly at least a related jurisdiction over the marine routes, albeit under ice cover for most of the year.[2]

In late 1969, Panarctic Oils' decision to expand its exploration programme confronted Ottawa with the option of maintaining or abandoning control of the operation.

The following chart illustrates the importance of this decision for exploration work in the Arctic islands. Under Assumption 2, in

LAND PERMITTED FOR OIL AND GAS EXPLORATION, BY AREAS BY CONTROLLING COUNTRY
(50% resident membership of common shares issued and outstanding)

Controlling Country	Assumption 1 Acres	%	Assumption 2 Acres	%
Canada				
Mainland	22.3	15.5	22.3	15.5
Arctic Islands	96.9	41.7	67.5	29.1
Marine	4.5	18.4	4.5	18.4
Total	**123.7**	**30.9**	**94.3**	**23.6**
United States				
Mainland	93.4	64.9	93.4	64.9
Arctic Islands	98.4	42.4	111.7	48.1
Marine	11.1	45.5	11.1	45.5
Total	**202.9**	**50.7**	**216.2**	**54.0**
United Kingdom				
Mainland	8.9	6.2	8.9	6.2
Arctic Islands	9.8	4.2	21.7	9.3
Marine	0.5	2.1	0.5	2.1
Total	**19.2**	**4.8**	**31.1**	**7.8**
France				
Mainland	7.6	5.3	7.6	5.3
Arctic Islands	20.9	9.0	23.5	10.1
Marine	0.3	1.2	0.3	1.2
Total	**28.8**	**7.2**	**31.4**	**7.8**

Source: CALURA, 1969

which the federal Government would terminate its participation in Panarctic Oils, land held by Canadian companies and individuals in the Arctic islands would drop from 96.9 to 67.5 million acres, lowering the percentage to 29.1 from 41.7. On the mainland and in marine areas, the funding made no difference; but the Task Force argued that the situation on the Arctic islands was critical. 41.7 per cent was almost equal to American-controlled lands and Canada had no option but to take the risk. Officials noted that some large integrated companies such as Shell and Fina also had direct involvement with their Governments and that Cabinet's action would not alarm industry. The Department of Indian Affairs and Northern Development, whose Deputy Minister sat as a Director on Panarctic's Board, pleaded for rapid Cabinet action.

Nearing the climax of Canadian-American confrontation over northern sovereignty, the Cabinet was persuaded not to abandon supporting evidence of effective occupation. On January 22, 1970, it approved increased funding to retain a controlling interest in the enterprise.[3]

2. THE DIPLOMATIC CONFRONTATION

The Panarctic decision, important though it was, was only one event in a growing drama in the Capital. The difficulties in dealing with Washington on the question of northern sovereignty increasingly consumed the attention of the Department of External Affairs throughout 1969. In the midst of a massive reorganization itself, and with new leaders in both countries, it made a first and unsuccessful attempt to downgrade the issue diplomatically. By achieving the correct level of participation in the 1969 S.S. *Manhattan* voyage; by calming Canadian public opinion; and by coordinating increased activities in the North to dramatize Canadian ownership and effective occupation, External Affairs hoped to avoid bilateral talks with Washington altogether and to avoid also the necessity to speak on the issue in the House of Commons. A major airing of the question in Parliament was likely to be messy.[4]

A blind eye was turned to the U.S. State Department's diplomatic snub — its refusal to request permission from the Canadian Government for American icebreaker support in

Canadian northern waters. Instead Ottawa decided to treat "working relationships" with the American Coast Guard as the equivalent of such official permission.

It therefore took the initiative in suggesting that Coast Guard vessels of both countries accompany the S.S. *Manhattan* in northern waters, both in Canada and in Alaska. Such joint arrangements involving both the oil companies and the two Governments would make it difficult for the United States to refuse cooperation and might avoid a confrontation. Since the oil companies at least had approached Ottawa, this partial solution might offer a basis for future cooperation; it could be taken as a recognition of Canadian jurisdiction and just possibly might prepare a basis for future cooperation with Washington. When, later, Mitchell Sharp indicated that Canada had "concurred and cooperated throughout" in the *Manhattan* experiment, he was referring only to these measures taken unilaterally in Ottawa in response to American unwillingness to cooperate with Canada.[5]

For its part, the Task Force on Northern Oil Development recommended in its first *Memo* to Cabinet a series of measures, symbolic and substantive, to reinforce Canadian claims. The Department of Transport was to cooperate as fully as possible in the S.S. *Manhattan* trials; the Canadian Coast Guard icebreaker, the *John A. Macdonald*, was detailed to provide support for the ice-strengthened tanker. The Governor-General found himself touring the eastern and central Arctic April 22 — May 4, 1969.

Second, the Task Force strongly recommended that Canada immediately initiate a polar ice-breaker programme to maintain a superior capability in Arctic waters, even though the American icebreaker *Northwind*, accompanying the S.S. *Manhattan* was an unimpressive vessel (and in fact failed dismally). Unless Ottawa demonstrated its commitment to uphold Canadian jurisdiction in the Arctic it would encourage another challenge when fortune might not favour Canada. The question was not *whether* to build polar ice-breakers — it was *how many*.

Third, the Task Force recommended an immediate stepping-up in the activities of the major Departments active in the North, particularly Indian Affairs and Northern Development, Transport, and Defence. These programmes should ensure Canadian control of resupply bases and operations, as well as a Canadian-designed and operated navigational and surveillance system. All DEW line bases should be returned to Canadian control, and close surveillance maintained over foreign activities in Arctic areas.

Until May, 1969, External Affairs still hoped that the voyage of the S.S. *Manhattan* might pass without a major Canadian-American incident. It hoped that the American State Department might come around to recognizing Canadian jurisdiction in Arctic waters and that the working relationships between the two Coast Guards and between the oil companies and Washington would protect Canada's position in the North. But by the end of April the implications for Canada and for Canadian sovereignty of oil developments in Alaska were increasingly clarified as the American State Department steadfastly refused to provide this recognition and as public concern mounted both in the press and in the House of Commons. Sooner or later a statement from the Prime Minister had to be made and on May 15, 1969, Prime Minister Trudeau outlined the Canadian position. His statement has continued to provide a touchstone for Canadian policy on sovereignty in the North.

First, the speech attempted to clarify for the House the term "Arctic sovereignty" as if to provide background information on the subject to members of Parliament. In fact, Trudeau's speech was a closely studied document which was meant for Washington as well as for public consumption. It asserted that Canadian sovereignty over the mainland as well as the islands of the Canadian Arctic was well established and that there was "no dispute concerning this matter." Publicly the United States had not accepted this position, and American negotiators were rumoured to have raised it at the Ditchely Draft Conference on the law of the sea in 1971. Trudeau now nailed down the claim in Parliament. Second, Trudeau unequivocally asserted Canada's exclusive sovereign rights to explore and exploit the resources of the Arctic Continental Shelf. As he pointed out:

> Canada's sovereign rights over the Continental Shelf in the Arctic follow from Canada's sovereignty over the adjacent lands, and again there is no dispute on this matter. No country has asserted a competing claim to the resources in question; no country has challenged Canada's claim on any other basis and none can do so under international law. Foreign companies carrying out exploration activities on the Continental Shelf in

Canada's Arctic areas operate under Canadian permit and licence and in so doing expressly recognize Canada's sovereign rights.[6]

The next section of Trudeau's speech, however, was ambiguous and implied the real issue in question as a result of the voyage of the S.S. *Manhattan*. This concerned the Canadian position on the waters between the islands of Canada's Arctic Archipelago. The Prime Minister repeated the Diefenbaker Government's contention that Arctic waters were "our own." But then, crucially, he detracted from the force of that position by adding that "not all countries would accept the view that the waters between the Islands of the Archipelago are internal waters over which Canada has full sovereignty." Indeed, by going on to indicate the nature of the disagreement, the Prime Minister appeared to retreat from the earlier position, but also to provide an opening for a challenge:

The contrary view is indeed that Canada's sovereignty extends only to the territorial sea around each island. The Law of the Sea is a complex subject, which . . . may give rise to differences of opinion. Such differences, of course, would have to be settled not on an arbitrary basis but with due regard for established principles of international law.[7]

Trudeau's extended elaboration of the northern sovereignty issue, and his apparent determination to clarify issues puzzled both the leader of the opposition as well as T. C. Douglas of the New Democratic Party not least since the remainder of the speech went on to indicate Canada's concurrence and interest in the *Manhattan* project as well as the importance for Canada of the development of Arctic navigation. Indeed, the speech gave every indication that the United States and Canada were at one in the planning of the project:

. . . For these reasons the Canadian Government has welcomed the *Manhattan* exercise, has concurred in it and will participate in it. The oil companies concerned and the United States Coast Guard have consulted with appropriate Canadian authorities in the planning of the operation . . . .the government has also selected and appointed an official Canadian Government representative on board the S.S. *Manhattan* who will act as technical advisor and as a coordinator of Canadian support for the operation.[8]

Stanfield and Douglas sensed correctly that Trudeau was protesting too much about the value to Canada of the projected *Manhattan* trials. Why did Trudeau not simply reassert what was understood to be the earlier position? Stanfield urged the Prime Minister to be more forthright. He was disturbed by:

the manner in which the Prime Minister seems to have abandoned the position taken by previous Governments with regard to the assertion of our sovereignty.

And Douglas commented in a perceptive statement,

It seems to me that if the Canadian Government leaves this matter in an indefinite state we are almost inviting someone else to suggest that we do not have jurisdiction, and that this is a question upon which we are prepared to compromise. I think the Canadian Government ought to make its position clear beyond any shadow of doubt.[9]

It is unfortunate that Prime Minister Trudeau did not square with Parliament; or at least that one of his officials did not leak the facts to the press. However regrettable, selective leaks in matters of national importance help keep the public abreast of events. They also keep a government honest.

Actually, the decision to deceive the public was taken following a *Globe and Mail* article of February 26, 1969 that quite wrongly asserted that Canadian sovereignty would not be challenged by Washington in the North.

It was a hard choice. Canadian public opinion was aroused and would demand strong action if the facts of the situation were released. Pressure for a formal declaration of sovereignty was already apparent in the House of Commons Standing Committee on Indian Affairs and Northern Development. The Canadian public had long believed that the waters and ice between the Arctic islands were Canadian. It would not tolerate compromise if Washington's intentions and objectives were clarified.

In short, Ottawa's freedom of action would be curbed; its hand forced. The Government believed that the public mood was irresponsible and had to be contained. The only way to accomplish this goal, distasteful to be sure, was to deceive Canadians. The existence of a challenge was denied; the tone struck by the *Globe and Mail* was declared official policy.

Tailor-made answers to possible questions in Parliament on the subject resulting from the *Globe and Mail* article, prepared the following day, Feb. 27, 1969, by senior officials' for the guidance of Mitchell Sharp document this lamentable decision. Specifically the Minister was to indicate that "there is no foundation for the suggestion that the U.S. Government is challenging Canadian sovereignty in connection with these trials".

Ottawa's decision not to acquaint the Canadian public and Parliament with the fact of an explicit United States challenge was disastrously short-sighted. Eventually the truth must come out; political pain rarely diminishes with time. If there ever were a time for a clear statement of the national interest, the sovereignty crisis was one. Enclosing northern waters as internal Canadian waters with a formal declaration of sovereignty in Parliament would have clarified the status of the North once and for all. It would have defined it as a national security zone, recognizing its historic and geographic unity with the rest of Canada.

Of course the Canadian case was not iron-clad; External Affairs had frittered away opportunities for firming up northern sovereignty. A statement of the Hon. A. Hamilton before the House Standing Committee on Mines, Forests and Waters in 1958 represented a commitment to Canadian sovereignty over Arctic waters, and the Trudeau government fell back on it to bolster its case in communications with Washington:

> The area to the north of Canada, including the islands and waters between the islands and areas beyond, are looked upon as our own, and there is no doubt in the minds of this government, nor do I think in the minds of former governments of Canada, that this is national terrain.

Senior officials were also aware of the apparent determination of Pearson in 1963-64 to enclose the islands of the Canadian Archipelago with baselines using the Norwegian Fisheries case of 1951 as a precedent. Briefing material sent to External Affairs in August, 1969, to the relevant Departments described Pearson's approach to the American State Department; the latter's heated opposition to the move which might give Indonesia or the

Philippines similar ideas; and Pearson's decision to withdraw the move *providing* the United States would agree to finalize a policy position on outstanding Law of the Sea questions on the east and west coasts. The North was not then on the boil, so it had a much lower priority.

But the 1958 statement could be countered by other contradictory official comments; reputable international lawyers agreed that Canadian sovereignty over the mainland and Arctic islands, as well as jurisdiction over the continental shelf, was not in doubt, but that the status of the waters between the islands was far from clear. While Pearson's 1963-64 approach would have been accepted by the international community before 1968, given the relative economic unimportance of the North at that time, the situation had now been revolutionized by resource and transportation technology. By the same token, senior officials in Ottawa were divided: one group felt Canada would betray an earlier position if it did not adopt the Pearson strategy; the other that Canada could retreat because Pearson's position had not been tested or accepted as official policy. The same difference of opinion was revealed in the Cabinet and within the Liberal Party caucus.

Timidity, the Canadian curse, won out easily in Ottawa. This was the real significance of withholding the reality of an American challenge. Predictably timidity was the wrong approach.

Ottawa's hesitation to acquaint the Canadian public and Parliament with the true facts of the situation from the outset indicated to Washington that Ottawa was willing to compromise. The critical time to act was at the very beginning; by not acting, Canada's fear of the United States was underlined. Every country encounters situations in which it must stand firm; if it does not it loses respect among the nations. Northern sovereignty for Canada represented a core objective. Pearson had considered it reasonable even during the 1960s, a period of slow activity in the North. Now, with the breakthrough following the Alaskan discoveries in 1968, it was of much greater significance. But the Government backed off, as Pearson had done earlier, in the face of American opposition. Similarly, the Government did not even use the option of a formal declaration of sovereignty as a bargaining lever in communications with the American State Department following Trudeau's May 15, 1969 speech to the House of Commons.

Having presented a formal statement to the House of Commons, it was now incumbent upon the Department of External Affairs to communicate directly with the American Embassy. In June 1969 it set out the official Canadian position on the question of northern sovereignty, substantially repeating the line of argument adopted in the Prime Minister's comments. It explicitly underlined the Canadian view that the status of Canadian jurisdiction over the waters of the Arctic Archipelago was not affected by the *Manhattan* project. And in repeating Trudeau's sentiment about the mutually beneficial effects of the project it looked forward to a happy future of American-Canadian cooperation. The thrust of the Note was to avoid any indication that Canada had perceived any American State Department actions which could be construed as questioning Canadian sovereignty. Rather, it stressed the complementarity of Canadian and international responsibility and the Canadian determination to support scientific research and oil and gas exploration. However, on the important issue, the jurisdiction of the Northwest Passage and the waters between the islands, the Canadian Note merely repeated the 1958 position implying Canadian sovereignty but not stating it. However, the Note apparently went further than the Prime Minister's statement to Parliament in including a statement to the effect that Canada had inevitably the greatest interest in Arctic waters in the Northwest Passage, given historic, geographic, climatic, and economic factors. Nevertheless, by only implying rather than stating Canada's determination to uphold the 1958 statement and to declare sovereignty, it provided the State Department with a lever to pry open the Canadian position.

Having sent the Note, the senior officials waited anxiously for a reply, hoping that none would be received. It should be underlined that there is no evidence that Ottawa to this point had received an explicit threat from Washington. External Affairs' invitation to retreat was anticipatory based on fear and misgiving.

Unhappily for the Department of External Affairs, the American response was both clear and uncompromising. The State Department, while recognizing the Canadian claim to sovereignty over the Arctic islands and mainland, and the sovereign rights of coastal states over the Continental Shelf for purposes of exploration and exploitation of natural resources, refused to recognize Canadian jurisdiction beyond the three-mile limit. Thus it took precisely the position that Trudeau had invited in his May

15 speech. To Washington, the general principles of international Law of the Sea, including the right of innocent passage and freedom of the high seas, applied to the Arctic water areas. Washington could not accept Canadian pretensions that the waters between the islands were internal or territorial waters. The latter applied only within the three-mile limit, and the United States would insist on the right of unrestricted passage through channels in the Northwest Passage even within such territorial waters. The Northwest Passage was an international strait with total freedom of navigation, and the United States would consider any unilateral extension of maritime jurisdiction as prejudicial to its interest.[10]

The American reply indicated beyond a shadow of a doubt that the United States was prepared for a confrontation over the status of the Arctic waters. The ball was now, clearly, in Ottawa's court. Canada was confronted by the worst of both worlds: though it had thrown away a strong bargaining position it would face retaliation anyway. External Affairs groped for a position but could not agree on the substance of a reply.

3. COMPROMISE — THE ARCTIC WATERS POLLUTION PREVENTION ACT

Accepting the actual loss of Canadian jurisdiction in the high Arctic — whether over the territorial land mass, the islands, or the waters surrounding the Arctic islands — was perceived by both senior officials and the leaders of all political parties as intolerable and a certain defeat for the Government in office. Having decided to reject the Pearson position, the Government nevertheless realized that a formula to extend limited Canadian jurisdiction over the Northwest Passage and Arctic waters had to be found.

It boiled down in the end to a choice between a "Canadian" or a "North American" Arctic. Canada could not avoid this painful decision. External Affairs would have to weigh the costs and benefits of the various options and then unilaterally declare the one that was least objectionable to the State Department. Ottawa had to expect American retaliation, but it could perhaps limit it by adopting an approach which might obtain at least partial agreement or sympathy in Washington. Controversy raged within the Government as to the most palatable strategy to attain minimal objectives.

By the end of 1969, senior officials from other Departments, the Canadian public, and Parliament were becoming increasingly concerned by the failure of External Affairs to articulate a coherent Canadian position.

By January, 1970, it became clear that the issue would have to be resolved quickly to get the media off the subject and to accommodate an aroused Canadian public. The Department's position, resting on the advice of its legal affairs division, centred on the extension of the territorial sea to twelve miles. Limiting the initiative to one simple, yet significant, step appeared to have distinct advantages. First, it involved a simple amendment to the Territorial Sea and Fishing Force Act; no major new legislation would be required. Second a twelve rather than three mile territorial sea would consolidate the Canadian position over Barrow and Prince of Wales Straits in the Northwest Passage. Early in 1969 External Affairs had come to appreciate that these narrow straits were the key to the Northwest Passage and that, therefore, they must be the first target of Canadian legislation. Third, a twelve mile territorial sea was increasingly accepted in the international community; the United States retained a three mile limit but it could not oppose a Canadian move in that direction without similarly opposing a great many respected fellow coastal states.

It was taken for granted in Ottawa that the United States nevertheless would insist that "international" straits were not affected by an extension of the territorial sea; that Canada could not alter the international character of such straits by overlapping the channels with bands of territorial waters. But this was the fourth advantage: however the Americans might protest they could not bring the issue before the International Court, and it would not therefore be necessary to introduce a reservation withdrawing the legislation from the Court's jurisdiction. To those schooled in the Pearson tradition, the introduction of a reservation before the International Court represented a break with the past, a step not taken lightly.

The Department of External Affairs, however, encountered opposition to this strategy within the Privy Council Office and among Prime Minister Trudeau's advisors. Flushed by their new sense of importance under Trudeau the latter opposed such a plan on the grounds that the United States would be more willing to accept anti-pollution legislation as a device for protecting Canadian jurisdiction than the extension of the territorial sea.

Anti-pollution legislation was obviously attractive given the notoriety of recent tanker disasters such as the *Torrey Canyon* espisode. The Department of Fisheries and Forestry, as well as Indian Affairs and Northern Development were interested in promoting Arctic anti-pollution legislation, and actually had a draft of such legislation available. Such a tactic would have the advantage of world-wide popularity, and it would be an easy way to avoid public debate on the sovereignty issue itself. A favourable response could also be predicted from the more enlightened and influential segments of the American media and public opinion.[11]

The Canadian position, therefore, sought to steer a middle course which was functional and regulatory, in which jurisdiction was claimed for achieving specific purposes. The Arctic Waters Pollution Prevention Act, in explicitly rejecting a claim to sovereignty over Arctic waters, was to soften the blow for Washington. Ottawa could claim that the functional approach adopted for the North was a logical development of Canadian foreign policy; that it rejected a selfish acquisitive approach; and that it was in broad agreement with similar American initiatives in the past. Trudeau's group, for example, did not think that the United States would challenge anti-pollution legislation before the International Court. It felt strongly that tanker disasters, most recently at Chedubucto Bay in Nova Scotia where the *Arrow* ran aground in February 1970, were sufficiently eloquent.

The crunch came with the second S.S. *Manhattan* voyage in early summer of 1970. With Parliament and the press demanding a response, and with two strategies in conflict at the highest level, Trudeau chose both. Two bills, comprising amendments to the Territorial Sea and Fishing Force Act extending the Territorial Sea to twelve miles, and the Arctic Waters Pollution Prevention Act, were rushed before the House of Commons on April 8, 1970.

As in his speech of May 15, 1969 concerning the voyage of the S.S. *Manhattan*, so also in April 1970, Prime Minister Trudeau told the House of Commons that the proposed legislation, particularly the anti-pollution legislation, was based on the right of coastal states such as Canada to protect themselves against "grave threats to their environment" since existing international law did not adequately recognize the need of such states to protect themselves against irrevocable dangers posed by new developments in transportation technology.[12] He recognized that the legislation represented a unilateral initiative by Canada in that commercially-owned shipping would be subject to Canadian construction and navigation safety standards within zones extending up to one hundred miles off-shore. The protective measures were also to apply to the exploration and exploitation of the submarine resources of Canada's northern Continental Shelf.

However, Canada's action, though unilaterial, was not to be seen as contrary to international law; the legislation was merely an attempt to assist in the development of new concepts in international law and he specifically referred to the September 28, 1945 Truman Proclamation on the Continental Shelf. There was no question that Truman had acted unilaterally; there was also no doubt that it had been rapidly accepted and established in international law. The Canadian 1970 position therefore was firmly based on what might be termed the "American" approach to jurisdictional questions.

4. THE AMERICAN RESPONSE

The Department of External Affairs was well aware of the likely target of retaliation by Washington — restrictions on American imports of Canadian oil. Nixon's Task Force on Oil Policy, established in February, 1969 to review the oil import programme, had recommended cutting back oil imports to 615,000 barrels a day effective July 1, 1970 pending State Department negotiations regarding "measures looking toward a freer exchange of petroleum, natural gas and other energy resources between the two countries." The sovereignty issue could only exacerbate friction between the two countries which had been developing around the energy issue for years, and which Nixon's Task Force had explicitly linked to a continental energy policy.[13]

In these circumstances, External Affairs was torn between a desire to initiate discussions immediately to try to ease the crisis, and a wish to respond to an American initiative and therefore to appear reactive and defensive rather than aggressive. In early 1970, events moved quickly toward a climax, but External Affairs was paralyzed. They drafted a Note to deliver to the American Embassy, but they could not agree about *when* to deliver it.

The mounting pressure in Parliament and from the public for action was not lost on Washington. By the first week of March, the American Embassy in Ottawa knew informally that Canada would go ahead with legislation to "extend Canadian jurisdiction." Still there was no diplomatic Note informing the State Department of this decision.

On March 10, 1970, President Nixon now solved the problem in characteristic fashion. Convinced in any case that imports of oil from Canada should be linked with a continental energy policy, he brought the issue into action against the Trudeau Government's impending announcement to Parliament and the proposed legislation concerning northern sovereignty.

He announced a new and extraordinarily low limit of 395,000 barrels a day on Canadian oil imports for the period March 1 to December 31, 1970. A week later, Nixon telephoned Trudeau to indicate the likelihood of further retaliation should Canada go ahead with the anti-pollution legislation and the extension of the territorial sea to twelve miles. He was furious that Canadian public opinion was persuading Ottawa to adopt "uncooperative" measures, and that Canada was trying to spring something on the United States without adequate consultation.[14]

In his conversation with Trudeau, Nixon had indicated his intention to dispatch immediately a high level American team to Ottawa to clarify respective positions in the light of March developments. It arrived at 10:20 in the morning of March 20, 1970, and remained locked in frustrating debate with its Canadian counterpart until 7:30 that evening. Mr. E. Ritchie, Undersecretary of State for External Affairs, headed up the Canadian contingent of senior officials from the Departments most clearly affected. The Hon. M. Sharp was also present.

The Americans were firmly negative, indicating that such action by Canada would be taken as a precedent by other nations for a similar unilateral extension of territorial sovereignty and that they constituted a serious blow not only to American but also to Canadian security because of the restrictive effect such measures had on the movement of United States naval vessels. For their part, the Canadians outlined the nature and extent of political pressure in Canada together with commitments to Parliament and indicated that they had no option but to proceed under these circumstances. They reiterated the numerous occasions on which Washington had acted unilaterally in far more grave and legally precarious situations. Equally however the Canadians underlined their country's commitment to cooperate with the United States.

The American delegation's reply, however, remained negative. It shared the Canadian concern for domestic political pressure but the apparent Canadian strategy of "creeping sovereignty" could not be tolerated. Ottawa's actions were illegal and unacceptable and would result in serious economic and security problems for the United States around the world. Washington would not only refuse to acquiesce in an assertion of Canadian jurisdiction over Arctic waters, it would also take whatever lawful and "appropriate" steps it considered necessary to protect its position in these matters. The American team urged Canada to delay any legislation preparatory to an International Conference regarding Arctic problems of common concern to both Canada and the United States. It recommended that the International Joint Commission draw up an interim bilateral agreement pending a multi-lateral convention dealing with Arctic pollution and navigation. Indeed it invited Canada to join with the United States and the USSR in reaching a world-wide agreement on the breadth of the territorial sea, rights of passage in international straits, and the fishing rights of coastal powers.

They reiterated their objection to the extension to twelve miles of the territorial sea. Any interference with the freedom of passage through the straits of the Northwest Passage, even those no wider than three miles, was considered intolerable. While the implementation of pollution control to a twelve-mile limit would be considered satisfactory, the enforcement of anti-pollution legislation to a limit of one hundred miles was not. But even within such a twelve-mile zone of pollution control, the United States demanded full freedom of shipping in the case of international straits.[15]

After extensive discussions, the Canadians proposed a compromise which would involve the legislation then in the hands of the Cabinet going forward but with a series of agreements which would help avoid an impasse in the Arctic over anti-pollution legislation (such as the restriction of the legislation to cargo-carrying rather than naval vessels). But Ottawa was not successful in gaining American acquiescence to Canadian jurisdictional claims. Official American statements maintained their opposition to the assertion of Canadian control over the straits of the Northwest Passage, and to the Arctic Waters Pollution Prevention Act. Meanwhile, the Arctic sovereignty issue deeply affected Canadian resource policy in the North and related aspects of Canadian-American trade relations.

NOTES

1. *Oilweek*, September 30, 1968.
2. E. Gray, *The Great Canadian Oil Patch*, Maclean-Hunter, pp. 237 ff.; House of Commons, *Debates*, February 25, 28, 1967; Toronto *Globe & Mail*, February 5, 1970; Department of Indian Affairs and Northern Development, Report, 1967-68, Ottawa.
3. House of Commons, *Debates*, February 4, 1970. The 45 per cent share was maintained by increasing the federal commitment to $22.5 from $19 million.
4. Much information for this chapter has been compiled from interviews with officials in Ottawa and Washington. They will not be identified individually.
5. Toronto *Globe and Mail*, September 18, 1969.
6. House of Commons, *Debates*, May 15, 1969, pp. 8720-21.
7. *Ibid.*, p. 8721.
8. *Ibid.*
9. *Ibid.*
10. This theme has been repeatedly underlined by American authorities, reflecting the strategic and maritime interests of a Great Power.
11. Little research had actually been done on the environmental hazards of northern ecosystems. This proved embarrassing in negotiations with the United States. Compare with Ottawa's abortive intervention against the trans-Alaska pipeline in 1972. Again, Canadian officials had no hard data confirming their assumption that a Mackenzie oil pipeline was less harmful that the Alaska route to the northern environment.
12. The specific points of the legislation have been discussed at length elsewhere and will not be repeated here. R. B. Bilder,

"The Canadian Arctic Waters Pollution Prevention Act,"
Michigan Law Review, Vol. 69, 1970-71; J. A. Beesley, "The
Canadian Approach to International Environment Law,"
The Canadian Yearbook of International Law, Vol. 11,
1973; W.V. O'Brien and A. C. Chapelli, "The Law of the Sea
in the 'Canadian Arctic': The Pattern of Controversy," (Part
One), *McGill Law Journal,* Vol. 19, No. 3, 1973; (Part Two),
Ibid., Vol. 19, No. 4, 1973.

13. See Gordon Cleveland, *The Last Post,* Vol. 1, No. 3, pp. 11-
18, for a spirited analysis of Canadian oil developments at the
close of the 1960's. See also Shaffer, *op. cit.*

14. Compare American consultation with Canada in regard to
Washington's unilateral rejection of the financial recover-
ability principle in toll policy on the St. Lawrence Seaway.

15. U.S.A. Senate Sub-Committee on Coastal Guard and Navigation Hearings on U.S.C.D. Appropriations, 92nd Congress,
1st Session, 30 March 1971, provides a useful review of the
American position in the aftermath of the April 1970
legislation.

CHAPTER FIVE
Northern Pipelines

The major initiative of April 1970, protecting Canadian jurisdiction in the North, produced shockwaves in Canadian-American relations. President Nixon had threatened "serious trouble" should the legislation be introduced into Parliament. He had demonstrated Canada's vulnerability in trade relations. He was enraged personally by Prime Minister Trudeau's handling of the crisis. The issue was extremely sensitive, particularly in the months immediately following the Arctic Waters Pollution Prevention Act, and the extension of the territorial sea to twelve miles. After April 1970, therefore, Ottawa officials turned their attention to repairing the damage to Canadian-American relations caused by the sovereignty crisis.

Fortunately, much heat went out of the controversy when it became increasingly clear that the oil companies preferred pipelines to tankers for the transportation of Alaskan oil to markets in the continental United States.[1] While Arctic marine transportation would definitely increase in the future, the S.S. *Manhattan* trials had revealed serious problems confronting commercial traffic through the Northwest Passage from the Alaskan North Slope. Since no immediate repetition of the 1968-70 sovereignty crisis was likely to occur, Ottawa had an opportunity to catch its breath. A further American challenge could be expected at some future date but there was now an interval in which Ottawa could consolidate its position and develop policies to ensure a more effective presence in the Arctic.

The focus of the Canadian Government's immediate concern in

northern matters as they affected Canadian-American relations now turned to energy, trade, and pipeline policy. Here as well major decisions were required. First, the integrated oil companies were pressing for a firm government decision in principle on a Mackenzie gas pipeline. The purpose of the line would be the transportation of natural gas from Prudhoe Bay in Alaska to southern United States markets, and would be required soon after the oil fields came into production. American environmental law prohibited the flaring of natural gas. But if the gas were to be tapped and forced back into the formation to facilitate the oil flow, a production solution had to be found within a few years.

Second, applications for licenses to export 8.9 trillion cubic feet of natural gas to the United States were before the National Energy Board. The export of such an enormous volume of gas inevitably raised questions about Canadian reserves south of the 60th parallel and the wisdom of relying on much more expensive frontier supplies — if they existed at all. Both issues also raised major policy questions about their impact on Canadian-American relations since they would intensify the drift toward continental integration in the energy field.

The Task Force on Northern Oil Development as well as the Department of External Affairs perceived grave dangers in further straining relations with the Nixon administration or interest groups strongly supported in the American Congress. Canadian natural gas exports and the delivery of Alaskan natural gas to the American midwest market were two such major issue areas. Anxious not to provoke the United States again with "nationalist" policies, Cabinet approved the Northern Pipeline Guidelines in August 1970 and the export of 6.3 trillion cubic feet of natural gas in September. By November 1970 this action had cleared the air considerably in Canadian-American trade relations. Joint ministerial talks in Ottawa on oil policy produced a mutually satisfactory announcement:

> Arrangements should be worked out quickly to permit, in subsequent years, full and unimpeded access to U.S. oil markets for Canadian crude oil and petroleum products surplus to Canadian commercial and security requirements.[2]

These developments, in particular the approval of the Northern

Pipeline Guidelines, require detailed discussion given their far-reaching implications for the North and Canada as a whole.

1. THE PROBLEM OF APPROVAL IN PRINCIPLE OF NORTHERN PIPELINE GUIDELINES

Following the April 1970 legislation, senior officials on the Task Force on Northern Oil Development again faced a dilemma on northern pipeline construction. With the sovereignty crisis resolved, delays became more difficult to justify. Industry wanted more than guidance — it wanted a commitment. Much money was being allocated for research and engineering work on Mackenzie pipelines and industry expected as clear a statement as possible of Government intentions. The Alaskan experience had taught industry a lesson; the three oil companies involved had simply submitted a general route map, three soil sample sheets, and a $ 10.00 cheque to support their June 6, 1969 application for a right-of-way permit from Prudhoe Bay to Valdez, and had requested an answer before the end of July.[3] American pipelines had normally been built with this fast-action approach and it was not considered unusual to approach the trans-Alaskan system in the same manner in mid-1969. Less than a year later, after bitter experience and with the added complications of dealing with the Canadian Government, industry wanted to avoid another fiasco in the planning and construction of a pipeline system up the Mackenzie Valley from Alaska and the Mackenzie Delta.

But what kind of commitment could Canada give industry? The National Energy Board could not rule before a full application had been received; the Cabinet could only agree or disagree but not until the Energy Board had so ruled.[4] In theory at least, the Energy Board was a quasi-judicial body which heard evidence, studied applications for permits for pipeline rights-of-way with objectivity, and thereby determined the national interest within the terms of reference set out in the National Energy Board Act. Although in practice the National Energy Board collaborated closely with industry, and in the case of the Task Force on Northern Oil Development actually chaired the Pipeline Committee, it was essential for the Government to retain the fiction of National Energy Board impartiality for public consumption. Therefore Northern Pipeline Guidelines would be announced by the "policy" Departments — the Ministers of Energy, Mines and

Resources and Indian Affairs and Northern Development. The content of such guidelines would be extremely important for the development of a Mackenzie Corridor and would have the profoundest implications not only for the North but for the country as a whole.

Equally significant, however, would be the signal given to industry. Would Cabinet acceptance of Northern Pipeline Guidelines mean approval–in–principle? Second, how would approval-in-principle be interpreted by industry and senior officials on the Task Force on Northern Oil Development? What level of commitment would be involved in announcing Guidelines? These two questions were discussed at length in the Task Force.

On the first question all parties agreed that Northern Pipeline Guidelines represented approval-in-principle for the construction of a Mackenzie gas and/or oil pipeline. But the second issue, the nature of the commitment, was more complex and crucial as a determinant of Government-business collaboration in Canadian-American energy relations. A Mackenzie pipeline corridor would be the bell-weather of northern development as a whole. Ottawa's posture with the private sector on the Mackenzie would therefore set a precedent.

The Task Force recommended Cabinet approval-in-principle on the understanding shared with industry that it implied a far-reaching commitment to the Mackenzie Corridor. It simply will not do for the Departments of Energy, Mines and Resources, or Indian Affairs and Northern Development, to claim a different interpretation of approval-in-principle. Industry was assured (and it explicitly sought assurance on this point to minimize risks) such action by the Government of Canada implied "some pretty definite agreement that the system can and will be allowed to be used." The following aspects were involved in the decision:

a. *"Active" rather than "passive" promotion*: Cabinet acceptance of Northern Pipeline Guidelines would permit a new phase of industry-Government cooperation. Joint planning would proceed on the assumption of an early application approval and construction of the facility. The purpose of such planning would be to clear away outstanding technical problems and to answer *in advance* any adverse criticisms during National Energy Board hearings. It was particularly important to demonstrate that pipelines were the most effective mode of transportation for northern oil and natural gas. But it was not intended that other modes such as rail or air transportation alternatives would even be studied. The cover-up assignment was given to the Transport Committee of the Task Force.

b. *Collaboration with Industry*: the Guidelines would solidify relations between the Task Force and industry in all respects. They would now be "partners" in specific as well as general terms, gearing up together for the enormous task of constructing a Mackenzie pipeline and allocating specific jobs between the public and private sectors. A symbiotic relationship would emerge in which complete confidence and trust would replace a guarded reticence.

The central problem for the Task Force, apart from elaborating an acceptable regulatory structure, would be encouraging the competing groups — the Northwest Project Study Group; West Coast Transmission Co. Ltd; and the Gas Arctic Study Group — to pool their capital and expertise in a single consortium for the planning of a Mackenzie gas pipeline.[5]

c. *Timing*: the Northern Pipeline Guidelines of August 13, 1970 were based on the assumption that the schedule was tight. An application was expected in 1972 at the latest, perhaps earlier. Senior officials braced themselves for rapid action. This was hinted in the official announcement of the Guidelines on August 13:

"Knowledge of northern Canada's petroleum potential has been quickly expanding and major companies in the industry have publicly expressed interest in constructing pipelines. Some already have plans and research underway."[6]

d. *The Role of the National Energy Board*: the National Energy Board was expected to play an extremely important role in liaising with industry representatives and in finalizing the preparation of the application for rapid approval. Since the Pipeline Committee of the Task Force was the lynchpin of the operation and the inner core of industry—Government collaboration, the Energy Board, chairing that Committee, was at the centre of northern pipeline construction from the first. Few Canadians realized how doubtful a role this "independent" regulatory body played in northern policy-making at this time. Certainly Parliament remained unaware of the commitments entered into with the Northern Pipeline Guidelines of August 1970.

Approval-in-principle then was perceived by all members of the Task Force as a serious step indeed, from which the Government could not easily retreat later. A strategy of "passive" promotion had been recommended in the April 1970 *Memo* to Cabinet given the many unknowns confronting the construction and operation of a Mackenzie pipeline. So long as officials limited themselves to listening to promoters, perhaps even expressing interest, the Government was not compromised. But the moment that the Task Force changed its approach, and released to industry the conditions under which pipeline construction would be allowed in the North, industry had a commitment. For example, when Harvey Booth, President of Alberta and Southern Gas, presented a proposal in June 1970 to ministers and officials in Ottawa, the latter took great pains to ensure that he got no encouragement — until a policy position being prepared for presentation to Cabinet had been finalized. This document elaborated the Northern Pipeline Guidelines released in August 1970.

3. BREAKING THE LOG-JAM

The very seriousness of the situation, the knowledge that Northern Pipeline Guidelines would have a permanent impact on relations between business and Government in Canada, created an unwillingness to act decisively either for or against approval-in-principle. A shuffle in Energy, Mines and Resources, with Jack Austin replacing C.M. Isbister as Deputy Minister and Chairman of the Task Force, produced added uncertainty in the energy field. Against this, among senior officials, was a belief that somebody must come forward with a strategy to break the indecision. It had to be someone with "standing" in the Ottawa community. More precisely, to get the wheels in motion, he had to be among the dozen or so people who count in the Capital.

In fact, the top elite in Ottawa comprises a very small number of senior officials and Cabinet Ministers. Among them, the most influential senior officials occupy positions of enormous weight, reflecting and reinforcing the extreme centralization of policy direction in Ottawa. Talented, over-worked, and usually associated with the Liberal party, militantly "pragmatic," these dozen or so officials command far-reaching attention among political and business leaders. United not so much by ideological uniformity as mutual respect and confidence, they exercise a *de facto* veto power over decision-making in the capital. The necessary coalitions for policy departures on any aspect of national policy must be built within this group; a consensus, once achieved and recommended for Ministerial approval, carries formidable weight in Cabinet. Even in rare moments of Prime Ministerial initiative, the benevolent neutrality of the inner circle is necessary for policy implementation.

Heading the staffs of the Central Agencies, Treasury Board and the Privy Council for example, as well as the key departments and agencies (but by no means including all Deputy-Ministers) those officials guard the files and their political masters.°

The inner circle is Ottawa's conscience, steering the Liberal party down the broad middle road that has returned it to power election after election. They are in short, successful, and they know it. Business executives also appreciate success, and know who's who in the capital.

The Mandarinate in 1970, the central feature of Ottawa's power structure, were very much interested in the pipeline issue. When finally, a member of the group, the Deputy-Minister of Transport, took the initiative to find out what the consensus was on a Mackenzie pipeline, his colleagues responded favourably. The strategy adopted reflected the seriousness of the issue and aimed for maximum speed and efficiency.

Transport, which could, after all, claim a legitimate interest in northern development, intervened directly with Gordon Robert-

---

° This is not to say that these senior officials "rule" their Ministers. By definition, they exercise only influence, not power. In an open confrontation with a Prime Minister, as in the James Coyne affair, the senior official will lose. Eventually, also, a new Prime Minister will want, and get, his own men. Trudeau, for example, greatly strengthened the Prime Minister's Office and Privy Council Office staffs to provide greater policy review capability in the East Block. Cabinet procedures were also streamlined. But few new faces appeared. Any major reorganization takes time. In the short term a Prime Minister and his colleagues must work with what they have inherited. Both sides, senior officials and Ministers of the Crown, understand that mutual adjustments are always necessary. Normally things can be worked out.

son, Clerk of the Privy Council, on April 8, 1970, suggesting a meeting of senior officials at the Deputy-Minister level to discuss the policy questions facing the federal Government as a result of recent developments in Alaska and the North. Copies of the letter were sent to the Deputy-Minister of Finance, Simon Riesman; the Secretary of the Treasury Board, A. Johnson; and Marshall Crowe, Robertson's Deputy in the Privy Council office. The suggested membership beyond these individuals included the Chairman of the National Energy Board, the President of Northern Transportation Company Ltd.; and the Deputy Ministers of Energy, Mines and Resources and Indian Affairs and Northern Development. Should this group agree that the timing was right, Robertson would give it his blessing. Moreover, should a consensus be reached, his office would ensure an early decision within the Task Force on Northern Oil Development, the Inter-Departmental Committee on Oil, and the Cabinet. The meeting in fact was arranged for May 12, 1970, in the Privy Council office. Finance, Transport, the National Energy Board, Indian Affairs and Northern Development, Energy, Mines and Resources and the Privy Council Office turned out in force. Gilchrist, President of Northern Transportation Company Ltd. and Strong, on behalf of the proposed Canada Development Corporation, also attended.

This was decision-making in the classic Ottawa tradition. Ministers were briefed; they were not excluded. The senior officials were not acting "irresponsibly." Rather, the process of elite selection and the tradition of secrecy in policy-making blurred any meaningful distinction between "administrative" and "political" roles, between bureaucrats and politicians. The role of Marshall Crowe, who chaired the meeting, illustrates the point. As Deputy Secretary of the Cabinet and Deputy Clerk of the Privy Council since 1969, Crowe was approaching the height of his career after a successful period of service with External Affairs (1947-61), the Canadian Imperial Bank of Commerce (1961-7) and the Canada Development Corporation, where he was appointed President. November, 1971 to May, 1973, as well as its Chairman from May to October, 1973. In this capacity he attended meetings of Canadian Artic Gas after C.D.C. joined the consortium. Appointed Assistant Clerk of the Privy Council in 1967, he was caught up in the intense energy debate within the Inter-Departmental Committee on oil, particularly as it affected

Canadian-American trade negotiations in the area. Now, as Robertson's right-hand man, it fell to him logically to lead the discussion on approval-in-principle for a Mackenzie pipeline system. Three years later, however, Crowe was named Chairman of the National Energy Board, an "independent" regulatory body that would process an application to construct and operate a Mackenzie gas pipeline system. Whether his earlier activity on the Mackenzie pipeline question cast doubt on Crowe's suitability to assess the merits of the case before the Energy Board is a matter for Canadians to ponder.

4. THE MAY MEETING

The purpose of the May meeting was to assess alternative strategies to deal with increasing pressure from industry for governmental approval-in-principle. Given the assumption that a Mackenzie pipeline system was in the national interest, (and the Task Force on Northern Oil Development agreed that it was) should Cabinet encourage its promotion immediately? Or, should Ottawa discourage matters from proceeding too quickly?

There were several reasons for maintaining the more cautious approach followed to date, and these had been reaffirmed in the second Task Force Progress *Report* to Cabinet only a month before. Essentially, they added up to a concern about premature decision-making given the Task Force's lack of information. Caution would permit more data to be gathered and Ottawa would be in a better position later on to make an informal choice. Energy, Mines and Resources tended toward this view.

First, Energy, Mines and Resources argued that the outcome of the S.S. *Manhattan* trials was still not final and that it might be wise to wait until Humble Oil had announced definitely its intention of abandoning the tanker option for the transportation of Alaskan oil. It anticipated the failure of the S.S. *Manhattan* trials and it did not take too seriously at this point the possibility that the liquifaction of Alaskan gas would render a pipeline from the North up the Mackenzie financially unattractive.

The point was that Ottawa still did not know if the oil companies were experimenting with the S.S. *Manhattan* for the examination of transportation possibilities, or because the United States Navy and State Department were using it as a lever in conducting oil and gas pipeline negotiations with Canada. The belief in Ottawa that the American Navy was funding the operation rendered the latter a distinct possibility.°

Second and more important, no research had been done on environmental problems associated with either gas or oil pipelines up the Mackenzie. During the meeting, the Department of Indian Affairs and Northern Development maintained that a pipeline developer would have to demonstrate the level of damage to the northern ecology. Yet, when pressed, Hunt of Indian Affairs admitted that his Department might in fact be less stringent on environmental protection than Alaska. Northern Transportation Company Ltd. pointed out that speedy action was required since Canadian environmentalists were not yet as well organized as American groups.

Third, Ottawa had not yet conducted a study of the economic impact of a gas or oil pipeline on the Canadian economy as a whole. All agreed that it would have an enormous impact. The project might stabilize energy exports and Canadian-American trade relations but it might also have undesirable effects on the Canadian economy. The Department of Finance, however, was only beginning this fourth Task Force on Northern Oil Development study. Trudeau's anti-inflationary campaign counselled caution in advancing a project which would involve extremely expensive support services. Moreover increasing Canadian sensitivity toward foreign ownership raised some doubts about the depth of Canadian capital markets should Canadian equity control be demanded by J. J. Greene.

Fourth, Energy, Mines and Resources was concerned about "staking the national interest" on the North when oil and gas discoveries off the east coast might exceed northern finds. The second Task Force Progress *Report* had had this in mind when it

---

° The Task Force, in its first *Progress Report* to cabinet in March, 1969, had reported that oil companies who wished access to Arctic data resulting from the *S.S. Manhattan* trials could help sponsor the voyage with a $0.5 million fee. It therefore recommended as well that the Government of Canada buy in as well to share in this important information source. Despite repeated requests, extending to June, 1972, Humble Oil refused to release it to Ottawa.

Humble Oil's unwillingness to share its information with Canada tends to confirm senior officials' belief in U.S. Navy co-operation: as the most important experiment of its kind in northern waters, it was crucial in the design of icebreakers. The U.S. Coast Guard *Polar Star*, launched in 1974, was in In all probability designed on the basis of the *S.S. Manhattan* data bank. Canada, for all the millions it spent in assisting the two voyages, was left empty-handed.

endorsed a policy of passive promotion until threshold reserves of oil and gas had actually been discovered in the North. Energy, Mines and Resources counselled caution until the trade-offs between east coast and northern oil and gas development were rigorously examined. Despite Northern Transportation Company Ltd.'s insistence on the urgency of action, and the imminence of pipeline development, delays might well postpone pipeline construction well into the 1970s. Not much would be lost by sitting tight until the situation became clearer. Ottawa should make every effort to distinguish the particular needs of pipeline developers from the broader objectives of northern development.

It was good sound advice. Isbister unfortunately was on his way out. Jack Austin, his successor as Deputy Minister of Energy, Mines and Resources, was heading for the national Capital.

On the other hand, arguments were presented in favour of an immediate recognition of private sector demands. In the first place, a number of senior officials simply felt that "the Canadian Government owed it to industry to set out its philosophical stance." Industry and Government were partners in the development of the North and Ottawa should make clear the broad framework in which the private sector would be operating in the post-1968 era. A Mackenzie pipeline for obvious reasons was a key investment decision and industry wanted a decision right away.

Second, the benefits on the Government's side would be that planning could take place immediately in respect of support services on the assumption that the pipeline would be built. This would add some stability and predictability to departmental activities in the North. The posture of industry seemed to indicate that early northern pipeline construction was inevitable. In response to the possibility of an east coast discovery, Northern Transportation Company Ltd. argued that American market demands were growing so rapidly that all available supply sources in Canada would be under pressure. Canada was no place for the faint-hearted.

Third, the National Energy Board argued that liquefaction technology was more of a threat than Energy, Mines and Resources supposed. It was moving forward rapidly and Canada might lose a Mackenzie gas pipeline altogether if it refused to take a position now on northern pipelines. The option would be a gas pipeline through Alaska and the transportation by tanker of liquified natural gas to American mainland markets. Alaska would win out again, and Mackenzie Delta natural gas might flow west rather than south. Northern Transportation Company Limited and the Departments of Transport and Indian Affairs and Northern Development were all alarmed by this possibility, for they counted heavily on American capital underwriting the development of the North.

Fourth, the consensus of officials in Northern Transportation Company Limited, the Department of Transport, and the Energy Board was that commercial interests would dictate the initiation of the construction of a natural gas pipeline up the Mackenzie within the next five years anyway — unless Canada decided to reject it. According to Northern Transportation, a pipeline application might be submitted in the very near future judging from current industry behaviour and interests (Northern Transportation and Energy, Mines and Resources noted industry hints of a "great oil discovery" at Atkinson Point). If the commercial decision were imminent, it was in Canada's best interests to accept the inevitable and to look seriously at questions of foreign ownership and environmental protection before the rush was on.

Fifth, regarding the environment, Northern Transportation maintained that the oil companies could be trusted. They were not promoters in the commonly accepted meaning of the word but rather sound organizations staffed by responsible men. Their task was to look into the future and make decisions as new resources and technology became available. The oil and gas companies could be relied upon to ensure the protection of the environment if only because they had a vested interest in maintaining good public relations with Ottawa. Exactly why or how they were captive to Ottawa, rather than the other way around, was left unclear. Imperial Oil executives hardly lost sleep over the fear of expropriation.

Sixth it was felt that northern pipelines could hardly be detrimental to the Canadian economy as a whole. To be sure, the Economic Impact Study would not be available until mid-1972 but there seemed obvious advantages to the Canadian oil industry, Canadian trade, and the economic development of the North. If industry decided that a Mackenzie gas pipeline was commercially feasible and desirable, then the Canadian economy would receive a powerful stimulus.

As to inflationary pressures and government curbs on spending, it was already stated Cabinet policy to mark off the North as a special area of concern that deserved exceptional financial inputs for regional development. Moreover, regarding Greene's concern about Canadian equity control of the pipeline, Northern Transportation pointed out that industry partnerships with governments in major projects such as pipeline construction were becoming an accepted fact internationally and would not unduly affect the flow of capital into Canada.

Indeed, according to Strong, a Mackenzie pipeline having Canadian control would be easier to finance than any other project since it would be underwritten against firm supply contracts. Despite early fears, TransCanada Pipelines eventually had no trouble in getting the financial backing of Canadian investment houses. Temporary public assistance got things going until the Canadian underwriting community was mobilized to support a sure thing. There was then no inherent contradiction between Greene's demand for Canadian content and control and investor confidence in northern pipeline construction. Foreign capital would not be scared away. Indeed Strong, new Director of the Canada Development Corporation, felt that the Canadian Government might want "a piece of the action" at the beginning and raised the possibility of participating in the pipeline. He noted that a preliminary proposal from the Alberta Natural Gas Company had advocated an entirely Canadian controlled Mackenzie gas line with the Corporation obtaining 30 per cent of the stock. Interestingly enough, in May 1975, the Corporation, another "independent" body within the family of federal agencies, announced its intention to invest $ 100 million in Canadian Arctic Gas, before the National Energy Board approved the project. In the circumstances it was not surprising.

Neither the native people nor their land claims were discussed.

5. THE CONSENSUS

The May 12 meeting was not "policy" but it did focus the issue as a major national issue. Following the discussion, officials returned to their Departments to weigh the "evidence" and the finalize a consensus that had emerged at the meeting.

The crucial question was: could or should a decision in favour of a Mackenzie pipeline be made without more information? The answer depended entirely on assumptions about the Canadian economy and business-Government relations in general. If private sector decisions reflected the national priorities, if capital was presumed to be in abundant supply, and if politically a Mackenzie gas pipeline assisted Canadian-American relations, then active rather than passive promotion could be justified. But each of these assumptions rested on complex premises. Senior officials in May 1970 accepted them all. Thus a consensus emerged that the project was in the "national interest." Two steps remained in the policy process: Northern Pipeline Guidelines would have to be drafted without delay; and Cabinet must accept them.

6. THE PRIVY COUNCIL OFFICE TAKES COMMAND

Centralizing the responsibility for a policy position on northern pipelines in the Privy Council Office suggested its priority in Ottawa. It also ensured prompter action. The May meeting had already built a powerful coalition prepared to accept a positive posture on the Mackenzie. On June 17, 1970, the Task Force on Northern Oil Development set up a working group to draft a *Memo* to Cabinet outlining the terms and conditions under which private enterprise would be permitted to construct a Mackenzie Valley gas or oil pipeline.

Industry on its side reacted immediately by mobilizing support and maximizing its pressure on the Government. In June 1970 the formation of the Gas Arctic Systems Study Group was announced and a month later, the Northwest Project Study Group was formed.

June, 1970 Gas Arctic Study Group
Alberta Gas Trunk Line
Canadian National Railways
Columbia Gas System
Texas Eastern Transmission
Northern Natural Gas (joins August 1970, dropping plans for
                own pipeline)
Pacific Lighting Gas (joins September 1970, withdrawing from
                Mountain Pacific System).

July, 1970 Northwest Project Study Group
TransCanada Pipelines
Atlantic Richfield
Humble Oil
Standard Oil (Ohio)
Michigan Wisconsin Pipeline
Natural Gas Pipeline

Representations in Ottawa became intense; the scent of an approaching decision was apparent. Nevertheless, while the Task Force on Northern Oil Development laboured under its new assignment, decorum was preserved and conventions maintained. The Deputy-Ministers still held the lobbyists at bay: approval-in-principle, while impending, had not yet been granted.

By late July 1970 the Task Force working group, in consultation with the Inter-Departmental Committee on Oil had worked up a final draft of Northern Pipeline Guidelines. As adopted by Cabinet, they were as follows:

1. The Ministers of Energy, Mines and Resources, and Indian Affairs and Northern Development will function as a point of contact between Government and industry, acting as a Steering Committee from which industry and prospective applicants will receive guidance and direction to those federal departments and agencies concerned with the particular aspects of northern pipelines.

2. Initially, only one trunk oil pipeline and one trunk gas pipeline will be permitted to be constructed in the North within a "corridor" to be located and reserved following consultation with industry and other interested groups.

3. Each of these lines will provide either "common" carrier services at published tariffs or a "contract" carrier service at a negotiated price for all oil and gas which may be tendered thereto.

4. Pipelines in the North, like pipelines elsewhere which are within the jurisdiction of the Parliament of Canada, will be regulated in accordance with the National Energy Board Act, amended as may be appropriate.

5. Means by which Canadians will have a substantial opportunity for participating in the financing, engineering, construction, ownership and management of northern pipelines will

form an important element in Canadian government consideration of proposals for such pipelines.

6. The National Energy Board will ensure that any applicant for a Certificate of Public Convenience and Necessity must document the research conducted and submit a comprehensive report assessing the expected effects of the project upon the environment. Any certificate issued will be strictly conditioned in respect of preservation of the ecology and environment, prevention of pollution, prevention of thermal and other erosion, freedom of navigation, and the protection of the rights of northern residents, according to standards issued by the Governor General in Council on the advice of the Department of Indian Affairs and Northern Development.

7. Any applicant must undertake to provide specific programs leading to employment of residents of the North both during the construction phase and for the operation of the pipeline. For this purpose, the pipeline company will provide for the necessary training of local residents in coordination with various government programs, including on-the-job training projects. The provision of adequate housing and counselling services will also be a requirement.

The Cabinet Committee on Economic Policy and Programmes thought it a sterling effort and made only three significant changes. First, the draft rather naievely included references to the *Deputy-Ministers* rather than the *Ministers* of Energy, Mines and Resources, and Indian Affairs and Northern Development functioning as the "point of contact between Government and industry." This had to be suppressed at once, and the text was suitably revised.

Second, one recommendation of the joint Task Force — Inter-Departmental Committee on Oil group was not announced: that Canadian underwriting houses be given priority in respect to equity financing and primary consideration in respect to debt financing of northern affairs.

Third, J. J. Greene demanded the addition of the fifth Guideline regarding Canadian ownership, although several senior officials thought it "excessively nationalistic." He had outlined his position to senior executives of TransCanada Pipelines Ltd. which was forming the Northwest Project Study Group. In this discussion TransCanada Pipelines had indicated its difficulty in ensuring Canadian equity control over the test programs which would amount to between 12 and 14 million dollars. TransCanada was having trouble raising money for this purpose but American companies were willing to participate if they obtained a share in the equity. In reply, Greene said that he would prefer public funds to loss of Canadian equity control. He underlined that "pipelines would have to be even more sacrosanct in this respect than other segments of the economy including the sale of uranium mines."°

Senior officials' fears that Guideline 5 would discourage risk capital and depress the industry proved unfounded. Despite some industry opposition to the principle of Canadian ownership, the Northern Pipeline Guidelines opened a golden period of harmony with business in the planning and design of a natural gas pipeline system in the Mackenzie. If before August 13, 1970, the Task Force remained aloof from intense industry lobbying to avoid commitment, it now fell in behind the private sector.

7.EXPORTS: THE SHIFT OF EXPLORATION TO THE NORTH

In late August 1969, the Inter-Departmental Committee on Oil reviewed the National Oil Policy in the light of energy developments in Alaska and the Arctic as well as the tense state of energy negotiations currently underway with the United States. It endorsed the familiar orientation, one that would last until 1973. *First*, the division of the Canadian market would be upheld. *Second*, the strategy of buying cheap for the market east of the Ottawa Valley and selling as much as possible in the United States would continue. Therefore every attempt was to be made by the Inter-Departmental Committee on Oil to explore avenues to the acquisition of free entry for Canadian oil. *Third*, the Committee rejected any idea of an oil import tax or two price system for oil sales in the United States; instead it recommended bilateral discussions aimed at relaxing the quota system.

The drastic reduction in the American quota announced on March 10, 1970, impelled Canadian officials to redouble their efforts to obtain greater access. If the attempt to grant American

° The Cabinet Committee insisted further that the *Northern Pipeline Guidelines* not prejudice the Hon. Herb Gray's forthcoming policy paper on Foreign Investment. Apparently he was consulted on this matter.

companies a pipeline right of way along the Mackenzie Valley for Alaskan supplies was a part of this overall strategy, so also was the promotion of natural gas exports. As one observer point out, "It was widely recognized in both countries that Canada's trump card in any negotiations was an ability to supply additional quantities of natural gas to meet an energy shortage in the United States which was becoming increasingly acute.[8]

The connection between such a sale and the relaxation of the American quota on Canadian oil exports was drawn to Mr. Greene's attention. He denied it, assuring Parliament on June 11th that "there is certainly no agreement that any relaxation must be contingent upon a greater quantity of Canadian gas being made available."[9]

Greene was technically correct in his reply to the House of Commons. The promotion of natural gas exports fitted in to a broader Energy Board strategy of shifting the exploration focus in Canada to the North, and attracting the major companies to the area. Without an Energy Board commitment to exports to the United States, industry would not develop the North on the argument that domestic Canadian requirements did not justify the necessary required expenditures. In May 1970, Greene drove the point home to the Independent Petroleum Association of America in Denver, where he warned American oil executives that "Increased Canadian supplies would be available for export only if Canada's petroleum industry as a whole gets progressive growth incentives and assured stability of access to U.S. markets for cruide and gas liquids. Should this happen, it has been estimated that the Western Canadian Sedimentary superior basin, supplemented by our frontier areas, could have as much as 5.4 t.c.f. to export in 1990."[9]

Or, as he told the House of Commons Standing Committee on Natural Resources and Public Works a year later on May 11, 1971:

"Obviously, both in Canada and in the United States, we have conceived that the more open that market is the more it will provide the incentive for further exploration in Canada and thence, very likely in the future, we will have more Canadian oil and gas and, thence, even more to sell."

A similar case was made respecting northern pipeline construction: the huge costs together with the high volumes in large diameter pipelines demanded access to American as well as Canadian markets.

Four years later, when Ottawa entertained second thoughts about Canadian supply capabilities, Dome Petroleum Ltd. of Calgary, a large gas producer in western Canada and very active in Arctic exploration after 1970, articulated this basic premise in no uncertain terms. Northern pipeline planning as well as exploration was based on the assumption of exports to the United States.[10]

The full significance of the National Energy Board approval of applications to export 6.3 trillion cubic feet of natural gas in August 1970 is not grasped therefore if that decision (subsequently approved by Cabinet in September 29, 1970) is analyzed in isolation from the August 1970 Northern Pipeline Guidelines. Despite glaring signals that the state of proven gas reserves in Canada was precarious, the Energy Board approved the largest export sale in history denying only one applicant, Consolidated Natural Gas (a subsidiary of Northern Natural Gas), an export licence. Export commitments of a further 6.3 t.c.f. placed a heavy burden on existing supplies. But the Board went ahead by including frontier and uneconomic reserves in its assessment of supplies, creating the impression of massive "ultimate" resources:

"It seems to us that at this point in time we see such a huge ultimate reserve of natural gas in Canada with the industry still in its early stages of development and still requiring incentives, that is markets, that there is danger in repressing the development of production by showing too much concern based on a future surplus figure."[11]

There was also the certainty of improving Canadian—American relations by approving export applications, particularly when, as in 1970, the natural gas was underpriced. The Board did not want to get out of step with "the annuity and comity that has come to characterize relations between the United States and Canada in respect of trade in natural gas."[12] Here again was a favourite argument within business circles; again the Board endorsed it fully.

Since the Board's decision permitted exports of low-cost western natural gas rather than saving it for Canadian markets,

Canadian consumers complained that the home market was gravely compromised. Northern reserves were not yet established, but even if they were, they were "beyond economic reach," and certain to be far costlier to Canadian consumers while the best natural gas was being exported at bargain prices. Why not delay development of the North, stimulate exploration efforts further south, and conserve the country's best fuel supplies? Why subsidize American users? For whose purpose was the North being developed in any case? If this was the model of northern development, why not discuss it openly in Parliament, rather than conceal the real issues in proceedings before a regulatory body?

The Government was not yet prepared to confront these hard questions and took the line of least resistance. The sovereignty scare added an incentive to cooperate with the United States. Both the National Energy Board and the Task Force on Northern Oil Development advocated linking Canadian energy resources and pipeline facilities more intimately with the United States. Both viewed the retention of American goodwill a first priority. As it was, by turning down one application the Energy Board was blasted by industry as overly conservative.[13]

Exploration expenditures in the North reflect the importance of the 1969-70 turning point in industry orientation. Between 1968 and 1971 expenditures jumped from 386 to 1,324 million dollars.

Exploration Expenditures North of 60
(in million of dollars)

	1963	1964	1965	1966	1967	1968	1969	1970	1971
Geological and Geographical	6.5	9.0	8.1	5.8	10.9	24.0	36.9	40.0	45.0
Exploratory Drilling	6.5	10.5	13.1	10.5	7.4	8.8	32.8	55.5	72.4
Land Costs	0.6	0.6	1.5	7.8	4.8	5.8	5.9	10.0	15.0
Total	14.8	19.7	22.7	24.1	23.1	38.6	75.6	105.5	132.4

Sources: Canadian Petroleum Association; *Oilweek*, December 4, 1972.

8. CONCLUSION

The Task Force and National Energy Board decision in 1970 completed a unified approach to Canadian oil and natural gas development and export policy. The Arctic now became an integral part of North American energy relations and negotiations. Exports to the United States were stepped up from existing western Canadian fields, on the basis that large "probable reserves" in frontier areas existed surplus to Canadian requirements. Northern natural gas, in particular, therefore became a focal point of exploration attention; the Canada Oil and Gas Land Regulations, in turn, offered enormous incentives for industry to turn to the Arctic. Few Canadians were aware of the vast policy implications of National Energy Board and Task Force decisions in 1970 or that these decisions had been made. None of this was ever debated in Parliament.

The stormy days of March and April 1970 had been precipitated by Canada's initiative on Arctic sovereignty. Particularly in a period of recession, Canada required a stable economic environment, and that environment could not be facilitated by the kind of Canadian-American friction that had been generated in the spring and summer.

The major economic decision affecting the North in 1970 offered a framework that Washington and American industry could only applaud. Happy that the key decisions were now behind them, senior officials in the Task Force on Northern Development plunged into the real business at hand—assisting industry to build a Mackenzie gas pipeline. The cost was high—the future of the Arctic.

NOTES

1. In October 1970, Humble Oil suspended icebreaker tanker tests and opted for pipelines over marine shipping. Prior to the second S.S. *Manhattan* voyage, R.H. Vernon, a Humble Oil vice-president and head of the marine department operation had indicated that Humble "still feels the marine solution may be the best means" to move North Slope oil. *Oilweek*, October 26, 1970; April 13, 1970.

2. Quoted in Cleveland, *op. cit.* pp. 16-17.

3. *New York Times,* July 16, 1974.

4. "The Northern Canada Off-shore Drilling Meeting, December 1972," Canadian Arctic Resources Committee, *Northern Perspectives,* Vol. 2, No. 4, 1974. The statement accurately reflects the character of Government-business collaboration after 1968 regarding northern pipelines as well.

5. See Chapter 8 for an elaboration of this point.

6. Departments of Energy, Mines and Resources and Indian Affairs and Northern Development, *Northern Pipeline Guidelines,* (Ottawa, 1970).

7. Quoted in *Canadian Annual Review,* Toronto, 1970, p. 438.

8. House of Commons, *Debates,* June 11, 1970, p. 7996.

9. *Oilweek,* May 18, 1970.

10. "Frontier Searches Based on Premise of Exports," *Globe and Mail,* November 19, 1974.

11. *Globe and Mail,* March 23, 1973. Eric Kierans, a former Liberal Cabinet Minister, was recalling Government thinking at the time. See also John McDougall, "Regulation vs. Politics: The National Energy Board and the Mackenzie Valley Pipeline," in A. Axline, P.V. Lyon, et. al. (eds.), *Continental Community* (Toronto, 1974), pp. 250-73.

12. In P. Sykes, *Sellout: The Giveaway of Canada's Energy Resources* (Toronto, 1973), pp. 92-93.

13. *Oilweek,* November 2, 1970. D. Furlong, Director of the Canadian Petroleum Association, attacked the National Energy Board's export decision as being "overly conservative." The Association estimated potential natural gas reserves at 725 t.c.f. in 1970.

Part II

CHAPTER SIX
The Framework of Northern Development, 1970-72

If the period 1968-70 had witnessed the elaboration of a framework that established the chief contours of northern development, the second phase, 1970-72, witnessed intimate Government-industry cooperation to implement that pattern of development. The first was a period of crisis; the second was one of normalization and bureaucratic routine. In 1968-70 there was a great deal of public interest in the North; 1970-72 were, in contrast, quiet years, with, as yet, little serious opposition to the proposed Mackenzie Valley Gas Pipeline.

In fact, the two periods were strikingly different, each characterized by a distinct policy process. During 1968-70 the integration of the North into North America occupied the attention of senior officials and Cabinet Ministers in Ottawa, Alberta, and Washington. The Canadian public, although aroused, was never directly involved in (or even informed of) decisions. Northerners certainly were excluded. Rather the pattern was one of elite diplomacy, secret negotiations, and crisis decision-making. Nevertheless, the strength of the 1968-70 period was the combined attention of the inner circle on the related international, bilateral, and regional aspects of northern development after 1968: Questions relating to northern sovereignty, trade, and pipeline planning were considered together and alternative approaches were weighed. The framework that emerged was questionable to say the least, but it had been based on high-level action rather than drift.

The period 1970-72, in contrast, witnessed a swift return to the bureaucratic politics and administrative chaos of the pre-1968 era. The earlier panic and crisis were forgotten; agencies and departments returned to the task of carving out, expanding, and protecting their jurisdictions. Attempts to reform the Advisory Committee on Northern Development into an effective mechanism for implementing the Government's stated objectives failed. The consequent absence of leadership at the top magnified further the control of the private sector over the policy process.

1. THE TEAM DISPERSES

The achievement of relative stability in northern affairs by September 1970 took the heat off the North and released senior officials for fire-fighting in other crisis areas: the struggle against inflation; Quebec; the collapse of the aerospace sector; the unexpected blow delivered by John Volpe, American Secretary of Transportation, to the St. Lawrence Seaway Authority; constitutional and administrative reform; the August 1971 Nixon surcharge. These (and many other) developments demanded the vigilance of the top elite.[1]

Some by-products of the 1968-70 northern crisis themselves assisted in turning attention south. For example, the sovereignty challenge had underlined the need for greater surveillance and control in the high Arctic; the Department of National Defence, and the aerospace lobby, saw an opening for a new Long-Range Patrol Aircraft. With an expenditure forecast of some $1 billion this matter could be counted upon to consume much time and energy of senior officials prior to authorization.

The culprit again was the extreme centralization in policy formation in Ottawa. Without consensus at the top, programmes languished and forward planning ceased. Northern developments were no longer monitored; inter-relationships were not grasped. Neither the Department of External Affairs nor the Department of National Defence, for example, studied the American icebreaker programme in the context of a possible future challenge to Canadian jurisdiction. The Ministry of Transport, for its part, vetoed a recommendation from National Defence to establish a northern base, while holding back on a polar icebreaker programme.[2] External Affairs pressed forward in the area of international law to establish the Canadian jurisdictional claims of April 1970, but failed to assess other policy instruments to implement the so-called functional approach. Nor did Task Force on Northern Oil Development officials link resource ownership and delivery systems with the jurisdictional question. As before 1968, so also now, there was no time to define the Canadian interest in the North. The men at the top could not be everywhere at once.

Two other developments exacerbated this failure to elaborate Canada's stake in the North on a continuing basis, and to monitor new initiatives. First, new faces appeared; others disappeared. For example, the Deputy-Minister of Energy, Mines and Resources was replaced in the fall 1970 by a Trudeau man, Jack Austin, as close to industry as the Chairman of the National Energy Board, and determined to make a name for himself in Ottawa. His predecessor had been cautious in matters relating to northern oil development and had been among the last to be swayed into accepting the Northern Pipeline Guidelines. In contrast, Austin was keen to press forward with the private sector in the lead. As Chairman of the Task Force he wielded great influence in Ottawa. He became a close friend of Trudeau.

Austin's recruitment from the outside underscored the second new factor: the coherence of the old Pearson team was being eroded by Trudeau men. Certainly Trudeau's first administration had witnessed some new faces in prestigious positions in Ottawa. But only after his major personal electoral triumph in July 1974, when he returned with a majority government, could his closest friends and confidants move in definitively. Not until his own man could replace Gordon Robertson, Secretary to the Cabinet and Clerk of the Privy Council, would the personnel shift initiated in 1968 be decisive.

Nevertheless and progressively after 1968, Trudeau's appointees filtered into key portfolios in Departments and agencies, or influential positions in the expanded Privy Council Office and the Prime Minister's Office. Able senior officials inherited from the old regime had been moved around to new positions in Indian Affairs and Northern Development, the Treasury Board, Finance, External Affairs, Industry, Trade and Congress, and Transport. While relations between the old and new men were not yet strained — that would come in 1972 — and while senior officials all admired their advantages versus the Cabinet in Trudeau's reorganization of the Cabinet system, Trudeau's chosen friends edged forward.

In northern affairs, the change can be documented by reference to the key decisions in the period under discussion.

The centrality of the Privy Council Office in the April 1970 legislation has been noted. External Affairs had met with determined opposition from Trudeau's advisors. But in the decision regarding Northern Pipeline Guidelines, Pearson's inner circle could still operate as a mandarin group. During the discussions in 1971 concerning the Canadian alternative to the trans-Alaskan pipeline system, however, Austin and Lalonde, new men, would play the central role in policy initiatives. Increasingly the old guard was marked until a new team was assembled; the instability further undermined the capacity for united action at the top in Canada.[3]

2. THE FAILURE TO REVIVE THE ADVISORY COMMITTEE ON NORTHERN DEVELOPMENT

Even without the guidance of hard-pressed senior officials, an efficiently functioning Advisory Committee on Northern Development would have ensured some coherence in northern development. Many senior officials were agreed that the Advisory Committee should, if possible, be revived. Planning for the construction of a Mackenzie pipeline itself demanded a better coordination of northern activities. Indeed, as the pace of development quickened throughout the Arctic, especially in the Mackenzie Delta and the Arctic islands, senior officials could find little alternative to coordination through the Advisory Committee. There was no other interdepartmental agency to turn to for non-energy matters, short, that is, of a radical restructuring of the administration of northern affairs in general.

However, the reassertion of central direction in the Advisory Committee would have to come from a Department with greater freedom of action in Ottawa than Indian Affairs and Northern Development. This had become abundantly clear in meetings of the Advisory Committee in the 1968-71 period in which Treasury Board had refused outright to tolerate a significantly increased coordinating role for it. For example, at its 75th meeting, on

January 9, 1970, Indian Affairs and Northern Development argued that the Advisory Committee should establish positive guidelines for the implementation of northern policies. Criticism was immediate and bitter; Indian Affairs and Northern Development was charged with attempting to establish "overriding programmes."

In these circumstances, this Department received qualified support from the newly established Ministry of Transport (formerly the Department of Transport). With a dynamic Deputy-Minister interested in the North, and with a vested interest in the improved coordination of northern activities, Transport offered welcome diplomatic support in the complex political struggle among Departments and agencies in Ottawa. Above all else, Transport put in order its own northern operation with the creation of an Arctic Transportation Agency, and by going out of its way to improve the effectiveness of the Transportation Sub-committee of the Advisory Committee on Northern Development.[4] It also made every effort to upgrade bilateral relations with the Department of Indian Affairs and Northern Development. Cheered by such support, the latter drew its first real blood in July 1971 when Cabinet supported a more dynamic role for the Advisory Committee in the North.

Specifically, Cabinet advised that "Indian Affairs and Northern Development in consultation with the Advisory Committee on Northern Development should introduce improved arrangements for joint planning and coordination of all policies in programmes, including joint consideration of their financial implications." Here was something upon which to build; it appeared to put Treasury Board in its place.

The Cabinet seemed genuinely interested in northern planning. The July *Memorandum* went on to say, "the government's financial allocations for all purposes in the North should be the subject of regular, detailed and continuous inter-departmental consultation involving all departments and agencies concerned, the Treasury Board Secretariat and the Territorial government." The implications of programme expenditures were to be noted early in the planning process and "in order to measure the success of each program and policy towards the attainment of northern objectives, performance indicators must be developed and actual expenditures and physical programs recorded in relation to these expenditures."

The last point was the most important. Much would depend on the Advisory Committee's success in developing performance criteria to evaluate private and public sector activities.

An Advisory Committee working group on the financial implications of northern development policy eventually met on November 12, 1971 and was instructed to report by April 1, 1972. The working group's terms of reference did not, however, include the identification of private sector expenditures. Even provinces were to be excluded. The group was to limit its attention to federal and Territorial Government outlays, to categorize them as "direct," "indirect," or "general." "Direct" expenditures were those made either primarily for purposes associated with the Territories or a prorated amount for overhead expenditures. "Indirect" expenditures were defined as "that portion of expenditures made for national purposes which directly affects the Territories" (DEW, postal service, weather stations, etc.). General service expenditures referred to that portion of expenditures made for all Canadians which went to the Territories (sovereignty for example).

The working group found itself confronted by a basic dilemma — the categorization was not neat; many expenditures contributed to Indian Affairs and Northern Development's northern objectives only indirectly, and sometimes (as in the case of expenditures for petroleum and mineral development and transportation) ambiguously. Was the working group to attempt to make distinctions as to *purpose*?

The question was fundamental for it would determine whether the Advisory Committee would merely oversee a data gathering process or become a coordinating group with considerable impact on the decision — making process. Even data gathering was a considerable step forward; but the linking of financial programs and northern objectives with performance indicators, as the July Cabinet instruction had demanded, required that the Advisory Committee analyze as well as collect information.

The attempt failed. The working group reported that Government outlays (in support of oil and natural gas exploration) were nevertheless to be considered "direct" northern expenditures, even though they contributed little to the economic or social well-being of the North. Such activities as the DEW line which affected the question of Arctic sovereignty and the security of Canada, or the maintenance of Arctic weather stations, similarly were to be dealt with as northern expenditures. "The proportion of such expenditures contributing towards northern objectives would be part of the later analysis of the figures and not of the data-gathering process." Unfortunately, the "later analysis of the figures" was not brought within the Advisory Committee group's terms of reference. Performance indicators were not developed to guide government activities as a whole in the North. Although some Departments, such as Transport, were sensitive to the need for special standards in the North, and for developing criteria in the spirit of *Canada's North 1970-80*, the Advisory Committee was not able to achieve a directing role. Even the Ministry of Transport balked finally at Indian Affairs and Northern Development's growing pretentions. For example, at the 84th meeting on October 7, 1971 the representative from Transport complained privately that "for our own protection we must ensure that the financial influence of the Advisory Committee is purely consultative."

The reasoning was not based merely on jurisdictional jealousy. It also reflected the nightmarish administrative jungle that Indian Affairs and Northern Development had permitted the Advisory Committee to become.

Years of impotence together with the crisis atmosphere after 1968 inevitably generated an extensive proliferation of committee structures within the Advisory Committee on Northern Development. The process began in December 1968 when a coordinating committee was set up to maintain continuity between meetings. New structures now multiplied. Senior officials, even in Ottawa, were amazed at the proliferation of committees. In February 1972 yet two more new sub-committees appeared. The attached Chart gives an indication of the extraordinary structure that had developed by 1972.

If prior to 1968, minutes of the Advisory Committee meetings were rarely distributed, the monthly summary of proceedings of its various working groups and committees sinned in the opposite direction after 1971; they became a massive and meaningless compendium of northern items in no apparent order or priority.

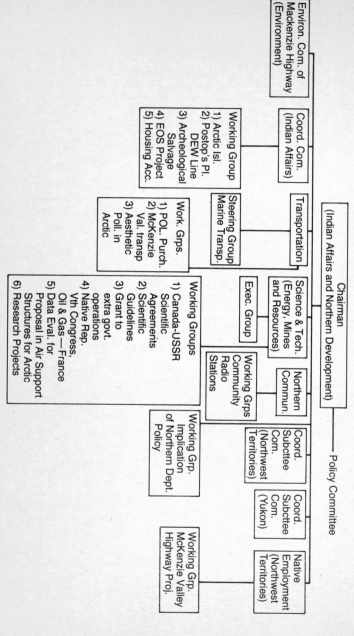

The Advisory Committee on Northern Development

Chairman
(Indian Affairs and Northern Development) ——— Policy Committee

Environ. Com. of Mackenzie Highway (Environment)

Coord. Com. (Indian Affairs)

Working Group
1) Arctic Isl.
2) Postop's Pl. DEW Line
3) Archeological Salvage
4) EOS Project
5) Housing Acc.

Transportation

Steering Group Marine Transp.

Work. Grps.
1) POL. Purch.
2) McKenzie Val. transp
3) Aesthetic Poll. in Arctic

Science & Tech. (Energy, Mines and Resources)

Exec. Group

Northern Commun.

Working Grps Community Radio Stations

Working Groups
1) Canada-USSR Scientific Agreements
2) Scientific Guidelines
3) Grant to extra govt. operations
4) Native Rep. Vth Congress, Oil & Gas — France
5) Data Eval. for Proposal in Air Support Structures for Arctic
6) Research Projects

Coord. Subcttee Com. (Northwest Territories)

Working Grp. Implication of Northern Dept. Policy

Coord. Subcttee Com. (Yukon)

Native Employment (Northwest Territories)

Working Grp. McKenzie Valley Highway Proj.

94

The great bulk became so obviously harmless that they were declassified to "restricted" from "secret." Cohesion and central direction simply could not be maintained within the organization.

Therefore in November 1971, a Policy Committee was formed. The idea was to achieve a forum where actual policy could be discussed, or as it was described "a committee at the Deputy Minister or Assistant Deputy-Minister level to deal with matters of a conceptual or policy nature." Here the ordering of priorities could be discussed above the rabble. Equally important, the reimposition of control at the top would help keep in check those individuals and groups within the Advisory Committee who were more native than the Inuit and who might misuse information. A closer watch over sensitive information stemmed embarrassing leaks, but at the cost of the original coordinating purpose of the Advisory Committee. It now became a mere holding operation.

Nevertheless, Indian Affairs and Northern Development used it to stall programs of other Departments and agencies that did not follow "established procedures." The effect was to slow down the policy process even more. For some Departments in a state of rapid development this limited their adaptive capacity in a constantly changing policy environment. While they might agree that more coordination was required, they insisted that the Advisory Committee not be permitted to paralyze their operations.°

But this could not be achieved, and a satisfactory compromise could not be found. Indian Affairs and Northern Development was determined to coordinate, but the Advisory Committee was not capable of effective action. Some Departments worked out bilateral relations with Indian Affairs and Northern Development that permitted reasonable cooperation, but this signalled a return to pre-1968 conditions. The Advisory Committee had failed again.

° For example, the coordinating committee of the Advisory Committee on Northern Development after 1970 became so over — centralized in terms of detail that it found itself time and time again incapable of implementing directives from the secretariat. A typical case — a memorandum to the effect that no new federal offices or units were to be established in the North without prior submission to the coordinating committee — produced severe strains with other bureaucracies in Ottawa.

3. THE OFFICIAL POLICY: CANADA'S NORTH 1970-80

Canada's North 1970-80, presented to the House Standing Committee on Indian Affairs and Northern Development in March 1972, appeared to open a new era; to Northerners, on the other hand, it merely meant more of the same. Unfortunately the native people, with their greater experience of federal policy-making, had the more accurate perception.[5]

Canada's North 1970-80 announced an official reordering of objectives and priorities in northern development. "In the course of its policy review during the past year," it read, "the Government affirmed that the needs of the people in the North are more important than resource development and that the maintenance of ecological balance is essential."[6]

After stressing that the Government's objectives in the North had now been decisively altered, moving "from defence to people programmes, from resource development to ecological problems," the document listed the Government's order of priorities for the period 1970-1980:

1. To put into rapid effect the agreed Guidelines for Social Improvement.°
2. To maintain and enhance the natural environment, through such means as intensifying ecological research, establishing national parks, and ensuring wildlife conservation;
3. To encourage and stimulate the development of renewable resources, light industries and tourism, particularly those which create job and economic opportunities for native Northerners;
4. To encourage and assist strategic projects (key to increased economic activity in the region or territory with solid economic and social benefits) in the development of non-renewable resources and with joint participation by government and private interests as generally desirable;
5. To provide necessary support for other non-renewable resource projects of recognized benefit to Northern residents and Canadians in general.[7]

° The Guidelines for Social Improvement include the following:

1. To create employment opportunities for native people in both the private and public sectors;
2. to provide intensive training, including on-the-job-training for native people in the public and private sectors;

But the policy statement was vague on how this reordering of objectives was to be accomplished. It was less a question of presenting a "blueprint" for northern development, than of defining the criteria to be used in evaluating "people" or "environmental" as opposed to "economic development" programmes. The Guidelines for Social Improvement placed the creation of employment opportunities for native people at the top of the list; yet Government support for non-renewable resource projects was well down on the ranking of Ottawa's northern objectives. How was this discrepancy to be weighed by people in the field?

The land issue raised even more difficult questions. If the "needs of the people in the North," were to be taken seriously, as *Canada's North 1970-80* claimed they were; if these needs were to become more important in government planning than resource development, then the settlement of native land claims would have to be ranked first in the Guidelines. Instead, the issue was not even raised, except indirectly in the final Guideline referring to safeguarding "the culture of the native peoples in the North."

Nor did the second objective, "to maintain and enhance the natural environment," affect far-reaching Government decisions in the North. Trudeau's announcement of the construction of an all-weather Mackenzie Highway in April 1972 seemed to document the official disregard for *Canada's North 1970-80* since it was made without benefit of environmental research. Similarly, and with even greater potential danger for northern ecosystems, Ottawa granted approval-in-principle for off-shore drilling in the

3. to intensify educational opportunities among the native people to create a cadre of skilled professionals in all fields;

4. to bring native people into executive and managerial positions "even at the risk of higher costs and some mistakes."

5. to improve mechanisms for effective consultation between native people, industry and government; for social and economic development of the bands; and for the hearing of grievances;

6. to maintain, as far as possible, traditional pursuits;

7. to create effective counselling services and "closest liaison with industry and effective cooperation as a group on the part of all government departments and agencies concerned with people programmes;

8. to strengthen communication links with the South;

9. to improve transportation links with the South;

10. to safeguard the culture of native peoples in the North."

Beaufort Sea in December 1972. No Government agency had evaluated the environmental hazards associated with such drilling in one of the most sensitive exploration zones in the world; and native people in the area had not been consulted despite the proximity of important lands and hunting grounds. The artificial islands in the Beaufort Sea on which the drilling was to take place were simply classified as land areas and licensed under the Territorial Land Use Regulations.[8]

In fact, the drafting and Cabinet treatment of *Canada's North 1970-80* prior to its release in March 1972 is most revealing.

The need for establishing a new official framework to plan northern development had become evident to many Ottawa bureaucrats following the dramatic events of 1968. The Department of Indian Affairs and Northern Development had been trying to get the attention of Cabinet since January 1970, when it had introduced a working paper entitled *Strategy for Northern Development* to the 72nd meeting of the Advisory Committee on Northern Development. Pushed aside by urgent matters relating to sovereignty, pipeline, and trade policy as they affected the North, the *Strategy* surfaced again only in the fall of 1970 when the pieces of the puzzle had fallen in place and the immediate crisis of northern development had been momentarily resolved. Even then, another great issue — the October 1970 crisis in Quebec with the Cross and Laporte kidnappings — postponed Cabinet consideration of the *Strategy* until late November. Only then did the Government consider Canadian objectives in the Arctic.

In other words, the formulation of a new approach to northern development was not perceived as a high priority by Ottawa decision-makers. Pipeline policy, for example, was not dependent in any way on a broader concept of the national interest: the Northern Pipeline Guidelines of August 1970 were drawn up before and entirely without reference to the on-going discussions that eventually resulted in *Canada's North 1970-1980*. Pipeline, trade, and sovereignty questions established the parameters of northern economic development and these decisions were reserved for the inner circle. Once settled, that is, once business and government had agreed on the future of the North in the economy of North America, the Department of Indian Affairs and Northern Development could try again.

In November 1970, the Cabinet accepted the general thrust of this Department's *Strategy* (now titled *Policy for Northern Development 1971-1981*) and instructed it to work toward a more detailed *Memorandum* It was this latter report approved by Cabinet on July 15, 1971, that emerged as *Canada's North 1970-1980* in March 1972. Since the draft was in final form by July 1971, and needed no further consideration, a question arises concerning the timing of its release. Native people and the Canadian public in general were waiting for an official statement; it had long been promised. Now it was ready, and still it was withheld for another nine months.

The failure to release *Canada's North 1970-1980* until March 1972 related to the government's determination to proceed with the Mackenzie Valley Gas Pipeline *before* settling native land claims in Treaty areas 8 and 11 involving the rights-of-way which would have to be negotiated for pipeline construction. It was agreed in November 1971 that it should not be made public, "for it would only create more dissent among the northern people."

Even after the pressure became too great to hold back a public announcement from the House Standing Committee any longer, the Cabinet had no intention of achieving a land settlement with the native people of the North before proceeding with pipeline construction.

4. THE UNOFFICIAL POLICY: THE ROLE OF BUSINESS IN NORTHERN PLANNING

The influence of business in the policy process associated with northern development increased in direct proportion to the lack of coordination in the public sector. Indeed, sterility and the octopus-like administrative structure of Indian Affairs and Northern Development and the Advisory Committee on Northern Development offered an ideal backdrop for vibrant Government-business interaction centered on the Task Force on Northern Oil Development. Issue-oriented, "temporary," and as yet relatively unbureaucratized, the Task Force could still operate as a parallel structure outside the established jurisdictions and procedures.

The real dynamic of resource planning in the North remained clear; effective power lay in the confidential relationships built up between corporate interests and the senior officials in the Departments of Indian Affairs and Northern Development, and

Energy, Mines and Resources, the Ministry of Transport, and the National Energy Board.

After 1970, collaboration between federal agencies and the private sector deepened. Officials were keen to demonstrate that Ottawa was a responsible partner; they sought more effective mechanisms to share information and to encourage confidence among existing and potential investors. The public and Parliament remained excluded.

While the centrality of the private sector in the North meant that the Task Force transmitted specific policies initiated by business for Government approval, corporate interests scored even more heavily in persuading senior officials of the wisdom of their assumptions concerning the future role of northern resources in the Canadian and American economies. "Rules of the game" were accepted: foreign control of resources; the primacy of exports; the consortium approach; the Panarctic Formula; and the exclusion of public participation — all of which established an unofficial framework of development quite different from that put forward in *Canada's North 1970-1980*. An understanding of this conflict between stated priorities on the one hand and the real world on the other is crucial to an appreciation of the primacy of continental resourse pressures following the Northern Pipeline Guidelines of August 1970. The "rules of the game" will therefore be studied individually.

a. *Foreign Control of Resources*: Apart from maintaining its 45 per cent equity participation in Panarctic Oils, insisting on "substantial opportunity" for participating in the "financial, engineering, construction, ownership and management of northern pipelines" (Northern Pipeline Guideline No. 5), and other minor initiatives such as the purchase of 18 per cent equity in Nanisivik Mines Ltd. at Strathcona Sound, Ottawa failed to take action after 1970 to reduce an unacceptable level of foreign control in the North. Of an estimated 544 million acres of potential petroleum—bearing sedimentary lands, only 20 per cent of the total average, mainly marginal areas, were not under permit by mid-1970. All the promising areas in the Mackenzie Delta, the Beaufort Sea and the Arctic Islands were already controlled by permitees. Panarctic Oils aside, foreign interests, particularly American, dominated the North by 1970.[9]

Under the terms of the Canada Oil and Gas Land Regulations of 1961, a free-entry system was adopted in which companies could be granted permits without the Department of Indian Affairs and Northern Development influencing the area of exploration, the type of development work, or the structure or ownership of the companies.[10] Simply by virtue of filing an application with this Department, and with minimal work requirements companies gained permits to a total of twelve years, after which they obtained the right of a twenty-one year lease, renewable for a term of twenty-one years from the date of commercial production. Royalty rates were set at 5 per cent for the first three years, rising to 10 per cent after this period. The leasing system and royalty rates under the Regulations were far more generous than Alaska, more generous even than Bolivia.

Ottawa decided in 1970 to suspend further permit — taking under the Canada Oil and Gas Land Regulations, but by then it was too late: all the best land was taken. Second, in a rare show of independence, the Oil and Gas Division of the Northern Economic Development Branch of the Department of Indian Affairs and Northern Development recommended altering the leasing system by issuing the so-called Oil and Gas Land Order No. 1, adopted in 1961. That extraordinary ruling had greatly enhanced the attractiveness to companies of the Regulations: the latter had entitled a permittee to lease only 50 per cent of his acreage, surrendering the rest to the Crown for sale at auction. The Order, however, gave him an opportunity to apply for leases in the remaining 50 per cent. In response to industry pressure, Indian Affairs and Northern Development announced a thorough review and redrafting of the Regulations, including another appraisal of its "unilateral" action respecting the Oil and Gas Land Order No. 1.[11]

The crucial fact of the review process through 1972, however, was the Department's concern, shared by senior officials, that changes in the Regulations not penalize existing permit holders. They had filed for permits with the expectations outlined in the Canada Oil and Gas Land Regulations of 1961. These expectations should be protected by ensuring that alterations not be retroactive. So argued industry, with customary effect.[12] By late 1972 the private sector was reassured. When the new royalty and

101

regulatory regime was finally announced in 1975, industry responded favourably.

Accepting the basic premise that the northern lands disposed of under the Canada Oil and Gas Land Regulations are public lands, Ottawa's unwillingness to change decisively the terms and structure of foreign control in effect denied the country any reasonable benefit from the exploitation of petroleum reserves. The royalty rates might enrich the companies, but how would the negligible income recovered by the Crown pay for the hundreds of millions of dollars of public funds required for pipeline construction support services. No doubt a few jobs would be created. Beyond that, petroleum exploration and production under these circumstances left little for Canadians, and even less for Northerners who would pay the environmental and social costs of resource exploitation for foreign markets. During 1968-70, with an explicit challenge to Canadian sovereignty, the Government expressed genuine concern over the high level of foreign ownership by maintaining control of Panarctic Oils. After the April 1970 legislation, the sensitivity to foreign economic control appears to have evaporated.

b. *Foreign Priorities — The Primacy of Exports*: The export promotion motive of the Task Force has been outlined in detail and the 1968-70 period requires no further elaboration. But the importance of the September 1970 sale of 6.3 t.c.f. of natural gas to American suppliers bears repeating: it linked natural gas exports to frontier supplies, and therefore had the effect of shifting the exploration focus to the North. The terms of the Canada Oil and Gas Land Regulations offered a powerful incentive to the private sector. The National Energy Board agreed to sell off proven reserves and low-cost fuel as a spur to exploration for high cost supplies in the North.

This extraordinary reasoning, saddling Canadians with future high cost fuels while their best western supplies were being exported at low prices was motivated by the Board's belief in large remaining reserves of Canadian natural gas, as well as the "prudent granary manager" approach adopted by the Board's evaluation of export permits.[13] According to former Cabinet Minister Eric Kierans, the National Energy Board was led astray by an uncritical acceptance of data supplied by industry:

The Board recommended the additional exports of 6.3 t.c.f. on the grounds that it estimated total Canadian reserves at 54 t.c.f. and total foreseeable Canadian requirements at 35.6 t.c.f. plus outstanding export contracts of 12 t.c.f., leaving a surplus to Canadian and export requirements of 6.4 t.c.f.. This was cutting it pretty close but the Board then went on to say that the historical gross additions to reserves had averaged 3.5 t.c.f. per year and this could be projected into the future . . . What the Cabinet did not realize, and were not told, was that the Board's own estimates and projections were based entirely on figures provided by the industry . . . With so much wealth, the Canadian Petroleum Association argued, Canada would be niggerdly and mean to begrudge so little to our friends and neighbours to the South. [14]

A year later, the Board discovered that industry's estimates had been grossly inflated and turned down further applications for the export of 2.66 t.c.f. of Canadian natural gas, on the grounds that not only did an exportable surplus in this volume did exist, but also a deficit of 1.1 t.c.f. loomed. It was an historic decision in revealing the weaknesses in the Board's assumption regarding Canadian natural gas exports: ultimate fuel reserves might be limited; further exploration south of the 60th parallel might yield disappointing results; proven reserves should not be squandered at will in low price exports; industry could not be relied upon for correct and appropriate statistics. It also forced the National Energy Board and the Task Force on Northern Oil Development to reconsider the export thrust of their activities in both the oil and natural gas sectors of the economy.

OIL EXPORTS: Throughout 1972, the Task Force remained preoccupied with the entry of Canadian oil to American markets. They failed utterly to foresee that the acute American oil shortage in 1972-73 would see Canada curbing the very exports pressed on that country so singlemindedly since the 1960s. In these circumstances, both the integrity and perceptions of senior officials must be rigorously examined. The Task Force's terms of reference specifically included forecasting North American petroleum supply and demand. Where did the failure lie — in the data, or in the disregard by senior officials of the information assembled?

103

The second Task Force *Progress Report* to Cabinet sent forward in April 1970 explicitly underlined future American shortages. Even with the delivery of Alaskan oil at full 48 " pipeline capacity, the oil shortfall could not be avoided. One assumption projected a gap of 1.8-2.5 million barrels per day (m b/d) in 1980; 4.8-5.1 m b/d in 1985; and 8 m b/d by 1990. The 1969 data released by the National Energy Board and which received wide attention were even more promising. The gathering crisis in United States energy requirements exceeding domestic supplies was well-known by 1970; Alaskan oil was not, and could not be, a long-term solution to American needs. The opportunities for Canadian exports to the United States were therefore excellent, and the Board projected a level of four million barrels per day by 1990.[15] The attached Chart summarizes Board assumptions in 1969.

If this were the case, the future market for Alberta crude was not in doubt — if Alberta had oil in that abundance. But did it? It was one thing to talk as industry circles did in 1970-72, of the "challenge of magnificent proportions" facing Canada to meet American shortages by stepping up Canadian production and exports.[16] It was another to do independent research to assess the reality of existing reserves. The Nation Energy Board report for its part foresaw massive supplies in Canada. The Task Force on Northern Oil Development was admirably situated to update Board statistics and to continue its early work in the area of assessing oil and gas supply and demand in Canada. Under the Chairmanship of Jack Austin, however, they lapsed. His willingness to accept industry statistics left little room for further research. No better opportunity could have been found for establishing a reliable inventory of Canadian hydrocarbon reserves in the context of Canadian-American trade relations. That industry executives could still lull senior officials into a deep confidence in the existence of hypothesized Alberta reserves of crude oil at this late date is inexplicable and inexcusable.[17]

A year later, in 1973, the game was up, and the perilous nature of Canadian oil reserves was revealed. Precious years after 1968 were lost in gathering reliable statistics and developing new technologies. While Ottawa may have been lulled to sleep by the energy cartel in North America for twenty years, the particular irresponsibility of Task Force officials from 1968 to 1972 requires emphasis. By abandoning promising research that might well have yielded reliable information concerning hydrocarbon supplies, they relinquished any claim to a position independent from industry.

NATURAL GAS: After 1970, the construction of a Mackenzie natural gas pipeline system appeared certain. On the American side, an informal agreement had been reached by west coast and mid-west interests that the former would not stand in its way and attempt to block its approval by relevant authorities.

But it was not at all clear how Canadian reserves of natural gas, particularly in the Mackenzie Delta, were to be incorporated into the project. Senior officials' knowledge of actual reserves located by the companies remained uncertain. By late 1972 a figure of 15 trillion cubic feet (half the "threshold" of 30 t.c.f. then considered necessary for pipeline construction) was being discussed. But no one could know for certain (indeed it was later shown to be much exagerated), since this information was carefully guarded by the private petroleum sector.[18]

The problem became acute when the National Energy Board discovered the perilous state of proven natural gas reserves in Canada south of the 60th parallel in 1971. With huge blocks of southern natural gas already committed to American markets, attention turned to the supply situation in the North. But here also, the Task Force found that the permittees had already signed away prospective discoveries in return for exploration funding. Imperial Oil Limited, for example, had negotiated a 10 t.c.f. sale of natural gas over twenty-two years to the Michigan-Wisconsin Pipeline Company of Detroit and the Natural Gas Pipeline of America. While the sale was made conditional on the Canadian Government issuing permits to build a Mackenzie pipeline and to export the gas, it represented an important political claim on northern supplies. Shell and Gulf had committed a further 8 t.c.f. to U.S. buyers, Panarctic Oils Limited and its partners were also lining up future American customers in exchange for financial assistance.[19] Customers in the United States were eager to buy; but did Canada have anything to sell? If not, the Task Force would be better advised to go slow on the Mackenzie Pipeline system and wait for the actual or proven reserve situation in Canada to clarify.

The matter was debated in the Task Force with particular force after the National Energy Board's 1971 decision to reject applications for further export permits. Without an independent,

U.S. Crude & N.G.L. Demand/Supply and Canadian Export Opportunity Analysis

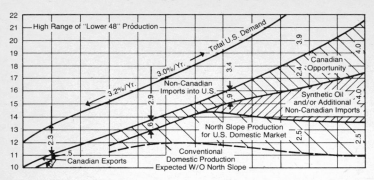

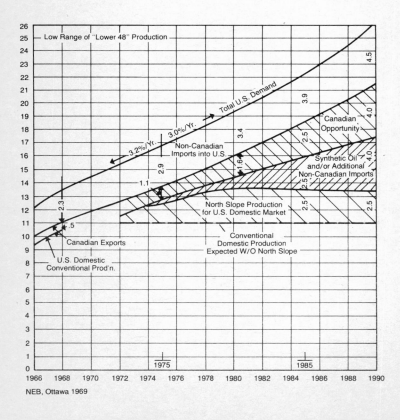

NEB, Ottawa 1969

data-gathering capability, senior officials lacked solid information. Again they were dependent on industry for their information. It came down to discussing the pros and cons of each others' hunches.

As in the case of oil exports, they plumped for the most optimistic assessment of Canadian reserves. In April 1972, the Task Force concluded that natural gas supplies in the North "must and will" relieve the restrictions on further export imposed by the National Energy Board. In taking this decision, it appears again that the Chairman of the Task Force was decisive in allaying doubts in the minds of several colleagues. Whether the Cabinet was informed of the decision remains unclear. But it had the effect of reaffirming the thrust of northern exploration and development and servicing the American export market.

Nor was the even more serious question posed concerning the national interest in pursuing the export of northern oil and natural gas. The development cost to the government of supporting the construction of a Mackenzie Gas Pipeline, excluding equity consideration, would be extremely high. Yet the Canada Oil and Gas Land Regulations were so generous to the foreign lease-holders (apart from other privileges, such as taxation benefits) that public expenditures would not likely be recovered, much less a significant rent collected. What was the purpose of these exports then? Whose interests did they serve? On this point the Task Force had nothing to report in 1970-72.

c. *The Consortium Approach*: The Canada Oil and Gas Land Regulations established the ground rules for northern exploration; their decisive modification was necessary if Canada were to gain anything at all from petroleum production in the North. However, any changes aimed at increasing effective royalty rates would be resisted by the companies, for obvious reasons. Under these circumstances, Ottawa's strategy (assuming of course that it desired the protection of the public interest) would most appropriately aim at private sector competition to avoid a common front of corporate interests backed by Washington. Consortia of this kind would exert formidable pressure on senior officials. Yet Ottawa chose instead to encourage these combinations so that they might plan together the pattern of northern resource extraction and delivery.

Senior officials actively promoted mergers of pipeline competitors on the Mackenzie. By June 1972, after considerable trouble in overcoming tensions between the Gas Arctic Study Systems Group (found in June 1970), and the Northwest Project Study Group, formed one month later, the Task Force had helped assemble Canadian Artic Gas Study Ltd., a formidable group of fourteen petroleum and pipeline companies, later expanded to a membership of twenty-seven.° In the Beaufort Sea it dealt with a solid front of the firms with proprietory interests in the area. The Arctic Petroleum Operators Association, formed in January 1970, aggregated the interests of firms in the high Arctic.

In practice, the consortia, including much the same membership whatever the area of interest, not only owned or controlled, but also coordinated northern economic activity. The petroleum and pipeline companies had financial reasons for pooling their resources given the magnitude of required investments. But as an additional benefit, a common approach gave them added bargaining power in dealing with Ottawa. For, barring a radical shift in Canadian jurisdiction, the regulatory system for the mining and petroleum sector throughout the North would be directed by Canadian officials in Ottawa. It was imperative for companies to retain as much influence in the capital as possible to ensure the continuation of their special rights and privileges, and to obtain maximum public assistance in the out-transportation of resources.

The Task Force was not in a mood to question the consortium approach. It preferred a stable economic environment to competition; consortia offered a mechanism to speed up the pace of northern development. Government support for Canadian Artic Gas Study Limited was the most important demonstration of the strategy because of the visibility and magnitude of the proposed Mackenzie pipeline system; the same approach, however, was foreseen for other northern projects as well.

d. *The Panarctic Formula*: The success of Panarctic Oils Limited after 1968 appeared to vindicate active federal participation in business ventures in the North. With 45 per cent equity in the company, and with direct influence over oil and natural gas exploration in the Arctic, Panarctic Oils Limited represented a new policy instrument for fulfilling northern objectives; it could at

° By 1975, it had been reduced to 19 members.

once ensure greater Canadian participation in resource development, strengthen Canadian jurisdictional claims, and provide an example of good corporate behaviour in its approach to the native people and the northern environment. At last Canada controlled a major oil company. Moreover it was under federal rather than provincial control. All Canadians might be proud. It is not surprising, therefore, that the Panarctic Oils Limited experience should be held up as a show-piece; indeed the "Panarctic Formula" quickly became a familiar slogan in characterizing federal assistance in northern economic development.

In some cases the 45 to 55 per cent funding formula between the federal Government on the one hand and a consortium of interested resource companies on the other was strictly adhered to. For example, in July 1970 a prominent Montreal consulting firm obtained a contract (without tender) for a joint federal-business research project on transportation alternatives in the eastern Arctic. The nine oil firms involved included Atlantic-Richfield, Humble, Mobil, Elf, British Petroleum, Home, Imperial, Pacific Petroleum, Commonwealth Oil and Canadian Industrial Gas and Oil. Information would be shared between the private companies and the several Government Departments involved. More specifically, the Department of Indian Affairs and Northern Development and the Northern Economic Development Branch had initiated the proposal. The former then used the "Panarctic Formula" to sell the idea to Treasury Board.

At other times the term was used by Government officials to refer to massive federal assistance for capital projects without demanding equity control. The Strathcona Sound lead-zinc development in Baffin Island, vigorously pursued by the Northern Economic Development Branch, involved heavy federal expenditures, particularly in transportation facilities, to permit large-scale production schedules for 1975-76. While the Government purchased an 18 per cent equity position, it was a minority holder, without the controls and direct participation maintained in Panarctic Oils. Nevertheless, the formula was invoked to obtain support for the venture. Apparently the term could also refer to "close cooperation" and "mutual assistance."

Federal cooperation with the Arctic Petroleum Operators' Association in studying the feasibility of Arctic shipping provides another interpretation of the Panarctic Formula. Having approached the Task Force on Northern Oil Development in August 1971, this Association was succeful in provoking the setting up of a special Inter-Departmental Steering Group to develop a shared information base for northern transportation systems and to investigate alternative approaches.[20]

Within the Steering Group, industry and Government set about to identify gaps in existing information and parcel out mutual responsibilities for covering them. The fundamental assumption of the exercise was confidence in each others' studies; neither side wished to duplicate research. In this case, then, the Panarctic formula referred to a *focus* of collaboration as well as funding.

As its interpretation by Government officials broadened, the Panarctic Formula came to symbolize a Government approach to private sector activity in the North as a whole rather than to any specific equity sharing formula or project assistance. It served as a signal to business that government-business *collaboration* rather than *conflict* was the first priority of Ottawa planners. Canadian, even Government, equity participation would not affect the behaviour of Panarctic Oils Limited in the "market place," nor would any other project involving federal assistance interfere with "commercial" decisions affecting the economic development of the North. Ottawa in any capacity was a reliable "partner."

Those individuals, including the Chairman of the House Standing Committee on Indian Affairs and Northern Development, who thought that Panarctic Oils Limited would be used as a policy instrument to implement Government objectives, were bitterly disappointed. The new company prided itself on its buccaneering spirit in the North. Not only did the company quickly distinguish itself by its disregard for the northern environment and its refusal to respond to the requests for consultation with native people in the exploration areas, but it also attached itself to powerful multinationals, particularly Tenneco; and sold its future discoveries to American customers in exchange for advance financial drilling assistance. The Minister of the Department of Indian Affairs and Northern Development had achieved a remarkable set of conflicting assignments: as Minister, he had committed himself to the priorities of *Canada's North 1970-1980*, to native rights and environmental protection; as the minister responsible for Panarctic Oils Limited, he participated in their violation.

e. *The Exclusion of Public Participation*: Not only did *Canada's North 1970-1980* underline an apparent Ottawa concern for "consultation" with the native people, but earlier the Trudeau Government's vague commitments to "the Just Society" and greater public participation had also promised a more open policy process. More than a few able Canadians had entered the federal service after 1968 considering that a new era had dawned.

The importance of the North in the first Trudeau years offered an ideal opportunity for Ottawa to implement participatory planning since neither the Yukon nor the Northwest Territories had provincial status. In fact, in certain respects, it was not possible for the Government to go back on its promises. The drafting of Territorial Land Use Regulations, for example, announced in 1969, impelled critics of the Department of Indian Affairs and Northern Development to anticipate bravely:

> The drafting of the Land Use Regulations marks a significant departure . . . recognizing for the first time that there are other segments of society besides industrial interests who have a legitimate interest in the area and thus a right to be consulted about legislative decisions affecting it. From the very beginning there was an attempt to involve conservation interests and have their representatives join those of government and industry in a working group on the draft regulations . . . The territorial councils in Yellowknife and Whitehorse were also consulted, and finally in an attempt to involve public opinion from beyond these special interest groups the regulations were published in Part I of the *Gazette* and public comment invited before their final promulgation![21]

Ultimately, however, the consultative process proved unsatisfactory. In the first place, the Inuit, Indian, and Metis were excluded — their interests were assumed to be represented by the Territorial Councils. Even by the standards of the day regarding consultation with native people in Canada, this lack of sensitivity was appalling and guaranteed native rejection of the Regulations..

Second and more important, public consultation did not involve a consideration of land use planning or management, but rather a more limited concept of land use control. Land utilization was crucial to the direction of northern economic development and of vital concern to Northerners. It offered an opportunity for Ottawa to exercise control in the protection of the public interest. The Minister of Indian Affairs and Northern Development recognized both the problem and opportunity in his address to the Tundra Conference of September, 1969:

> The problems that face us are critical but we have an almost unparalleled opportunity to exercise an ecological conscience in how we develop our northern resources. Laws and regulations after all are only tools to achieve a desired objective. They are important of course but so is the objective of wise stewardship of the land and the resources it supports. We also have an obligation to exercise wise stewardship for the benefit of indigenous people who presently depend on wildlife and fishery resources and for future generations of all Canadians who will want to study and to enjoy the northern environment.[22]

Nevertheless "the wise stewardship of the land and resources it supports" was not taken up in the Territorial Land Use Regulations as they ultimately emerged from seven drafts. The introduction of land management zones represented a considerable step forward despite well known gaps in enforcement of the Regulations. But the Regulations left open the merits of land use itself.

According to the Department of Indian Affairs and Northern Development, "the Land Use Regulations are designed to set formal rules to exploration and development activities on northern land, but in no way prohibits or excludes such undertakings." Land ownership, for example, was not affected by the Regulations. The private sector would determine both the nature, the pace and purposes of resource development. In these areas, which represented the real worry of native people and environmentalists, the "public" had no right to be involved in any way. Industry and Government would plan northern economic development.

Only industry participated in northern policy-making and its level of effectiveness was in direct proportion to the political impotence of the excluded groups. *Canada's North 1970-1980* and the lip-service given to participation in no way affected the centrality of business in the North and the dynamic of northern growth that conflicted with official promises.

If anything, the North after 1968 provided special opportunities for administrative discretion. An excluded native population, scattered and with few resources, offered little challenge to Indian Affairs officials trained in the habits of colonial Government. Senior Department officials administering the North were schooled in a tradition hostile to participation by the native people. One "protected" the natives; one did not "listen" to them. When it finally appeared that northern development had arrived, there was no disposition to view the Northerners as owners and managers of their historic lands. They were depressed outsiders with a high unemployment rate, requiring firm guidance (and jobs).

Moreover, legislation dealing with the North was and is geared to facilitate administrative discretion, delegating vast areas of rule-making to the Department of Indian Affairs and Northern Development and other agencies. Environmental protection legislation along the lines of the United States National Environmental Protection Act was resisted because it would provide an instrument for protecting the public interest and remove discretion in this area from the bureaucracy.

Compounding the exclusiveness of federal control and administrative discretion, was the monopoly over information relating to northern development. Neither the press nor Parliament had access to the ongoing discussions between business and Government regarding the disposition of northern lands and resources. Both could be manipulated to accept decisions long since finalized. The public was told to wait for the next election. Command over the "confidential" and "secret" files permitted the Government to conceal the real dynamic of northern growth by excluding Canadians from the policy process. In terms of major economic investment decisions in the resource field, this situation fitted in nicely with the concept of policy-initiation in the private sector, and Government agencies as transmission belts for these demands; in terms of planning infrastructure, it meant liasing intimately with industry to ensure respective roles were not out of line. Planning the $300 million transportation facilities required for the

* Changes in the Canadian Oil and Gas Land Regulations for example, would not have to come before Parliament or public hearings, leaving one of the most important variables in northern development effectively outside the scope of public enquiry.

construction of a Mackenzie pipeline demanded intimate Government-industry collaboration — in advance of Energy Board "public hearings," of course, since years of preparation were needed to create an adequate infrastructure for the project.

The other constituencies, native people, university researchers, and environmental groups, were denied any major policy role and did not have access to information. In 1970-72, the Government was highly successful in its control over information, and in developing close relations with industry while excluding other groups from the policy process. Groups such as the Canadian Arctic Resources Committee lamented their disadvantages as compared with business, but came up with few practical proposals to open the political process in Ottawa.

In place of informing the public concerning resource and pipeline matters and consulting with the groups affected, Task Force officials took it upon themselves to advise the Cabinet on the public interest. In the July 1972 *Progress Report* on the proposed Mackenzie Gas Pipeline, for example, they stated squarely that "the weight of public opinion in Canada is generally in favour of northern pipeline development." Also, provided that care was taken to ensure Canadian ownership and participation, senior officials perceived "community support" for the Mackenzie corridor. Jean Chretien's speech to the 18th Annual Association of Pipeline Contractors on May 11, 1972, entitled "Mackenzie Corridor: Vision Becomes Reality," had been well received and suggested continuing support in the business community for the undertaking. There even appeared to be evidence that the Canadian capital market would and could underwrite the construction of the proposed Mackenzie gas pipeline.

Despite the stated concern for "consultation" with the native people, there was simply no scope for a meaningful dialogue given the model of northern development that had emerged and been accepted after 1968. In both areas, native people and the environment, protection could take place only at the margin — that is, after the framework of development was already established by the central resource and pipeline decisions worked out in confidence between private executives and senior officials in

Ottawa. *Canada's North 1970-1980* merely advised administrators in the Department and agencies working in the North that within the broader framework they should be more sensitive to natives and the environment. Some were, but many officials found their role humiliating. In few areas of public policy in Canada was the discrepancy between the official line and the actual events as remarkable. It is not surprising that leaks of confidential documents became more frequent after 1972.

This situation would not change with a new document such as *Canada's North 1970-1980*, unless the senior officials and the private executives were replaced, or forced under pressure from the public to alter the framework of northern resource development itself. Between 1970 and 1972, little pressure of this kind existed, although opposition was gathering.

NOTES

1. In March 1970, Minnesota Senator W. Mondale and fourteen other midwest senators sponsored a bill to "forgive" the St. Lawrence Seaway debt leaving only operating and maintenance costs to be met annually by tolls. Similar bills had failed in the past two Congresses, but the Nixon administration had pledged itself to overhaul American maritime policy. Public Law 91-469, October 21, 1970, introduced in Section 43 a (2) an amendment to Section 5 of the St. Lawrence Seaway Development Corporation Act (PL 358, May, 1954) which stated (among others) that "the obligation of the Corporation to pay the unpaid interest which has accrued on such obligations is terminated." The swift action threw the Canadian St. Lawrence Seaway Authority into confusion, because it eliminated any incentive on the American side for raising tolls. Canada had built five-sixths of the Seaway.

2. By 1975 the concept of a DND northern base was again under discussion.

3. Walter Stewart, *Shrug: Trudeau in Power* (Toronto, 1972). The Supergroup concept, although important in stressing the lack of accountability of the Trudeau government, failed to note the inherent instability within the top elite itself.

4. E. J. Dosman, "Transport Policy in the North: Organizational Goals and Policy Environment," in K. W. Studwicki-Gizbert (ed.), *Issues in Canadian Transport Policy* (Toronto, 1974), pp. 441-71.

5. *Canada's North 1970-80: Statement of the Government of Canada on Northern Development in the 1970's*, presented to the Standing Committee on Indian Affairs and Northern Development, March 28, 1972.

6. *Ibid.*, p. 6.

7. *Ibid.*, p. 29.

8. Canadian Arctic Resources Committee, *Northern Perspectives*, vol. 2 No. 2, 1973. James Woodford "The Imwerk Incident", *Canadian Forum*, June-July, 1973.

9. See Chapter 3, p. 42-46 and Chart. CALURA, *Report for 1971* and Statistics Canada, March 1974 underscore the extent of foreign control, particularly American, in the mining sector as well.

10. Pearse (ed.), *op. cit.*, pp. 80-98.

11. *Ibid.* pp. 88-89 "The 5 per cent for the first three years is unprecedented. Furthermore, the 10 per cent thereafter is to be compared with a 16 2/3 per cent rate in the United States offshore areas and a 20 per cent effective rate in Alaska."

12. Industry lashed out at what it considered Ottawa's "breach of faith." It "had felt quite secure in its belief that none of the changes would be retroactive." Instead, "Having given away rights to most of the nation's potential oil and gas areas on most generous terms, the Government of Canada has now cast itself in the role of "Indian giver" by demanding the return of half of the acreage." *Oilweek*, May 18, 1970.

13. By late 1974 nothing had been done about the changes in the oil and gas regulations promised in late 1970. *Oilweek*, May 18, 1970.

14. Eric Kierans, "The Day the Cabinet was Misled," *Canadian Forum*, Vol. LIV, March 1974, p. 4.

15. National Energy Board, *Energy Supply and Demand in Canada and Export Demand for Canadian Energy, 1966-1990* (Ottawa, 1969).

16. *Oilweek, October 12, 1970.*

17. See Bregha, *et al.*, *A Case for Delaying the Mackenzie Valley Natural Gas Pipeline.* York University, June, 1974,

for an excellent discussion of Ottawa's ready acceptance of statistics from industry, with predictable results.

18. Toronto *Globe and Mail*, November 8, 1974. Industry sources now referred to 7 t.c.f. Note also Canadian Arctic Resources Committee, "Gas From the Mackenzie Delta: Now or Later," Conference Proceedings, May 23-24, 1974.

19. Judith Maxwell, *Energy From the Arctic: Facts and Issues* (Montreal, 1973), p. 23. Other companies such as Gulf Oil Canada Ltd. and Dome Petroleum also received advance loans. This flow, which amounted to $700 million by 1974, was virtually ended in that year when the Federal Power Commission in the United States decided that American consumers were unlikely to receive frontier gas from Canada, and excluded such payment in rate calculations. Toronto *Globe and Mail*, February 9, 1974; *Financial Post Survey of Oils*, November 30, 1972, 1973, 1974.

20. By July 1971 the Arctic Petroleum Operators Association was sufficiently cohesive to request the Task Force on Northern Oil Development to initiate a joint study of harbour and transportation alternatives in Arctic waters.

21. G. Beakhust and P. Usher "The Regulation of Land Use in the North," unpublished manuscript (Ottawa, 1973).

22. Quoted in *Ibid.*, p. 3.

CHAPTER SEVEN
Planning the Mackenzie Pipeline 1970-72

Although economic initiatives by industry were encouraged in the North as a whole (in the Arctic Islands as well as the mainland Northwest and Yukon Territories), all senior officials in the 1970-72 period perceived the huge task of constructing a Mackenzie Valley natural gas pipeline as the central Government-industry effort into the mid-1970s. Not until late in 1972 did significant attention shift to the feasibility of pipelines or the marine transportation of hydrocarbons in the high Arctic. Even then, the matter was taken up only when it appeared that planning for the Mackenzie pipeline was in the final stages.

Pipeline planning on the Mackenzie, in short, offered the chief immediate focus for inter-departmental planning 1970-72 in the Canadian North. It dominated Government-business relations, providing a common preoccupation. Community development, land and water management, and transportation studies were initiated to accommodate the needs of a Mackenzie gas pipeline[1]. No one in Ottawa doubted that the North was on the verge of a dramatic expansion of economic activity; no one doubted where the action was.

There seemed to be little time to lose. Indian Affairs and Northern Development in November 1970 thought an industry decision to construct a natural gas pipeline might be forthcoming *within six months*. It was imperative that the Task Force on Northern Oil Development prepare suitable support structures as soon as possible.

The August 1970 Northern Pipeline Guidelines had cleared the way for uninhibited Government cooperation in the project. "Tailoring to possible demand" as a senior Indian Affairs official succinctly put it while planning a meeting with Arctic operators in December, 1972, became the working slogan within the Task Force in the period 1970-72. There was now to be no withholding of information from industry; contractors' and consultants' requests for information or their reports were to be forwarded directly to the consortia planning the construction of the pipeline. Before August 1970, such an intermediary role would have appeared inappropriate. Now all barriers to discretion fell. Between August 1970 and fall 1972, satisfactory progress could be reported in the planning of the Mackenzie Corridor.[1]

1. ALTERNATIVES TO THE PIPELINE

The proposed Mackenzie pipeline system represented a major undertaking and would have incalculable effects on the North and Canada. It would seem normal, therefore, to examine alternatives to a pipeline system for transporting Alaskan and northern natural gas to United States markets.

Task Force officials didn't see the need for studies of this kind, however. They were aware that individuals like Richard Rohmer were keen to explore exotic transport ideas, including giant resource carrying aircraft, LNG (liquified natural gas) pipelines, and submarine or semi-submersible tankers for use in the North. Similarly, they knew that the Queen's University Institute of Guided Ground Transport was exploring the feasibility of an Arctic railway as an alternative to pipelines.

Rohmer in his *Arctic Imperative* had stated that:

It would seem that the owners are hypnotized by the pipe, the only method to use so far as they are concerned. In fact, they have done absolutely no research on alternative modes such as the railway or air, and have concentrated strictly and simply upon the pipeline methodology both for oil and gas.[2]

The same is true on the Government side in 1970-72; the Task Force simply could not accept the possibility that an Arctic railway (the least fanciful alternative in its view) could transport oil or natural gas more efficiently than a 48″ pipeline. Energy

Mines and Resources, immediately prior to the Task Force July 1972 *Memo* to Cabinet, dismissed the notion out of hand. The Queen's University study had just been released (June 1972).[3]

Piecing together information from various sources, Energy, Mines and Resources estimated on May 9, 1972 that for a 2 million barrel per day capacity, a double track railway with 19 trains of 168 cars each carrying 93.7 tons of oil would be required. They would pass each other from either direction at 35 minute intervals, and require a total manpower of 4533 personnel. It scoffed at the notion that such a system came into question in the transportation of northern supplies.

The Transport Committee of the Task Force was therefore given the thankless job of developing a paper to accompany the July Memo in which the various alternatives would be briefly reviewed and which would conclude with the assertion that pipelines were more efficient than other modes. Transport received no special funding for its "research" which was *pro forma*, and done in-house by its Policy Planning and Special Projects group. It was dutifully attached as an appendix and raised no questions at the Cabinet level.

No senior officials questioned the essential wisdom of northern pipelines at this time, or doubted their merits over other forms of transport. The Ministry of Transport issued a brief press release on June 8, 1972 which referred to on-going "studies" of the rail option. But this was a sop to Queen's University only. The more accurate reflection of Ottawa opinion was the absence of any mention whatsoever of a railway option in the *Northwest Transportation Plan 1972*, February 1972:

> The major transportation requirements in this part of the study area the Mackenzie Basin and the North Slope is related to the potential for oil and gas on the North Slope. Recent gas discoveries near the mouth of the Mackenzie, coupled with major oil and gas discoveries in the Prudhoe Bay area of Alaska, have caused developers to seek routes by which these products can be moved to market economically. Oil appears to lend itself best to one of two transportation alternatives, tanker or pipeline, while a pipeline is the only feasible transportation system for gas.[4]

2. PIPELINE PLANNING AND LAND NEGOTIATIONS

When Atlantic Richfield announced the discovery of significant petroleum reserves on the North Slope of Alaska, the Alaskan State Administration came under pressure to formulate a concrete position respecting native land claims. Two years before, in response to native objections, Stuart Udall, American Secretary of the Interior, placed a freeze on Alaskan land allotments pending an Indian claims settlement. By so doing, Washington and Alaska went on record as supporting a land settlement with the native people prior to the construction of a trans-Alaskan pipeline. In turn, they obtained the support of the Alaskan Indians and Inuit.[5]

In contrast, Canada refused to accept the principle of a prior land settlement. Unlike the Americans, Indian Affairs in Canada had learned nothing, and its position simply reflected a reflex to limit Indian land claims in the North whenever valuable resources were discovered. In fact, the signing of Treaties 8 and 11 covering some 400,000 square miles of the traditionally occupied areas of the Northwest Territories had been related directly to resource discoveries. Treaty 8 was signed in 1899 three years after the discovery of gold in the Yukon. Treaty 11 was signed in 1921 after discoveries of oil by Imperial Oil at Norman Wells in the summer of 1920. Both treaties in short were initiated by federal Governments seeking to extinguish Indian claims to land in light of significant resource development.

The Prudhoe Bay discovery added an enormous impetus to native awareness of the significance of land claims and land management in general in the protection of their livelihood and indeed survival in Canada.

After 1968, northern native people realized not only that the stakes were big, but that developments would have irreversible effects on their culture and economic future. In the Yukon, where 900 natives of Ilingit descent would share directly in the Alaskan settlement, the Yukon Native Brotherhood was formed in October 1968. The mood was catching, reinforcing a growth in Indian consciousness throughout Canada that became apparent some years before.

The August 1970 Northern Pipeline Guidelines had included the provision that Northerners must be trained and employed for construction and operation of any pipelines. At that time,

Panarctic Oils employed only six Eskimos. The Guidelines, however, offered an insight into Ottawa's thinking, in that they omitted any reference to land claims or a land settlement. They were not even preceded by a general statement of Government policy. This latter came only in *Canada's North, 1970-1980* almost two years later. By that date the Indians, Inuit, and Metis of the North had taken long strides forward in organization.

In January 1970, the Committee For Original Peoples' Entitlement was formed after the Atkinson oil discovery (of January 1970) in the Mackenzie Delta, indicating that an organizing drive among the native people was underway. In February, the Indian Brotherhood of the Northwest Territories was incorporated as a non-profit benevolent society. Although it had existed in name since the summer of 1967, it emerged three years later as an increasingly effective spokesman for Treaty Indians in the North. With the first natural gas discovery in the Mackenzie Delta in 1971, there appeared greater confidence among Northerners as well that considerable wealth lay beneath their ground, as well as in Alaska. It increased the determination of native people to obtain a land settlement just as it stimulated the appetites of the integrated oil companies and senior officials in Ottawa. In August 1971, the Inuit Tapirisat of Canada was founded to speak for the 17,000 Eskimo in Canada. The idea had emerged in July 1970 at the Coppermine Conference to discuss problems of the Eskimo. One month later the Yukon Association of Non-Status Indians was formed.

These groups obtained tremendous moral support when the Alaskan Native Claims Settlement Act was finally adopted in December 1971 providing the most generous land settlement awarded to any native group in any area of North America in the long history of European settlement of the Continent. The settlement provided $ 462.5 million in direct cash, along with $ 500 million in future mineral rights and 40 million acres of land. One Canadian expert termed it " . . . one of the most imaginative pieces of legislation in American history."[6] The Alaskan settlement now became a basic minimum for Canadian Indians and Inuit. Yet the Trudeau Government explicitly rejected the recognition of aboriginal rights.

As local self-government and economic development proceeded, Indians, Inuit, and Metis were rapidly becoming more sophisticated politically. Communities were developing structures that aggregated their interests and strengthened the drive for greater self-determination. The white population in the same communities and the whole pattern of racial exclusiveness of the North were not successfully disseminating a positive image of Canadian citizenship throughout the Territories. The native people remained separate and distinct; and they wanted their land.

Senior officials among themselves had to admit also that Indians and Metis were now better organized. The first reference to possible extensive delays in pipeline construction was volunteered in a Task Force meeting in summer 1971. Yet Indian Affairs and the Task Force remained determined to go ahead with pipeline construction in the Mackenzie, without a land settlement. They simply refused to countenance the loss of time involved in lengthy negotiations with the native people.

The Task Force, to its credit, requested Cabinet approval for this strategy. Its July 1972 *Report* to Cabinet presented the position in the bluntest possible terms: Pipeline construction does not prejudice Indian rights under Treaties 8 and 11; the settlement of land claims, therefore, is not a prerequisite to the approval of pipeline applications. As a result, the Government should commit itself to no more than "consultation" and "the protection of the rights of northern residents." The natives should not be encouraged into Alaskan-type assumptions. Cabinet agreed (July 14, 1972).

The essence of the matter was timing: if Canadian Gas Arctic could move quickly, it would move through National Energy Board hearings before actual confrontation could develop. And once approved, the promise of employment would divide native organizations.

3. PREPARATIONS TO JULY 1972

By the time of the July 1972 *Progress Report* to Cabinet, the Task Force felt in a position to conclude that "preparations for the construction of a gas pipeline from the Mackenzie Delta area of Northern Canada and Prudhoe Bay are now reaching an advanced stage," and that planning was proceeding on the assumption of pipeline construction "during the middle years of the decade."

Such a timetable foresaw concluding the work of the Task Force by late 1972, or at the latest, spring of 1973; an application for a Certificate of Public Convenience and Necessity from the National Energy Board in 1973; and the initiation of construction in winter, 1973-74, or less optimistically, 1974-75. Matters were well in hand.

More specifically, the Task Force had confronted two sets of problems in planning for the pipeline in 1970-72. There was first the conceptual issue, designing a regulatory structure for a Mackenzie pipeline corridor that would be consistent with the broader regulatory apparatus respecting northern development. Senior officials referred to this process as "defining the national interest." Second, there was the urgent task of preparing logistics support for pipeline construction, and assisting industry in the selection of an appropriate route.

The National Interest: The northern regulatory structure had operated at three levels:

sovereignty: the body of regulations associated with the control and surveillance of foreign activities in the North.

energy: regulations designed to ensure adequate safeguards, standards, and financial conditions for oil and gas development in the North.

land and water use: measures to protect the northern environment as they affected the lands and waters of the Arctic.

Now a fourth was added, pipeline regulations, which must be consistent with the others. Sovereignty, energy, and land and water use regulations had all been reviewed after the events of 1968[7] so that considerable deliberation went into the question of pipeline regulations.

All Task Force members agreed that the Northern Pipeline Guidelines were not specific enough, and that at least some points would have to be elaborated. By July 1972, they had reached a consensus on the areas in which the "national interest needs to be defined in more detail than the August 1970 Guidelines."

Native People and the Environment: Just as a prior land settlement was rejected so also the Task Force in its discussions ruled out environmental legislation similar to the United States National Environmental Policy Act enacted in 1970. Advanced legislation of this kind provided stringent safeguards, and it had teeth. Instead, faced by public pressure, the Task Force opted for Expanded Guidelines for Northern Pipelines, tabled in the House of Commons, June 28, 1972. They contained three headings — Pipeline Corridor Guidelines; Environmental Guidelines; and Social Guidelines. While some revisions were foreseen as a result of public briefs on the Guidelines, the Task Force considered its work in these areas as accomplished by July 1972.

Native Employment: Following the August Northern Pipeline Guidelines, a Committee on Native Employment under the Advisory Committee on Northern Development was set up to ensure work opportunities and available work skills. Suitable progress had been made by 1972. Beyond that, the Task Force underlined its determination that there be maximum opportunity for the employment of Canadian talent wherever it was located, and the establishment of pipeline construction expertise in Canada at a world scale level.[8]

The remaining work centred rather on financial, ownership and Canadian content guidelines. While the issues were not seen as unusually complex, policy decisions in several areas would be required before pipeline applications could be received. Each posed questions.

Right-of-Way Terms: The applicant would have to apply to the Department of Indian Affairs and Northern Development for a grant of right-of-way under the Territorial Lands Act. Would hearings be appropriate? The Task Force thought not. Would, however, the concept of terminable grant and right of way help satisfy native organizers, the media and economic nationalists?

Ownership: Maximum Canadian ownership was popular throughout the country. J.J. Greene himself popularized the notion of equity control over a Mackenzie pipeline. But there was some doubt about the effects of the various levels of control on the economy as well as the ability of capital markets in Canada to underwrite the project. In July 1972, the Task Force recommended a safe generalization, that "maximum Canadian ownership be pursued yet causing least disturbance to the balance of payments." Under any plan, the majority of Directors, chief executive and financial officers must be Canadian.

The Task Force agreed that informed advice from eminent Canadians in the private sector would be required to finalize recommendations in this area. Therefore the creation of a national advisory Council was announced in September 1972 to coordinate the financing of a Mackenzie Valley natural gas pipeline, specifically the appropriate level of Canadian control and financial participation.[9]

Canadian Content: The Task Force recommended that the question of Canadian content was important and that whatever specific financial and institutional arrangements were adopted, the use of Canadian materials, equipment and supplies should be maximized. It advised the formation of a special Inter-Departmental Committee on Industrial Supply.

The July 1972 *Report* undoubtedly marks the highpoint of optimism about the early construction of the Mackenzie line. Benefits "of considerable magnitude" were foreseen for Canada; the worst problems appeared already surmounted. The native and environmental "intervenors" were contained.

4. LOGISTICS AND THE SELECTION OF THE CANADIAN ROUTE

The August 1970 Northern Pipeline Guidelines had introduced the concept of a Mackenzie corridor. It indicated that one gas and one oil pipeline would be permitted, but was imprecise beyond that as to its specific aspects, particularly the actual route from Prudhoe Bay and the Mackenzie Delta. Immediately following the acceptance of the August 1970 Guidelines, Government Departments, particularly Transport and the Department of Indian Affairs and Northern Development, initiated studies to determine, with industry, the optimal route, and the optimal mix of support facilities: road, barge, and air.

Providing support services for a project as vast as the construction of a Mackenzie natural gas pipeline represented a major interdepartmental effort. Moreover, transport planners foresaw serious distortions if the Government concentrated on logistic support to the exclusion of long-range, inter-modal problems in the Mackenzie River valley. It is fair to conclude, however, that planning in this area was "on schedule" as well by July 1972.°

° But the Task Force thought that Alberta might give trouble on throughput arrangements, pipeline tariffs and rates of return. Since northern gas would (inevitably) be more expensive, Alberta producers would also want higher

By November 1970, Alberta Gas Trunk and Canadian National Railways announced the initiation of two major studies dealing with pipeline logistics and the Corridor concept. The latter was to deal with all aspects of a possible gas and oil pipeline, highway, railroad, and waterway approach. It provided a stimulus to Government Departments to work out respective roles. It was imperative that Transport and Indian Affairs cooperate closely. The first step taken, therefore, was the setting up of an interdepartmental working group to recommend a pattern and schedule of transportation activities to meet the needs of the concerned Departments. The study would also have the useful effect of identifying necessary policy areas such as the choice of building an all-weather Mackenzie highway, long promoted by Indian Affairs, or expanding the fleet of Northern Transportation Company Ltd.

In the 1971-72 period the Ministry of Transport's Arctic Transportation Agency became increasingly active in coordinating logistics planning for the pipeline period, while Indian Affairs' Northern Roads Committee studied surface transportation requirements. The Pipeline Committee of the Task Force, for its part, monitored on-going logistics studies in consultation with the three competing gas consortia.

By July 1972 the following gains could be noted:

The groundwork was laid for a comprehensive review of air transport requirements. In March 1972, an in-house report, "Aviation Requirements for pipeline construction in the NWT," made an important contribution to air transport development for the Mackenzie Corridor.

A pioneering study was implemented on a user-charge policy on the Mackenzie to ensure a measure of cost recovery on river improvement projects. Whether industry would accept the principle remained unclear.

The Mackenzie Highway Sub-committee of the Interdepartmental Committee on Northern Roads was making useful progress on an integrated traffic model which would measure the implications

well-head prices in domestic as well as American markets. "There will be no disposition on the part of producers or the Alberta Government towards a two-price system."

of different sources of pipe and construction schedules in the Mackenzie network.

It was possible to project for the consideration of Cabinet in July 1972 that support services associated with the construction of a Mackenzie natural gas pipeline would approach $ 300 million.

Transport planners, however, were faced with two difficult areas of uncertainty. First the decision in favour of a Mackenzie Highway was made without reference to on-going work on logistics support for the pipeline. Without warning therefore the planning framework was altered. Northern Transportation Company Ltd. was frustrated, convinced that barge costs were much lower, and that the pipeline companies were counting on moving most of their materials by water rather than highway. In July, 1972, it complained in a letter to senior officials that the operating cost per ton mile of barge transport was approximately one-half that of the highway even when the road-bed costs were donated and the cost of the company's dredging programme included. Even if the highway were built, 50 per cent of the pipeline traffic would still be handled on the river. But it was not successful in reversing the decision.

The decision to proceed with an all-weather highway added a new problem. Some members of the Mackenzie Valley sub-committee set up by Indian Affairs' Northern Roads Committee were edgy about environmental hazards associated with the project, as well as native opposition to the road. Others, who urged speed, were dismayed that environmentalists "were calling the tune" in the Committee, and were concerned that road planning was not being coordinated carefully enough with industry. They urged colleagues not to get out of step with the pipeline companies; a crash program at the end must be avoided. The July Cabinet *Memo* could indicate that "pipeline planning is now proceeding in parallel with Mackenzie Highway work and the schedule calls for use of the completed highway in pipeline construction."

The second difficulty was that experienced in persuading the competing groups interested in building a natural gas pipeline to merge. Greene, Minister of Energy, Mines and Resources, had made no secret of his determination to seek a common effort by the consortia. One .had remained aloof from the beginning (Trans

Mountain) but Northwest Project Study Group and the Gas Arctic consortium disagreed vigorously over markets, financial and management principles, and route selection.

The most probable explanation of the difficulties which the various groups had in coming together lies in the often bitter competition which had existed among certain firms, and the incestuous network of corporate and marketing relationships which existed within each group. For instance, TransCanada and American Natural Gas of the Northwest Study Group had been locked in a fierce competition with Northern Natural Gas of the Gas Arctic Group over access to Alberta gas and the American midwest market ever since the 1950s. During the Energy Board export hearings in 1970 TransCanada had intervened to prevent Consolidated Natural Gas Ltd (98.5 per cent owned by Northern) application for 1.5 t.c.f. Consolidated was turned down completely, while the other three applications were approved in full. Since TransCanada was a founding member of the Northwest Group, and Northern Natural Gas joined Gas Arctic in August, 1970, their rivalry was bound to affect inter-consortia cooperation.[10]

Moreover, Gas Arctic and the Northwest Group fundamentally differed over route concepts. The former had a marked west coast orientation and therefore favoured a southerly route into Alberta, possibly using existing Alberta Gas Trunk rights-of-way. The latter, Northwest, was basically composed of utility companies serving eastern Canadian and American midwestern markets. The preferred route from Alaska and the Arctic along the Mackenzie River would be more direct, across the top of Alberta and then diagonally down to Emerson, Manitoba.[11]

Compounding these difficulties were genuine difficulties over the feasibility of Canadian ownership and the use of Canadian or American engineers. Relations from the first were marked by an air of suspicion that was not easily dissipated.[12]

In terms of interdependent corporate and marketing relationships, the connections even within the Northwest Group are very instructive. Since the mid-sixties TransCanada and American Natural Gas were involved in a joint ownership of Great Lakes Transmission. TransCanada marketed gas to Great Lakes which in turn sold the gas to Michigan Wisconsin Pipeline, a subsidiary of American Natural Gas. TransCanada sold gas directly to Natural

Gas Pipeline Co., a subsidiary of Peoples Gas Co. The three founding members of the Northwest Group were therefore bound together in an intimate complex of corporate and marketing networks.[13]

Not until June 1972 did Gas Arctic and Northwest Project Study Group work out a satisfactory compromise and combine to form Canadian Arctic Gas Study Ltd.° This heartened Task Force officials and permitted them to indicate to Cabinet that the merger, and the possibility of Trans Mountain joining it, increased the likelihood of an early application before the National Energy Board. But the lateness of the decision to merge, increased the possibility of a costly crash programme to complete logistics preparations prior to construction.

The effects, however, were immediate. Canadian Gas Arctic established its own task force in Vancouver which by September 1972 was studying ten alternative pipeline routes including the social and environmental hazards associated with each. Now the

° The member companies in Canadian Arctic Gas Study Limited (1974):
Alberta Gas Trunk Line Co. Ltd.
Alberta Natural Gas Co. Ltd.
Atlantic Richfield Co.
Canada Development Corporation
Canadian National Railway Co.
Canadian Pacific Investments Ltd.
Canadian Superior Oil Ltd.
Canadian Utilities Ltd.
Colorado Interstate Gas Co.
Colombia Gas Transmission Corp.
Consumers Gas Co.
Exxon Corp.
Gulf Oil Canada Ltd.
Imperial Oil Ltd.
Michigan Wisconsin Pipeline Co.
Natural Gas Pipeline Co. of America
Northern and Central Gas Corp.
Northern Natural Gas Co.
Numac Oil and Gas Ltd.
Pacific Lighting Gas Development Co.
Panhandle Eastern Pipe Line Co.
Pembina Pipe Line Ltd.
Shell Canada Ltd.
Standard Oil Co. (Ohio)
Texas Eastern Transmission Corp.
TransCanada Pipe Lines
Union Gas Ltd.
Source: *Financial Post*, Survey of Oils, 1974

Government's traffic model could develop some sophistication. Detailed discussions began concerning the source of pipe; shipment destinations; dock facilities; stockpiling costs; and possible construction date. Initial progress following the merger was promising enough to dispel doubts concerning extensive delays.

By fall 1972, the Task Force on Northern Oil Development had been in operation for four years. During this period, its chief preoccupation had been the construction of a Mackenzie pipeline, oil or gas, or both. It looked as though its chief task was near completion. There had been bad moments, for example when, without consultation with Canada, American Secretary of the Interior Morton released a statement concerning the selection of a transportation corridor for that route:

> Finally, one of our orders withdraws 1.2 million acres as an addition to the existing transportation and utility corridor already under withdrawal. This long, narrow strip runs from the Prudhoe Bay area along the South edge of the Arctic National Wildlife range to the Canadian Border. It could be used for a natural gas pipeline and for other utilities.

Washington's reason for selecting this particular route was to avoid crossing the tract of land set aside as a National Wildlife Range, hoping to avoid a further confrontation with conservation groups. Unfortunately, the American utility corridor had to link up with the trunk line down the Mackenzie, and abutted on a sensitive area in the Yukon. As one official remarked:

> What the Americans appear to have completely overlooked is that Canada also has some very definite views on the location of a pipeline corridor on the Canadian side of the boundary. For example, the obvious extension of the U.S. corridor into Canada would pass in the vicinity of, or through, the community of Old Crow and the particularly sensitive Old Crow flats. Not only would such a corridor on the Canadian side raise the problems of the community of Old Crow, and the Old Crow flats, but also the perhaps even more important problem of the recent claim by the Indian people of Old Crow to practically all of the Northern portion of the Yukon.

There had also been delays. But in general, the Task Force had performed well under pressure, and was approaching the end of its first mission. One more Cabinet submission was required in spring 1973 to clear away remaining issues and then the Mackenzie pipeline was in the lap of the National Energy Board. An application from Canadian Gas Arctic could be expected to coincide with the approval of ALYESKA'S trans-Alaskan oil pipeline application, since North Slope gas production would go onstream with crude deliveries.

With the planning of the Mackenzie corridor in its last stages, the focus of the Task Force could now shift to the Arctic Islands where existing discoveries had been located and would also have to be brought to market. The optimism was misplaced. Only a few months later the proposed Mackenzie pipeline was on the defensive.

NOTES

1. Note Transport Canada, *Northwest Transportation Plan* (Ottawa, February, 1972).
2. Richard Rohmer, *The Arctic Imperative* (Toronto, 1973), p. 131.
3. Canadian Institute of Guided Ground Transport, *Railway to the Arctic* (Kingston, 1972).
4. Transport Canada, *op. cit.* p. 5
5. P.L. 92-203; 85 Stat. 688 (U.S.), December 18, 1971. Compare Peter A. Cummings, "Native Land Rights and Northern Development," *Alberta Law Review*, Vol. XII No. 1, 1974.
6. P. Cummings, "Our Land—Our People: Native Rights North of 60°", in D. Pimlott, et al., *Arctic Alternatives* (Ottawa, 1973) p. 104.
7. See above for details on sovereignty, energy and land regulations.
8. A petroleum industry committee on the employment of native people was formed in December 1969, to coordinate Government-industry training for resource development. *Toronto Globe and Mail*, December 9, 1969.

9.   *Oilweek*, September 18, 1972.

10.   *Oilweek*, October 12, 1970.

11.   Rohmer, *op. cit.*, pp. 85-86.

12.   *Toronto Star*, September 23, 1972.

13.   *Globe and Mail*, July 25, 1967; May 9, 1969; June 18, 1969; June 20, 1969; June 14, 1972; May 23, 1969. *Financial Post*, April 12, 1969; April 19, 1969; May 17, 1969.

CHAPTER EIGHT
The Political Awakening: The Failure of the Canadian Alternative

Like Banquo's ghost, the dream of luring Alaskan oil as well as natural gas down the Mackenzie River Valley rather than a trans-Alaskan pipeline system haunted senior officials of the Task Force on Northern Oil Development. But there were dangers. Promoting a Mackenzie oil pipeline in the teeth of Alaskan, American west coast and industry opposition could strain Canadian-American relations. Since the framework of northern development had been premised on harmonious trade and energy relations between the two countries permanent damage could not be ruled out. First and most directly, the expected initiation of oil and gas development in the North depended on the willingness of American authorities to permit entry of Canadian supplies. Senior officials were acutely aware of American leverage over the oil industry in Canada.

Indirectly, the "Canadian alternative" controversy, if not carefully contained, would heighten public interest in northern energy developments throughout Canada. Senior officials feared that too much interest would make it difficult to keep "politics" out of northern development. The framework for development selected by Government and business after 1968 was vulnerable.

A politicization of Canadian public opinion could score a breakthrough in the social, economic and environmental aspects of northern development. Should affected groups, particularly the native people, discover that Ottawa was not honouring the priorities set out in *Canada's North 1970-1980*, their dissatisfaction might increase and precipitate political action. Any political action would embarrass Ottawa. Above all, Ottawa must conceal the decisions-in-principle concluded with the private sector regarding pipelines and gas exploration for these would reveal the extent of Task Force collaboration with corporate interests.

In the Mackenzie and elsewhere in the North, new political factors might emerge with significant potential for delaying, altering or even curtailing resource development programmes. Significant delays in the construction of a natural gas pipeline down the Mackenzie could mean that the trans-Alaskan pipeline system might be completed by the consortium supporting that route before the Mackenzie system would be available to bring out North Slope supplies. This concept of an all-American route for Alaskan natural gas was being hinted at in industry circles in the United States. Canada might "lose out" altogether. Any number of unanticipated factors could upset the momentum of northern development and trade relations with the United States.

Officials had to admit to a dilemma. A "correct" level of public awareness in northern affairs was essential to protect Canadian interests in the North. The sovereignty crisis had required a careful orchestration of public opinion to keep it under control. The public must be made to realize that the Arctic was "Canadian;" but it should not learn that the United States had actually challenged that jurisdiction. Planning for the Mackenzie Corridor similarly demanded a careful balancing act. Environmentalists and native people had to be given the impression that everything possible was being done in their interests. Given the increased concern throughout the country regarding foreign control of the economy, economic nationalists would have to be appeased.

The particular sensitivity surrounding the "Canadian alternative" question lay in potential west coast pollution as a result of tanker traffic between the Alaskan port of Valdez and the Cherry Point refineries in Washington State upon completion of the trans-Alaska pipeline. Here was a potent instrument for orchestrating Canadian public opinion in bilateral negotiations with Washington. In fact the debate over the "Canadian alternative" proved of great importance in awakening public interest in Canada to the momentous developments taking place in northern Canada.

1. NEW HOPE FOR THE ''CANADIAN ALTERNATIVE''

The discovery of oil at Prudhoe Bay, Alaska, in January 1968 had raised the question of its transportation to mainland United States markets. There were three possibilities: oil tankers via the Northwest Passage to east coast markets; a trans-Alaskan pipeline to an ice-free port in the Pacific, with trans-shipment by tanker along the west coast to the lower forty-eight states; and a Mackenzie Valley pipeline which would link Prudhoe Bay reserves and American markets via a continental route. The early encouragement given by the National Energy Board to pipeline proposals along the Mackenzie; Ottawa's enthusiasm over the formation of the Mackenzie Valley Pipeline Research group; and the decision to forge ahead with the August 1970 Northern Pipeline Guidelines represented efforts to promote not merely a natural gas, but also an oil pipeline along the Mackenzie Valley. If, by August 1970 a natural gas pipeline system appeared the more likely, the Task Force had by no means given up on beating out the trans-Alaskan oil route and thereby winning both prizes.

The difficulty, however, lay in the apparent disinterest of industry in a Mackenzie Valley oil pipeline system, or the "Canadian alternative" as it became known. The decision of Atlantic Richfield and Humble Oil in favour of the Alaskan route in 1969, and the formation of the ALYESKA consortium to build the 48″ pipeline to Valdez was greeted with considerable dismay in Ottawa. Moreover, the immediate ordering of the pipe from Japan, even in advance of approval by the United States Federal Power Commission and Secretary of the Interior, indicated the determination of the consortium to proceed as rapidly as possible with the trans-Alaskan pipeline system.

By July 1969, while the companies were poised to begin the construction of the trans-Alaskan pipeline, Atlantic Richfield, British Petroleum and Humble also announced they would conduct a feasibility study concerning a large diameter pipeline from Puget Sound to Chicago or a delivery system for Alaskan crude. Since the Nixon Administration was known to favour the trans-Alaskan route, given the visible economic impact of the project on the American west coast states and the attractions of a delivery system under full American jurisdiction, prospects seemed excellent. However, having gone ahead without government clearance the ALYESKA consortium had generated a great deal of domestic opposition.

From the beginning, ALYESKA had run into heavy political weather. First the native people unconditionally demanded a land settlement prior to the construction of the pipeline. The State of Alaska supported their claim to equitable consideration of their aboriginal rights. Together with the strength of the native cause in the courts, there was simply no alternative but to take up this question in order to lift an injunction curtailing further work on the trans-Alaskan system. However, this was merely a delaying factor; the native people were prepared to accept a settlement. And by the spring of 1970, it appeared that a generous land settlement could be obtained in exchange for extinguishing aboriginal claims. In this area, therefore, ALYESKA would face no more difficulty.

More serious were the environmentalists who were determined to halt construction of the trans-Alaskan system. They had worked out a well-organized strategy to delay construction for as long as possible or indeed preclude it altogether. Scientific opinion supported their claim that the oil pipeline would traverse an exceptionally dangerous, earthquake prone region where major pipeline breaks would have an incalculable effect on the Alaskan environment. Similarly, it became clear that ALYESKA had not yet done the necessary scientific and engineering studies to cope with the hazards of pipeline construction and operation in the Arctic. On this basis, Judge Hart in 1970 had granted an injunction preventing pipeline construction.[1]

Unlike Canada, the United States had developed effective legislation for environmental protection. Congress and President Nixon approved the National Environmental Policy Act and Environmental Impact Guidelines in 1970 and 1971 respectively, which set down stringent standards for pipeline construction. Clearly, environmentalists had found friends in Congress as well as the media. The legislation added another valuable weapon for pipeline opponents which contained considerable potential for continued court action over construction of a trans-Alaskan pipeline system.

Moreover, if ALYESKA surmounted environmental obstacles under the National Environmental Protection Act or the

Environmental Impact Guidelines, environmentalist foes could further delay construction over questions relating to pipeline rights of way under the Mineral Leasing Act. In order for it to proceed, the right-of-way would have to be widened by an Act of Congress. Thus the courts could stop the trans-Alaskan pipeline on either an environmental or right-of-way finding even if the project were approved by Rogers B. Morton, Secretary of the Interior.

Morton had been known to question the wisdom of a trans-Alaskan pipeline system in private, and it was well known that various other American agencies shared a skeptical attitude toward the ALYESKA consortium. The position of the courts was by no means clear and Congressional opinion was not yet tested. Not much could be taken for granted.

The struggle was most intense in the Congress. The nub of the controversy was a struggle between the midwest states which would benefit most directly from a Mackenzie route and the west coast interests which backed ALYESKA. Both groups were powerful in Congress, with the ALYESKA project backed by the United States Merchant Marine, west coast Senators and Congressmen, the construction industry and the State of Alaska. Alaska in particular resented any Canadian initiative in favour of a Mackenzie oil line that would deprive that state of the economic benefits of pipeline construction and tanker shipments from the port of Valdez. The controversy was so heated that Nixon was rumoured, according to External Affairs officials in Washington, to have considered delaying approval of the trans-Alaskan line until after the 1972 Congressional elections. The Canadian Embassy in Washington thought it an open question if the Gordian knot could be cut at all.

Nor could Embassy officials get a clear reading from the corporate world on the respective routes as the impasse continued. Transport officials had reported as early as April 1970 that an energetic promotion effort by the Canadian government might conceivably secure the Mackenzie route over ALYESKA. They had formed this opinion in conversations with American petroleum economists and Washington officials associated with energy matters. The Mackenzie route appeared to be as economically feasible as the trans-Alaskan; it was also a more secure route for eastern and midwestern American markets. Moreover, since the large natural gas potential of Prudhoe Bay rendered a gas pipeline along the Mackenzie Valley increasingly likely, economics of scale might be realized in a corridor comprising two pipelines. The August 1970 Pipeline Guidelines, elaborating the corridor concept, had explicitly indicated the potential for an oil, as well as a natural gas, pipeline from the North.

But in the early months of 1971 business leaders were playing it close to the chest. The Department of External Affairs calculated that they still favoured the ALYESKA proposal but mainly on political grounds. It questioned the possibility of their achieving a sufficiently satisfactory Canadian-American agreement to protect corporate interests; industry could not be expected to pursue the Canadian alternative without a formal inter-governmental agreement sufficiently attractive and definitive to permit the integrated oil companies "to plan realistically." External Affairs believed that any such agreement would have to include the availability of Canada's northern oil and gas potential for American markets if industry's cooperation were to be gained.

A March 9 1971 communication from the Embassy spoke to this problem at some length. Regarding uncertainties in industry circles concerning the conditions to be "imposed" on Canada as a "price" for permission to construct a Mackenzie Valley oil pipeline system, it indicated:

"In this context one hears the frequent comment that the corporate interests could scarcely be expected to pursue the Canadian alternative in the absence of an inter-governmental agreement sufficiently definitive to permit the companies to plan realistically. At the same time there is recognition that the oil and gas potential Canada's northern reaches would have to be given consideration in any bilateral agreements. The emphasis on inter-governmental arrangements is probably nurtured by the experience the ALYESKA companies who committed themselves to TAPS without having first cleared with the U.S. national government."

The American State Department concurred in the need for a formal treaty protecting corporate interests in a March 1971 memorandum on this subject. But it too outlined the difficulties of building sufficiently binding guarantees into any such agreement. According to Embassy officials the State Department felt that the Canadian Government might impose conditions as a price for permission to use a Canadian right-of-way for an Alaskan pipeline.

The chief concern for business leaders was the price of further delays. They wanted a decision one way or the other although in 1970 they leaned somewhat in favour of ALYESKA. This at least was the conclusion of External Affairs as communicated to Ottawa and the Task Force on Northern Oil Development. Could a determined Canadian initiative save the Canadian alternative and foil the trans-Alaskan route?

Tempting as this thought was, it had the makings of another major problem for External in its relations with the United States, only a year after the sovereignty crisis with the April 1970 legislation. The earlier crisis had illustrated familiar characteristics of External Affairs' behaviour under Mr. Sharp: lack of foresight and preparedness; inability to deal decisively with Canadian-American bilateral relations and therefore a reflex to wait and respond to an American initiative; a frantic desire to restore "the political culture" of relations following the crisis; and a tendency to forget unpleasant episodes so that nothing was learned. The April 1970 legislation, although a panic response and a retreat, was nevertheless a step in the right direction. Ottawa's posture in the debate with the United States over the Canadian alternative, in contrast, was a disaster and a national humiliation.

2. CANADIAN OPTIONS

By early 1971, it became clear to senior officials and External Affairs that Ottawa, for political reasons, would have to take issue publicly with the proposed trans-Alaskan pipeline system. Hearings on this system, held in February 1971 in Alaska and Washington, revealed strong opposition to the project; they also crystallized Parliamentary and press reaction in Canada to the dangers of west coast pollution. In March, in particular, the media took up a motion put forward by Mr. J. Baldwin (Peace River):

> That this House opposes the trans-Alaska pipeline and tanker project because of the ecological dangers posed by this project to the people, towns and cities of British Columbia and the national resources of Canada's western seas and coasts and that this House therefore urges the Government to immediately institute an independent economical and ecological feasibility study of alternative routes.[2]

There were, however, degrees of opposition. First, the

Government could restrict its protests to the west coast pollution issue in the event of heavy tanker traffic from the Alaskan port of Valdez to the Cherry Point refineries. The Province of British Columbia and public opinion in Canada in general were increasingly aroused by this pollution threat. The Canadian Wildlife Association and David Anderson, a Liberal Member of Parliament from British Columbia, sought entrance as litigants among the environmental groups confronting ALYESKA. This was granted on May 11, 1972. But already in February 1971, Ottawa felt under sufficient public pressure to request bilateral discussions with the United States in this regard.

Second, Canada had the option of formally promoting a Mackenzie Valley option to the trans-Alaskan pipeline. It would be a more radical step, but it was reported to be a favorite speaking tour theme of J.J. Greene, Minister of Energy, Mines and Resources. In January 1970, in Vancouver, he apparently informally proposed that the ALYESKA consortium give up its efforts in favour of a Canadian system that had significant advantages over the American counterpart. Ecologically it was more favorable; financially it was less costly and would open up Canadian oil and natural gas supplies in the North. Nor would a Mackenzie oil pipeline undermine American security requirements: Canadian use of American landbridges in its energy network and the NORAD agreement underlined the absence of a Canadian security threat. On the environment question, J. Davis, Minister of Fisheries and Forestry, concurred in March 1971 that an oil pipeline (alongside a Mackenzie gas pipeline) up the Mackenzie Valley was entirely feasible. Despite reports of conflicting opinions within the Government and a denial of any Canadian commitment to an oil pipeline, the Toronto *Globe and Mail* worried on March 23, 1971, that:

> No matter what Mr. Greene says in a letter elsewhere on this page, no matter what any of them say, it is apparent that the Cabinet will do anything to persuade U.S. oil interests to take its pipeline down the Mackenzie Valley. Its performance with respect to tankers down the B.C. coast does not suggest that our Arctic will be very safe.[3]

The difficulty here was the tactical one of persuading either industry or the United States Secretary of the Interior of the virtues of the Canadian alternative. Green and Davis did not speak for the Government, and no official representations on this point had been made in Washington. Consideration of such a move, however, could not be delayed indefinitely and, on March 24, 1971, the chief executives planning the trans-Alaskan route explicitly confirmed their indication to proceed with the project.[4] A direct approach to the American State Department was now the only alternative if Canada were to stop this pipeline.

At a meeting of the Task Force on Northern Oil Development held to assist External Affairs prepare a position for the impending talks, External Affairs expressed the view that Canada was on strong ground on the west coast pollution issue. An initiative in this area could in no way be construed by Washington as interfering in an American domestic squabble, something senior officials agreed that Congress would view darkly. They further agreed that Washington would view direct Canadian advocacy of the Canadian alternative in this light. The Secretary of State argued that, at least in the early stage, Ottawa should concentrate on estimating and publicizing the dangers for Canada of the west coast tanker route, and let Canada's invitation to build a Mackenzie oil pipeline as expressed in the August 1970 Northern Pipeline Guidelines sink in without active promotion. With direct discussions with the State Department restricted to the west coast danger, bilateral negotiations would be initiated which, in the event of genuine corporate interest in pursuing the Mackenzie alternative, could lead to inter-governmental understanding in this area. At the same time, the Task Force would maintain contacts with industry to impress upon companies the advantages of the Mackenzie route and the interest of the Canadian Government in pursuing it. It was a careful strategy designed to persuade gently and to avoid a confrontation with the United States.

Industry was well aware anyway of Canada's position; External Affairs argued that restricting the discussion to the west coast issue was the wiser and safer course to follow rather than actively pursuing a Canadian alternative over the ALYESKA application. It was better to hint massively than to club with a sledge hammer. On the basis of External Affairs' reasoning, the Task Force agreed with the strategy, and accepted the establishment of a small sub-committee to study the dangers and possible remedial measures involving oil shipments from Alaska.

The brutal fact as of March, 1971, was that the Task Force had not done sufficient research to document any claim that the Canadian alternative was environmentally or financially more attractive than the Alaskan system. Indeed, the Ministry of Transport argued within the Task Force that the environmental hazards associated with tanker shipments along the west coast to Cherry Point were by no means clear and could not be taken for granted.

In these circumstances, the Canadian Secretary of State's advice to keep the two issues separated appears well conceived. It would have been better if Canada had maintained that posture. But even the west coast pollution issue was potentially messy. The Canadian Government had every right to protect the British Columbian coastline against the potential effects of tanker traffic to the Cherry Point refineries, but it had to be internally consistent to be persuasive with Washington.

Ottawa did not object to equally hazardous oil tanker movements off the Canadian east coast through the Canso Straits, and it had not yet formulated a coherent policy on the likely ultimate requirements for oil shipments out of the Canadian North. The point was underlined by Thornton Bradshaw, President of Atlantic Richfield Oil Company, in a press release on June 22, 1972, following Rogers B. Morton's endorsement of a trans-Alaska pipeline system over the Canadian alternative. "Canada," he said "is quite willing to accept risks of oil operations when its own interest benefits."[5]

This proved correct. The oil shortage of 1973-74 following the Middle East war of October 1973, witnessed massive Canadian tanker traffic out of the port of Vancouver, on the one hand, while Ottawa continued to fire its heavy artillery at the pollution dangers of American shipping off both coastlines. No action was taken to develop a coherent policy after 1971, despite the stated concern about west coast pollution.

3. CRISIS

The summer of 1971 produced no new major developments on the issue of the Canadian alternative. There was little evidence that External Affairs' strategy was convincing the oil companies to choose the Mackenzie route over ALYESKA. Indeed, the chief event in Canadian-American relations was the August 15, 1971, import surcharge imposed by Washington without consultation, and universally interpreted in Ottawa as brutal and unilateral.

One immediate, if not necessarily permanent, effect of the Nixon initiative was to encourage senior officials in Ottawa to be less trusting and more forthright in Canadian-American relations, and to be less constrained to maintain the extreme caution that had characterized the Canadian approach to bilateral relations with the United States to that time. From the point of view of northern development, and Canadian oil policy in general, the surcharge affair made Canadian officials even more anxious than before to secure the American market for western crude oil by the construction of northern pipelines linking Alaska and United States mainland markets. Ottawa must press forward with the Canadian alternative rather than acquiescing in the trans-Alaskan pipeline system. This reaction helps to account for the change of policy that became apparent in September 1971.

On August 31, 1971, the Canadian Embassy in Washington reported its impression that an opening still existed for the Canadian alternative. Embassy officials reported that while they had little to go on, enquiries about the Mackenzie route were still being received. They felt that Ottawa should consider taking up the matter again to give guidance for their responses. With the exception of outlining the process for formal application for a pipeline certificate from the National Energy Board, and assuring enquirers that approval for an application would not take much time, officials were not able to comment substantively on Ottawa's position respecting the Canadian alternative and ALYESKA. Could Ottawa therefore be more specific? The Embassy initiative was sufficiently persuasive for External Affairs to take the matter up again in the Task Force on Northern Development. Would being "more specific" mean departing from the former careful strategy designed to keep the issues separated in favour of a more active role in pressing for the Mackenzie route?

The Chairman of the National Energy Board responded to External Affairs' dilemma by suggesting as little change as possible in the approaches adopted as a result of the deliberations within the Task Force earlier in the year. A firm position on the west coast pollution issue had not yet obtained results. It should be maintained to ensure public support for the Government, but it ought not to be linked to the Canadian alternative. He advised that Ottawa simply communicate to the American State Department that the Task Force was continuing discussions with representatives of the American oil companies concerning the Canadian alternative; that American authorities had suggested these talks; and that these discussions would be pertinent to any Canadian decision. But he advocated instructing the State Department that studies undertaken by the National Energy Board had shown the costs associated with the trans-Alaskan pipeline system to be much higher than for the Canadian alternative. It would therefore be worthwhile for the United States to consider this difference carefully before approving the ALYESKA proposal.

The Ministry of Transport concurred and added another reason for caution: the supporters of the trans-Alaskan pipeline, including the State Department, were drawing Canada into the controversy to drum up support in Congress for that route. Official Canadian promotion of a Mackenzie route would hurt that prospect in Congress, for it would be interpreted as an intervention in American domestic politics. The route selection, according to the Ministry of Transport, would be resolved by the Administration's view of respective political advantages. Political arguments rather than environmental or economic criteria would be decisive. The State Department and President Nixon favoured the west coast interests and the strongest argument in favour of the trans-Alaskan pipeline was the argument concerning the security of an all-American route. Any hint of Canadian interference would help defeat the midwest Congressmen and their lobbies.

It would be risky if there were fewer unknowns, according to Transport, but the Canadian position was extremely exposed and could easily backfire if it became clear that Canada had not done its homework. The Ministry of Transport reiterated its concern that the Task Force simply did not have reliable information on the following central issues:

1. The proven or probable oil and gas reserves of the Canadian Arctic, or even reliable information from industry concerning their exploration programmes.

2. The concessions which Canada would have to make to the United States to get the Canadian alternative accepted. This was a thorny point, and External Affairs was not of much

help. But it would be essential to know this since the issue would spill over into Canadian politics if the United States responded favorably to an Ottawa initiative in support of a Mackenzie oil pipeline.

3. Knowledge of techniques for building an oil pipeline down the Mackenzie. While Northern Transportation Company Limited was certain it could move the pipe and construction supplies, where would these come from — Canada or elsewhere? Did Canada have the engineering and labour skills required for this task? At the very least, the Task Force ought to have worked out a timetable indicating the specific dates at which such equipment, techniques and skills would be available.

4. The impact on the Canadian economy of the construction of a Mackenzie oil pipeline. So far the Task Force still had little idea of the effects of a natural gas pipeline much less an oil line, on the Canadian economy. Pending a report headed by the Department of Finance, due in mid-1972, senior officials had agreed among themselves that these effects would be positive. But this had been on the assumption of a single pipeline rather than a corridor containing both lines. Would an oil pipeline be going too far? "Is Kierans right?" asked Austin, Chairman of the Task Force, in a letter to Ritchie, Undersecretary of State for External Affairs, on September 9, 1971, outlining the pros and cons of lobbying for the Canadian alternative in Washington. Apparently he was wrong.

5. The environmental impact of a Mackenzie oil pipeline. The Task Force really had no reliable information available here. A crash research programme was only beginning on the environmental effects of the proposed natural gas pipeline. This gap in evidence was really crucial, since Canada's case rested on its claim that the Mackenzie route was less dangerous environmentally than the trans-Alaskan pipeline system.

6. The type and intensity of environmentalist opposition to northern pipeline construction in Canada. If the Alaskan case was any example, significant protests might develop, even

though Task Force officials still reckoned that opposition groups were not as well organized as in the United States and would therefore be easier to handle.

7. The availability of Canadian capital and rates of return for the construction of northern pipelines. Senior officials had assumed that there would be sufficient capital for the construction of a natural gas pipeline. But would the limited Canadian capital market be able to sustain the construction of a Mackenzie corridor including both an oil and a natural gas pipeline? Again, in the absence of the Department of Finance report, there was no firm basis for judgement on this issue.

8. Native opposition to northern pipeline construction in Canada. The Alaskan case suggested that native groups would demand a comprehensive land settlement prior to the initiation of pipeline construction. Senior officials in Canada, in contrast, assumed that this would not be necessary; that pipeline construction could begin prior to such a land settlement. However, native opposition was growing and it was by no means certain what the courts would decide in a test case. If a challenge emerged and the courts proved difficult, the construction of a Mackenzie pipeline could find itself confronted by a serious delay prior to the settlement of native land claims.

All these issues needed research badly before an aggressive approach in favour of a Mackenzie oil pipeline could be launched. The Ministry of Transport therefore agreed fully with the National Energy Board that External Affairs should limit itself to a progress report on the Canadian alternative. Meanwhile, research on the above issues should be expedited so that a clear Canadian position could be formulated in the near future. If industry or Washington in the meantime changed its mind as a result of American domestic pressures and requested Canadian cooperation in the early construction of an oil pipeline along the Mackenzie, Ottawa's bargaining power would be greatly enhanced.

This low key approach failed to gain acceptance at the Cabinet level. Eventually, both the National Energy Board and Transport allowed themselves to be persuaded into linking the issues of west coast pollution, the Canadian alternative, and Canadian oil policy in general. The chief impetus appears to have come from the Department of Energy, Mines and Resources and the Prime Minister's office. Working first on the Secretary of State for External Affairs, they built a coalition from among Deputy-Ministers in Finance, Industry, Trade and Commerce, and the Privy Council Office. Under this pressure, the Deputy-Ministers in Transport and the Chairman of the National Energy Board yielded.

On October 28, 1971, the Interdepartmental Committee on Oil recommended the following statement for Cabinet consideration.

> That the Secretary of State for External Affairs communicate with the United States and advise, publicly, that we were seeking the opportunity of discussing the Canadian alternative with U.S. governmental officials.

This was interpreted by senior officials as not letting the Canadian alternative "die on the vine." They were acutely aware of the implications of their actions. This point is worth underlining, since these issues raised fundamental questions regarding the integration of the Canadian and American economies.

First, there was the political problem of an initiative which Washington would interpret as interference in its internal affairs. As the Chairman of the Task Force on Northern Oil Development pointed out on September 9, 1971

> It would amount to joining issue in a major controversy within the framework of U.S. domestic politics and Canadian-American relations.

The problem was that Ottawa could not find an unobtrusive way of laying an official foundation under Section 102 of the United States National Environmental Policy Act to delay consideration of the ALYESKA proposal until the Canadian alternative had been properly examined. Given this, Canada would have to use the blunt instrument of a public diplomatic note. It would be resented. "Would," asked Austin, the Task Force Chairman in his September 9, 1971 letter to the Secretary of State for External Affairs, " the political costs be too high whatever resulted?" He referred pointedly to the pipeline debate in 1956 in the House of Commons which, however much out of context, vividly demonstrated the point.

Second, a public Cabinet offer to build the Mackenzie oil pipeline with the well-known knowledge gaps in the Task Force on Northern Oil Development on this subject, would mean that the following crucial decisions concerning Canadian-American relations would have to be faced by Cabinet:

1. *Canadian National Security*: Canadian security would be affected by a land bridge between Alaska and the mainland United States carrying a strategic resource. It was further assumed that Canadians would accept this increased dependence. Any resulting problems would be outweighed by the benefits of secure export markets.

2. *Trade*: The chief problem of the Canadian oil industry for Ottawa planners after 1968 was the American export market. The rationale of the Mackenzie pipeline had from the first been the promotion of Canadian exports; this remained the chief objective, despite the fanfare over the west coast tanker issue. But did Canada have limitless supplies of oil to export? Pressing the United States for adoption of the Canadian alternative would involve a firm, long-term export commitment for Alberta crude.

3. *Northern Reserves*: Canada would have to be prepared to commit future petroleum reserves in the North for export to the United States as a concession for building the Mackenzie alternative. The Interdepartmental Committee on Oil saw no problem here since the promotion of exports to the United States formed part and parcel of Canadian oil policy since 1961. The American State Department had made it perfectly clear that the construction of a Mackenzie oil pipeline would have to be accompanied by a treaty which took into consideration Canadian reserves in the North.

4. *National Priorities*: Senior officials and the Liberal Government assumed the early construction of a Mackenzie gas pipeline to be in Canada's national interest. Now the undertaking was vastly expanded by including an oil pipeline as well as a national priority.

These were not trivial issues and there were others: Would Canada agree, for example, to less stringent environmental standards than Alaska? But the four main issue areas would bind Canada to the security and energy interests of the United States more tightly than ever, and they prejudged Canada's own oil reserves required for her own needs.

Yet Cabinet agreed. To be sure, it found it difficult to decide on the wording of a draft letter for Donald MacDonald, the new Minister of Energy, Mines and Resources, to deliver to Rogers B. Morton. The matter had been discussed in Cabinet on November 16, 1971, but no decision was reached and the Interdepartmental Committee on Oil was advised to keep the matter under supervision. Now, action was approved.

Even in his first interview with the press on February 21, 1972, Mr. MacDonald had underlined his belief in the Mackenzie corridor system including an oil pipeline. In March, he had discussed the Canadian alternative with his counterparts in Washington, arguing for combined efforts on the Mackenzie as a more attractive venture than the trans-Alaskan route. While he failed to convince, he nevertheless came away determined on a last ditch effort.

The opportunity soon came, as the date of the formal ALYESKA consortium application to the American Secretary of the Interior approached. The day after the submission, May 4, 1972, MacDonald's letter to Rogers B. Morton, drafted with much care by the Interdepartmental Committee on Oil in consultation with the Task Force on Northern Oil Development, was delivered in Washington, and published in the Canadian press. It represents the final word on the inherited assumptions dating back to 1968 and the discovery of oil in Alaska. The statement of advantages is a final summing up of the misperceptions of Ottawa senior officials and Cabinet Ministers in this period. The letter urged Morton to:

> Give consideration to additional recent information concerning a pipeline route through Canada as an alternative to the trans-Alaska pipeline.

MacDonald assured Morton that a Mackenzie oil pipeline would enhance the energy security of the United States. It would also have the distinct advantage of supplying directly the midwest (a rapier thrust into the Congressional struggle between the midwest and west coast interests). Happily, Canada had an interest in the energy security of the United States and could supply interim American needs "by extra-Canadian crude as required." The impression was given of massive reserves in excess of Canadian needs.

American midwest opinion applauded the arguments made by MacDonald:

> What is wrong with the suggestion of Representative Aspin of Wisconsin that if the United States can't afford to wait until a Canadian pipeline is built, it might make up the deficit by lowering the present import quota on Canadian oil. The line that presently carries oil from Edmonton to Chicago, he argues, could accommodate 300,000 more barrels a day, which the Canadians would be only too glad to deliver.[6]

Further, according to MacDonald, the Mackenzie route would avoid the west coast pollution danger, "an area which, if not solved by wisdom and reason today, could produce increasingly difficult and negative influences on a whole range of issues in Canadian-American relations."

In contrast, MacDonald went on, a Mackenzie route would be less environmentally hazardous than the trans-Alaskan pipeline. Thirty new studies not discussed in the ALYESKA submission, now seriously out of date on environmental research in Canada, could be made available to the American Department of the Interior. Moreover, MacDonald went on to add:

> If Canada is to allow the disturbances occasioned by a gas pipeline for which an application is expected in late 1972, than the incremental factor of a second pipeline in the same corridor is not as significant as a totally new pipeline route would be.

Further, the United States might be interested to note a significant new factor — Canada's decision, announced on April 28th, 1972, to build an all-weather highway along the Mackenzie (for which, he might have added, no advance environmental research had been carried out). As for timing, there was no reason why the National Energy Board and Cabinet could not approve a Mackenzie route "expeditiously."

MacDonald's intervention is extraordinary from several points of view. The letter contained statements that are indefensible in view of the facts of pre-pipeline planning in the Mackenzie Valley. There was next to no work done on environmental impact, rights-of-way, Canadian content, Treaties 8 and 11, foreign ownership, or financing. Indeed, the preliminary report of the Finance Committee of the Task Force on Northern Oil Development would shortly reveal extremely strong reservations concerning the construction of a single gas pipeline. There was nothing at all to substantiate the claims made by MacDonald in his letter — in particular, that the National Energy Board would entertain an early application in 1972, and give approval by the end of the year.

Most important of all, Ottawa's objective of securing free entry for Canadian oil products in American markets retained all its validity at this point. Indeed, the capacity of Alberta's oil fields was underlined as a fundamental advantage to the United States if it opted for the Canadian alternative to the trans-Alaska line. Only a few months later Ottawa imposed export restrictions on oil.

Even American Under Secretary of State Irwin, who (as External Affairs reported to Ottawa on May 11, 1972) lashed out at the Embassy for what he termed a blatant interference in American domestic affairs, expressed doubt to his Canadian colleagues that Canada really could deliver the promises made in MacDonald's letter. Underlining Washington's growing concern about an energy shortage in the fall, he asked how Canada, split into two markets, and, more dependent on off-shore sources than the United States, could make such far-reaching claims.

Equally intriguing is the failure of the Nixon Administration to respond to MacDonald's initiative. What it apparently failed to appreciate, was that Canada was offering the United States a continental oil policy package without having thought through the consequences. The Canadian alternative was not merely an access route to Prudhoe Bay; it was a lever to secure future access to energy sources. Moreover, the Canadians were offering this from such a weak position that the United States could exact extremely advantageous conditions. This was noted by David Freeman, former Science Advisor to Nixon and a formidable authority on energy policy in the United States:

> The notion that we cannot afford to wait for the completion of the Canadian energy corridor is a false notion that is detrimental to obtaining a secure source of energy for the U.S. in the 1970's.[7]

The American Administration, in turning aside Ottawa's offer, missed an opportunity to establish an iron-clad umbrella over

Canadian energy resources in a lopsided bargain with a Canadian Government incapable of forward planning.

But like Ottawa, Washington reacted to immediate political pressures preparatory to the Congressional elections of November 1972. The administration was responding in the first instance to a variety of special interests: The ALYESKA consortium, the United States Merchant Marine, Alaska and west coast Congressional and business pressure. The highly charged atmosphere did not facilitate long-range planning.

Intelligent observers, such as Freeman, realized that there was more at stake in the Canadian alternative than an interest group tug of war. The future security of the United States demanded a long-range policy designed "to encourage Canadian development" when American energy shortages reached "the critical point." The ALYESKA application, therefore, was a "procedural sham:" the Department of the Interior had made up its mind long before, on political grounds, without assessing the long-term supply problems facing the United States.[8]

Ironically, Ottawa did not perceive Canada's good fortune in confronting a policy process that, like the Canadian, failed to develop long-term policy objectives. After Morton's acceptance of the ALYESKA application over the Canadian alternative, officials felt rejected by the State Department's refusal to submit the matter (even the west coast pollution issue) to the International Joint Commission. External Affairs felt that it had been abused by ALYESKA supporters, who, as predicted, made much of "foreign interference" in American politics.

So ended Ottawa's hope for a Mackenzie oil pipeline from the Alaskan North Slope to American markets as an alternative to the trans-Alaskan route. The Mackenzie Valley Pipeline Research Group presented Ottawa senior officials with a final "over and out" on December 19, 1972.[9] The briefing underlined that the project was entirely feasible and might be built at a later date should further oil discoveries materialize in the Mackenzie Delta or Alaska. The trans-Alaskan pipeline, however, could accommodate the proven 9 billion barrel reserves at Prudhoe Bay. Although the Canadian media picked up the Canadian alternative concept in early 1973 for a brief period before the final Congressional approval of the trans-Alaskan line, officials in Ottawa dropped it after Morton's rejection in June 1972.

The failure to defeat this route realized the worst fears of Task Force officials. Without having produced any positive results in Canadian-American energy relations, the incident focused public attention on northern development. The press and Parliament were in an uproar over the west coast pollution issue and had been led (by the Government) to link developments on the Mackenzie with those affecting west coast shipping. It gave aid and comfort to groups struggling to interest southern Canadians in the dangers surrounding a Mackenzie natural gas pipeline. The period witnessed the formation of an effective opposition, the necessary prelude to the public debate on the North that broke through after the Canadian general election of October 1972.

NOTES

1. William T. Lake, "The National Environmental Policy Act," Proceedings of the Workshop on the Philosophy of Environmental Impact Assessments in Canada", *Environment Protection Board* (Winnipeg, 1973), pp. 11-24

2. Quoted in *Arctic Alternatives, op. cit.* pp. 4-5.

3. *Toronto Globe and Mail,* March 23, 1971.

4. See Rohmer, *op. cit.* p 93.

5. Thornton S. Bradshaw, *Press Release,* New York, June 22, 1972.

6. *Washington Post,* May 16, 1972.

7. Ibid.

8. Ibid.

9. A year and a half later, however, five members of Mackenzie Valley Pipeline Research Co. reactivated the concept in the Delta project. See Chapter 9.

CHAPTER NINE
Prelude: The Environment

For the first two years after 1968, the Task Force on Northern Oil Development was able to avoid serious public opposition to northern pipelines on environmental grounds, but senior officials in Ottawa were keenly aware of the political importance of this factor from the outset. The trans-Alaskan pipeline system had been stalled in its tracks by a well organized and tenacious group of American environmentalists. Since, in the first instance, the Task Force was a lobbyist for a Canadian pipeline network in the North, perhaps as an alternative to the Alaskan route, and since the environmental issue would be much the same in the event of the construction of a Canadian pipeline, Canadian officials involved could not help but draw parallels.

Throughout 1969 and 1970 Washington officials and American oil representatives candidly warned Task Force officials that a Canadian alternative would encounter public opposition no less severe than the trans-Alaskan system. The Task Force disagreed, arguing that environmentalist groups in Canada were not as well organized as in the United States, but privately they were bothered by the Alaskan pipeline nightmare. The concern was instrumental in persuading the Task Force at this stage to forego research on possible environmental hazards of oil and gas pipeline construction and operation in the Canadian Arctic, since research activity might generate unseemly public interest and rally potential opposition.

Nevertheless, the absence of data put the Task Force at a disadvantage in claiming that a Canadian alternative along the

Mackenzie was less hazardous than the trans-Alaskan system, and that oil and gas pipelines would not seriously impair the Arctic eco-systems. Since officials in Washington's Department of the Interior were perfectly aware that Canada had not done its homework, the Minister's credibility in negotiations in favour of the Canadian alternative was severely undermined. In the absence of Canadian research, there was simply no way of comparing the relative merits on environmental grounds of the two proposed pipelines.

Questions posed by industry were scarcely less embarrassing. In this early phase of Task Force activity, the integrated oil companies were seeking answers concerning the environmental safeguards which Canada would impose in the event that an oil pipeline along the Mackenzie was constructed. During the critical meeting of May 1970 in the Privy Council Office, the Department of Indian Affairs and Northern Development conceded that Canada might be willing to impose less stringent standards than the Alaskans. This extraordinary admission, however, did not spur the Task Force to undertake a research programme. The August Guidelines must be seen in this perspective. According to the Sixth Guideline, an applicant would have to satisfy the National Energy Board that suitable environmental protection could be ensured during the construction phase and operation of the pipeline; but without specific guidelines or data, the National Energy Board was incapable of evaluating pipeline applications.

In short, the conservation and environmental protection agencies in the federal Government, whether in the Department of Indian Affairs and Northern Development, the Department of Forests and Fisheries, the Department of Energy, Mines and Resources, or the Ministry of Transport, were in subordination to the resource emphasis represented by the Task Force on Northern Oil Development.

This atmosphere helps explain the essentially instrumental nature of the Arctic Waters Pollution Prevention Act of April 1970. The legislation arose neither from a belief within the Government that the environmental protection of the Arctic basin was a first priority, nor from a well-researched and documented position. Rather, it was introduced as a policy instrument to protect Canadian jurisdiction in northern waters. However, the fact that the Trudeau Government opted for this strategy was a political event of the first importance, for it focused public attention on the environmental question in the North. It was a stimulus for citizen groups to organize on pipeline and resource issues as well. In this way it contributed to the Task Force's problems after 1970.

1. THE AUGUST GUIDELINES AND THE ENVIRONMENTAL REGULATIONS

The Task Force on Northern Oil Development was not totally unconcerned about environmental considerations. Following the acceptance by Cabinet of the August 1970 Guidelines, and at the urging of Austin (Energy, Mines and Resources) and Howland (National Energy Board), the Pipeline Committee of the Task Force agreed to set up a sub-committee on ecological problems. Composed of officials from the National Energy Board, Energy, Mines and Resources, and Indian Affairs and Northern Development, the overall aim of the sub-committee was to plan and coordinate a Government-industry approach to environmental and ecological problems associated with the project. The Task Force Chairman did not want the matter to gravitate beneath the National Research Council's umbrella Associate Committee on Geo-technical Research (specifically its Sub-committee on Pipeline and Land Use Technology in Northern Terrains); as a potentially key political issue, it was essential that the environment issue remain under the control of the Task Force and that business and Government officials alike recognize the Task Force as the coordinating unit for all concerns related to northern oil and gas development.

The overwhelming industry orientation of the sub-committee — none of the individuals on the committee had any particular knowledge of northern eco-systems and all were considered to have close links with industry — is surprising only if the purpose and nature of the unit are forgotten. For the sub-committee on ecological problems was not itself to undertake research in the area of northern environment, but rather to ensure effective liaison with industry. Industry was expected to provide the research; the Task Force did not doubt that this research would be of suitably high quality. An autonomous research unit, the Environment Protection Board, funded by Canadian Gas Arctic and set up in September 1970, satisfied the Task Force that industry was concerned about independent and high quality environmental research. The sub-committee had neither funds nor staff for research activities nor did it apply for any. The conclusion must be that the Task Force was prepared to accept without further question the quality of research being performed by industry and by the various other Government departments.

From the sub-committee's point of view, the key to the situation and the reason for urgency lay in the projected timetable for pipeline construction that was presented to the Task Force at this time. The Pipeline Committee foresaw approval for the pipeline at the Deputy-Minister level by mid-1971 with hearings before the Energy Board that fall. By June 1972, the projected hearings would be completed with the necessary land tenure and certificates of convenience and rights-of-way obtained by industry. Since initiation of the construction phase was foreseen in the fall of 1972, it was essential that the Pipeline Committee work out a common business-Government approach on all matters as soon as possible so that the necessary preparation for public hearings would be completed by fall 1971.

Specifically the terms of reference of the new sub-committee were: a) to serve as the point of contact for the Task Force Pipeline Committee between business and Government on environmental questions; b) to draw up guidelines related to corridor selection; c) to elaborate on the guidelines to be followed by industry as indicated in general terms in the August Guidelines; d) to identify environmental problem areas; e) to disseminate information within the Government; and f) to identify federal legislation and regulations related to northern pipeline activity and recommend additional legislation.

Without staff and with the sub-committee members heavily engaged in studying other aspects of pipeline development, particularly engineering problems, little progress was made in the succeeding months. It also reflected the low level of concern for environmental questions within the Pipeline Committee itself. There is simply no evidence that senior officials in the fall of 1970 felt under any great pressure to elaborate guidelines on environmental matters. However, during the winter of 1971-72 the formation of public groups concerned with the environmental implications of northern oil and gas development proceeded rapidly.

2. THE MOBILIZATION OF PUBLIC PRESSURE AND THE TASK FORCE RESPONSE, 1971

The rapid development of public interest in environmental matters related to northern pipelines in the winter of 1970-71 coincided with increasing Task Force confidence in an early application to build a natural gas pipeline from Alaska and along the Mackenzie River Valley to the United States. It was not greeted with enthusiasm. Indeed by March 1971, for the first time, senior officials considered the formation of opposition in Canada, similar to that against the trans-Alaskan pipeline to be a distinct possibility, with all the attendant delays and legal expenses. The media, it was feared, would not hesitate to cooperate in dramatizing apparent Government inconsistencies.

A major Task Force response was therefore considered essential to calm public concern that the Government was not doing enough on this aspect of northern pipeline construction. On March 17, 1971, the Task Force Chairman formally invited R. F. Shaw, Deputy Minister of the Department of Fisheries and Forestry, to participate in the group. Referring him to the House Debates of December 20, 1968, which accompanied the formation of the Task Force, the Chairman indicated that the new Committee of the Environment which he would head could ensure that the environmental responsibilities of the various departments and agencies in the North would be brought together more effectively. In this way also, the Task Force, on behalf of the Treasury Board, could provide the appropriate allocation of research funds for the several departments most immediately concerned "as we tackle one of the most important problems facing the Government." After outlining briefly the other four committees, the Chairman assured the Deputy Minister of the authority of "this important interdepartmental group for all matters of a research, legislative and administrative nature related directly or indirectly to northern oil development."[1]

In fact, the new Environment Committee was a belated recognition that problems of ecology deserved serious Government attention in respect of northern oil development. In effect, the Task Force was attempting to upgrade environmental matters within its own organization replacing the former sub-committee with a full-fledged committee headed by a Deputy-Minister.

161

Second, by giving the Department of Fisheries and Forestry the coordinating role in the preparation of "guidelines for maintaining environmental quality in the construction and maintenance of oil and gas pipelines in the Arctic," the Task Force and the Government would present a new posture: it would appear to be diluting the industry orientation of the previous sub-committee membership in favour of an official with an unmistakable environment mandate in his regular portfolio.

The formation of the new committee and the invitation to the Department of Fisheries and Forestry recognized that public interest in the North had reached a point where the legitimacy of any pipeline decision by the National Energy Board would be questioned in the absence of greater attention to environmental questions.[2] Letters to Members of Parliament; diverse representations to Ministers; Opposition questions in Parliament; together with unmistakable evidence that non-profit groups such as Pollution Probe at the University of Toronto and the Canadian Arctic Resources Committee were highly motivated and enjoyed considerable support, signalled heavy political weather for the Government if the Task Force chose to ignore the question.

However, there was also growing pressure from within the Ottawa bureaucracy for action. An official communication from the Minister of Fisheries and Forestry in spring 1971 had informed the Task Force Chairman that he had read the winter issue of the Canadian Wildlife Federation publication and supported its claim that the Task Force was misleading the Canadian public into believing that the Government was conducting large scale research into environmental problems associated with northern pipeline construction.

The letter caused some concern within the Task Force and added impetus for upgrading environmental concerns. Furthermore, officials felt that some units within Indian Affairs and Northern Development were known to be "soft" on environmental matters relating to economic development and would in the nature of things use public interest in the North as a lever for promoting their own demands.

Both outside and within Government circles, therefore, increasing attention was being directed to the North. In February a Task Force official remarked that Canada had better follow the example of the United States in attempting environmental guidelines for pipeline construction in the North. A decision followed very quickly after this admission of failure. In May 1971, in an extraordinary measure, the Cabinet gave approval to a $5,000,000 research program dealing with environmental aspects of northern pipeline development.

But even before the new proposed Committee could meet, the initiative was again seen to be inadequate. In June 1971, the Task Force proposed a further upgrading of environmental matters, and a linking of environmental and social problems involved in northern pipeline development. A new Social and Environmental Committee of the Task Force was proposed, together with an Advisory Group of outside experts to assist the Task Force in its work in this area. The novel features of the proposed new Committee were its large projected research program, its management structure and the concept of an Advisory Group.

a. *Structure*: From a tiny four-man sub-committee of the Pipeline Committee, the new June proposal outlined an exuberant structure which could not possibly be attacked as "inadequate" by public bodies. Chaired by the Department of Indian Affairs and Northern Development, the committee would encompass a massive research programme under a director (environmental-social programme-northern pipelines); a programming unit; senior and social environmental advisors; and no fewer than five Coordinating Committees (the Departments of Environment, Indian Affairs and Northern Development, and Energy, Mines and Resources, and the two territorial governments). Moreover, the director of the Social-Environmental Programme would be assisted by the Advisory Group and a special liaison committee formed with the National Energy Board. The following table gives an indication of the scope of the new structure.

b. *Advisory Group*: The Advisory Group concept was a direct response to public pressure and a formidable attempt to allay public suspicions that environmental matters were receiving short shrift by the Government. The Cabinet *Memorandum* outlining the usefulness of the proposed body made this perfectly clear: the criticism of the apparent inactivity of the Task Force in protecting the northern environment, especially with regard to possible pipelines, and the expressed concern that public groups did not have an opportunity to bring their views to bear on northern

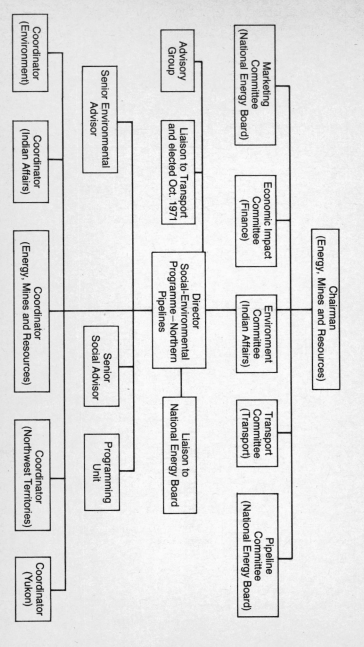

Task Force on Northern Oil Development

pipeline problems, suggested the usefulness of an Advisory Group which would provide expertise as well as a sounding board for Task Force ideas. In addition, it would focus public opinion to provide a direct input into the policy process. The alternative, according to the memorandum, was to receive fragmented advice from special interest groups which would necessarily be conflicting and, therefore, not altogether satisfactory.

A further advantage would be the increase in public confidence that would flow from the participation of citizen groups in planning and the Task Force stressed the importance of an active public relations campaign to emphasize citizen participation. The membership was projected at about twenty and to include groups across the political spectrum — from the Inuit Tapisirat, through the Canadian Wildlife Federation and the Canadian Arctic Resources Committee, into clearer sailing with the Canadian Pipeline Joint Advisory Committee and Imperial Oil. The Department of Indian Affairs and Northern Development was to foot the bill for its activities.

c. *Programme*: The terms of reference for the new Environment Social Committee went far beyond those of the defunct sub-committee. It was designed: 1) to serve as the point of contact between industry and Government; 2) to identify environmental and social problems in pipeline construction and development; 3) to recommend and coordinate agency inputs; 4) to recommend guidelines which the Task Force would pass along to industry at its discretion; 5) to identify and recommend routes based on these considerations; 6) to develop draft terms for the disposal of pipeline rights-of-way; 7) to make recommendations for meeting questions regarding the Indian problem and more general aspects; 8) to assess environmental and social aspects of proposals for pipeline construction.

More important than the mandate was the stated intention of directing a programme of research and developing a coherent management structure. Indeed, the new committee requested not merely final approval for the $ 5,000,000 provisionally approved in May 1971 but also a further $ 10,000,000 to fund a three year crash programme of environmental research in the Canadian Arctic. A $ 15,000,000 allocation represented a striking departure and, to some members of the Task Force, a somewhat heavy handed attempt by the Department of Indian Affairs and Northern Development to strengthen its bid for leadership on environmental matters within the Task Force. Both the chairman of the Social-Environmental Committee and the Director of the Social and Environmental Programme were to be seconded from the Department.

In fact, the new committee had not worked out research priorities for the funding of the long list of projects that had been thrown together at the last minute and appended to the Cabinet document. Good reasons existed for a more careful look at the operation of the programme, both in terms of financial review and research priorities. Defended, however, on the grounds of developing a strong, integrated programme and ensuring inter-agency coordination of northern environmental research, and put forward as a last ditch effort "as we approach the time when firm applications to proceed are obtained from industry," the programme was approved by Cabinet against misgivings among many senior officials. Such was the perceived political pressure that so slim a proposal could find Cabinet support. It was a direct product of public pressure and was reluctantly put forward in an atmosphere of crisis. Now the Task Force had an environmental impact committee with a hugh budget for research.

d. *Assessment*: The organizational and budgetary breakthrough achieved in October 1971 was not indicative of a shift in priorities or assumptions within the Task Force regarding pipeline development in the North. Indeed, injecting so large an amount of money into northern pipeline research (rather than, say, comparable research dealing with Sable Island in Nova Scotia) tended to commit the federal Government even more openly to a pipeline along the Mackenzie. The Task Force consensus remained that Ottawa could and should oblige industry by clearing away outstanding obstacles as quickly as possible. There was never any doubt that environmental questions would, at the very most, delay pipeline construction for only a short period of time. Inevitably there would be some environmental damage (Task Force officials estimated the probability of a break every hundred miles) but this was to be minimized by demanding safeguards. In the end, however, the cost of protecting the environment had to be weighed against the competitiveness of Canadian frontier oil and gas in Canadian and American markets. Industry would be in the best position to indicate to the Task Force how far to go in protecting the environment.

There is no evidence that senior officials in the Task Force wavered in the assumption that industry could be relied upon to protect the environment in northern pipeline construction and that the environmental question should not obscure the economic factors related to pipeline construction. No policing of industry studies was recommended. The chief worry until fall 1972 was the activity of public groups and various trouble-makers in the Departments of Indian Affairs and Northern Development and of Environment who might attempt to stop the pipeline using the strategy of opponents to the trans-Alaska pipeline.

A typical attitude was expressed by a senior official in the Northwest Territories Government who was briefed on the environmental situation in early 1972:

> We are approaching the problem with open minds and the basic premise that the pipeline will be built but that the environmental and economic balance must also be protected. This will impose certain obligations and there may even be restrictions on pipeline people, but in the end we will have a pipeline as well as our natural environment and economic balance. We should all benefit.

In general, there was little enthusiasm for the new environmental programme in the Task Force, but officials accepted the probability of a one-year delay, and realized they would have to come to terms with it.

The Advisory Group concept, as adopted by the Task Force, was innovative in the context of northern pipeline planning, but senior officials privately foresaw a very limited role for this new body. The Task Force had to provide evidence that the Government accepted citizen participation in planning, but the substantive functions of the Advisory Group were to remain carefully confined.

First, its formal activities were to be very limited. It was to meet with the Committee on request and the meetings were to be chaired by the Committee Chairman. Second, although it was to advise on the progress of on-going research in the Arctic and on additional research required (as well as the terms and conditions for actual construction and the pipeline route selection), only two annual meetings were forecast with one brief trip a year to the Mackenzie delta. Per diem expenses were limited to $50 for a total projected annual budget of $49,500.00. The price of participatory democracy is not high.

Finally, the Advisory Group was not to have access to confidential information. The danger of improper use of information was explicitly underlined and the records of the Task Force would not be made available to the Advisory Group. A clear line had to be drawn between avoiding the impression that the Task Force was not interested in public participation and providing extremists with a forum to disseminate their views. Thus the July 1972 Memorandum to Cabinet, the mark of optimism in a speedy construction of gas pipeline already one year delayed, concluded that environmental considerations might delay construction for as much as a year but could not stop northern pipeline development.

3. THE EXPANDED PIPELINE GUIDELINES, JUNE 28, 1972

The Expanded Northern Pipeline Guidelines drafted by the new Task Force Social-Environmental Committee and tabled by the Hon. Jean Chretien on June 28, 1972, demonstrated the point well enough. Hastily thrown together, the Guidelines gave little indication of detailed Government research, and they ruled out effective criticism of the merits of a Mackenzie Pipeline itself. Indeed, the expanded Guidelines, in an attempt to elaborate those aspects of the August 1970 Northern Pipeline Guidelines specifying the "corridor" concept, and the requirement that applicants must protect the environment and people of the North, were more like a set of maxims or a code of good behaviour than clear directives or stipulations of use to engineers in the field.

The width of the "corridor" was left studiously vague:

The concept of "one trunk oil pipeline and one trunk gas pipeline" within a "corridor" was enunciated with the intention of confining environmental and social disturbance resulting from trunk pipelines to a *narrow zone*, thus limiting insofar as possible the geographic area involved in these disturbances and leaving as much as possible of our northern lands in an undisturbed state. On the other hand, it is recognized that restriction of both oil and gas pipeline construction activities to a *narrow* "corridor" would lead to increased intensity of land use and the possibility of unacceptable environmental and social disruption. ... Thus caution will be required in defining specific routes or "corridor" boundaries. (Italics added).[3]

The Environmental Guidelines listed concerns which applications for a pipeline right-of-way would have to satisfy — safety and integrity of the pipeline; effects on the terrain and vegetation; matters relating to river and lake crossings; effects on wildlife, etc. The tenth and final Guideline stressed that industry develop a monitoring system "to ensure operational performance in keeping with the above-stated environmental concerns."[4]

The fundamental problem lay in the statement introducing the Environmental Guidelines: "Any certificate issued will be strictly conditioned with respect to applicable statutes providing for the protection of the environment." In fact, Ottawa in general and the Task Force in particular did not have sufficient hard data available to draft adequate standards. Senior officials in the Task Force, other than those from Indian Affairs and Northern Development, were, in fact, mortified by the potent weakness of the Guidelines in this respect. Thus, the first Guideline really asked the question that the Guidelines as a whole supposedly answered, in outlining

. . . that a pipeline be constructed, operated and abandoned in keeping with good engineering practice to ensure its safety and integrity, in the interests of good environmental management and the reduction of environmental damage.[5]

But what was "good environmental management"? On this point, neither industry nor environmentalists obtained any enlightenment whatsoever. Instead, they got a list of concerns that the Canadian Arctic Gas consortium would have to take up in their submission.

At least three other major problems in the Expanded Guidelines caused dismay among Task Force officials who felt them vulnerable to public challenge. First, the Government had already decided and announced the building of an all-weather Mackenzie highway to support pipeline construction without prior socio-environmental research. The Guidelines therefore inevitably sounded somewhat hollow, and public groups such as the Canadian Arctic Resources Committee immediately seized on this inconsistency. In fact, the case of the Mackenzie Highway decision remains a rallying cry for all environmentalist groups interested in the North.

Second, the 1972 Guidelines focused attention on a thorny point that raised questions among Government lawyers. Did the National Energy Board have authority under the Act to deal with social and environmental concerns in pipeline construction? The Act itself was silent on this matter. The problem had never come up before, so that no precedent could be referred to. But now the proposed Mackenzie gas pipeline raised the issue in an acute form; the project was national in its importance and implications for the country as a whole, and hard decisions would have to be made. For example, if the Energy Board was competent to pass judgement on environmental matters, what criteria would it employ for determining rights-of-way, the terms of land-tenure agreements, and so on?

An alternative procedure would be to hold a second set of hearings dealing with the application from the Department of Indian Affairs and Northern Development under the Territorial Lands Act, for tenure of land comprising the pipeline right-of-way. From the Task Force's point of view, however, this course of action should be avoided. It wanted speedy action, on the assumption of an early application. A second set of hearings would slow down the process. Also senior officals realized that public hearings dealing with the right-of-way issue would be harder to control than National Energy Board hearings where the technical nature of the discussion could more easily overwhelm critics, particularly with adequate Board preparation on likely questions. Substantive policy issues, such as the details of pipeline construction, alternative modes of transportation, financing arrangements, and matters relating to supplies and markets, could be transformed into technical and regulatory problems.

The land issue had better be kept away from the public, both in the North and in Ottawa, because the inter-relatedness of basic policy areas could not so easily be camouflaged in technical jargon. Moreover, the Task Force exercised much less of a monopoly over land-use data than information relating to the pipeline and resource industry. The broadened focus of a second set of hearings, would centre attention on the project in its entirety rather than on the individual component parts, and force a judgement on their inter-relatedness rather than in isolation from one another. A

170

"regulatory" problem would almost certainly be transformed into a "policy" problem. The potential for disruption was considerable; procedurally the Government was very vulnerable.

This fear explains the third vexing problem with the expanded Guidelines — they too obviously ruled out meaningful public participation. It was one thing to adopt a model of northern development that excluded the public; it was quite another to parade it. The expanded Pipeline Guidelines assumed that the merits of an immediate Mackenzie gas line were established beyond doubt, that it would be built, and that all that remained were minor technical problems. The Minister's introductory comments on June 28, 1972, therefore appeared unnecessarily provocative:

> The Government's purpose in expressing these latest views is to give further guidance to industries engaged in research and planning in connection with northern pipelines and to afford the opportunity to northern residents, and all others concerned, to make observations on the guidelines proposed.
>
> In particular, the government is ready to sit down with representatives of the native peoples involved, invite their views on the guidelines proposed, and reflect these views wherever possible.
>
> Comments from individuals or groups not represented on the advisory group of the Task Force on Northern Development might address them to the Director, Environmental-Social Programme of the Task Force on Northern Development.[6]

In effect, the Task Force claimed that it had solved the problem of consultation with affected groups through the setting up of the Social-Environmental Committee, and, in particular, the establishment of the Advisory Group. But given the magnitude of the project, and the irreversible environmental consequences of a Mackenzie gas pipeline, was not the Cabinet or at least a Parliamentary Committee a more relevant focus for questions than a senior official? It would take an immense act of faith on the part of any group or individual to put money on the Advisory Group. The whole thing was too bald, a poor exercise in public relations. It also failed. The inconsequential nature of public participation in the Task Force was typical of all aspects of

171

northern development. But pipeline planning, as J. J. Greene (and before him C. D. Howe) had stressed, was dangerously unpredictable.

4. THE ADVENT OF PUBLIC-INTEREST GROUPS

A symptom of public concern about the North was the formation of public interest groups to monitor Government and industry planning for northern development. Pollution Probe at the University of Toronto had a broader focus that extended beyond the Arctic but it nevertheless was keenly interested in gathering and disseminating reliable information on the actual progress of resource exploitation as it affected the northern environment. Other groups and individuals organized conferences and working groups on the subject. The press also demonstrated a keen interest in northern pipelines after the trans-Alaska pipeline system hearings in February 1971, not least in the context of the ensuing Parliamentary debate over the Canadian alternative.

Nevertheless neither these organizations nor the press possessed the necessary focus or capabilities required for an effective public watchdog over Government and business activities in the North. This task required a single-minded concentration on the Arctic, a long-term commitment, as well as short-run objectives, and a credible research competence to give it legitimacy among established opinion-makers across the country. In this sense the establishment of the Canadian Arctic Resources Committee marked a new stage in the mobilization of informed debate concerning northern economic development. According to the organizers of the new group:

> We were concerned that Canada badly needed an organization which could provide a pair of eyes to look in on the North in a more perceptive way than any existing citizens' organization was capable of doing; which could act in an "Honest Broker" capacity to attempt to ensure that the things that needed to be done in advance of development of whatever type, got done; which could help bring to the surface the question of what was to be done about the claims of the native people; and which could help overcome the barrier to factual information existing between the Canadian public and the Government on matters

that pertained to development, the native people and the environment.[7]

The Canadian Arctic Resources Committee's first project — to assemble experts in the various disciplines, economists, demographers, lawyers, engineers, environmentalists, and native rights experts in order to establish "areas of strength and weakness in existing knowledge, on needs and priorities, and on the potential impact of development on the environment or the people," — was very successful. Both the preparatory work and the meetings (Carleton University, May 24-26, 1972, in cooperation with the Arctic Institute of North America) exhibited professionalism as well as commitment. With the publication of *Arctic Alternatives*, the proceedings of the May 1972 meetings, the Committee became a political factor of some importance in northern development. The further addition of several extremely visible scholars made it difficult for Government Departments and agencies to ignore its existence altogether. The concession to environmentalists granted during 1971-72 was related directly to the increasingly informed public discussion centring around the Committee.

By late 1972, senior officials in the Task Force, but particularly in Indian Affairs and Northern Development, were annoyed at the coverage in the media devoted to the least attractive aspects of the northern framework of economic development:

a. The Canadian Oil and Gas Land Regulations (1961) and foreign ownership of resources virtually ruled out any financial benefits to Canada from the export of Arctic oil and gas. In fact, the Canadian Arctic Resources Committee was preparing a Conference on this subject. "Cornucopia For Whom?", for December, 1972.

b. The United States was well in advance of Canada in the recognition of native claims and aboriginal rights.

c. Canada possessed nothing as adequate as the American National Environmental Protection Act for safeguarding the northern environment in the event of pipeline construction. Administrative discretion was all-pervasive in the Canadian North.

d. Public participation in northern policy-making was virtually impossible and completely ineffective. Neither the native people nor Parliament nor the press could crack the information monopoly of Government and business. The armour of the bureaucracy was impenetrable, short of calculated leaks. Indian Affairs and Northern Development could not command the necessary documents and briefings required for satisfactory investigation. Effective public hearings or other methods to ensure citizen participation were a first priority in northern development.

Before 1973, groups such as the Canadian Arctic Resources Committee and Pollution Probe had obtained a following and built a firm base of operation, but they remained frustrated by their identification in Government circles with the radical (ineffective) fringe of Canadian politics. Task Force and particularly Indian Affairs officials dismissed them out of hand as " . . . outsiders whose romantic idea of Eskimo culture is running behind a smelly old dog team." They were caricatured, along with native organizations, as hostile in principle to economic development.[8]

The charge was wholly incorrect. Native people, whose traditional way of life was being rapidly undermined, and environmentalists, who perceived the dangers of uncontrolled resource and pipeline development, objected to the model of economic development set in motion by Government and industry after 1968, particularly within the Task Force. They did not object to economic development itself, indeed they welcomed it — if it could be related to the needs of Northerners and Canada as a whole, if time were permitted to preserve the human and environmental aspects of the region.

So long as they remained isolated from more powerful allies, their growing influence could not be decisive, and their demands for greater public involvement in the Mackenzie pipeline debate could be ignored or minimized. Public interest groups by themselves could not break the established inertia of the Task Force on Northern Oil Development. They required the broad base of support throughout Canada that could only come from far-reaching changes in the political and economic environment of the country.

During the winter of 1972-73, the context of northern development changed dramatically. The Trudeau Government suffered a sharp rebuff at the polls in October 1972 and Canadian-American relations soured. The assumptions underpinning the framework of northern development in 1968-72, the inherited beliefs from simpler days, were now tested, and found wanting.

NOTES

1. *House of Commons Standing Committee on National Resources and Public Works* , May 26, 1971.
2. The new Department of the Environment into which the Department of Fisheries and Forests would be merged, was officially announced in early summer, 1971.
3. Government of Canada, Department of Indian Affairs and Northern Development, *Expanded Guidelines for Northern Pipelines*, June 28, 1972, pp. 7-8.
4. *Ibid.*, pp. 13-17.
5. *Ibid.*, p. 14.
6. *Ibid.*, Foreword and p. 3.
7. *Arctic Alternatives, op. cit.*, p. 8.
8. *Toronto Star*, June 23, 1973.

CHAPTER TEN
Breakthrough

Although opposition to the proposed Mackenzie Valley natural gas pipeline had formed before 1972, it had centred largely on social and environmental questions. Few objections had been raised about its possible implications for the Canadian economy as a whole. It is therefore of interest to note that the first serious questions about the financial and economic wisdom of the project surfaced within Government circles rather than from outside pressure groups; and that the controversy centred on Canadian-American economic relations in general rather than narrow financial grounds.

After 1968, certain key Ottawa officials, particularly in the Department of Finance, progressively lost confidence in the so-called "special relationship" that had characterized Canadian-American relations after World War II. The contribution of foreign corporations in certain sectors of the economy had proved negative. In aerospace, for example, the third largest export component of manufactured goods in the late 1960s, a crisis ensued in 1969 when the parent firms, General Dynamics and Hawker-Siddeley, lost interest in Canadair Ltd. (Montreal) and De Havilland Ltd. (Toronto). Canada's experiences with such famous joint ventures as the St. Lawrence Seaway and the Columbia River project were not particularly pleasant. More recently, the August 1971 surcharge reminded officials that the level of economic integration achieved with the United States did not guarantee special treatment.

In particular, they had been stung often enough by 1972 to

realize that further large scale capital projects in the order of a Mackenzie gas pipeline could seriously damage the Canadian economy. The increasingly close ties between the Canadian and American economies which had appeared during the 1960s as "interpenetration," now had developed into "imperialism." Integrating the North into that structure, to serve primarily American interests, looked less attractive than it had only two years before.

Hard-headed realists, these officials were in no way sentimental about native rights and the Arctic environment — any environment for that matter (except perhaps Rockcliffe Village in Ottawa). They merely objected to the pattern that had been developing in Canadian-American relations.

1. THE ECONOMIC IMPACT REPORT JUNE-DECEMBER 1972

The key event within the Task Force which reflected these doubts was the tabling in June 1972 of a Preliminary Report of the Economic Impact Committee, chaired by the Department of Finance. Despite its formidable influence in the Ottawa community, Finance had maintained a low profile within the Task Force in the period 1970-72. It had, of course, actively contributed to the conceptual decisions regarding northern economic and pipeline planning in 1970. But the other Task Force members — the National Energy Board; Energy Mines and Resources; Indian Affairs and Northern Development; and Transport — were more visibly committed to ongoing pipeline (and resource) planning. Among these, in turn, Energy Mines and Resources and Indian Affairs and Northern Development were in the vanguard. Both Ministers had publicly endorsed the proposed natural gas pipeline in the Mackenzie Corridor.

The Preliminary Report of the Economic Impact Committee was very nearly a finished product and contained the central arguments that later discouraged Task Force officials. They boiled down to three outstanding points:

1. Normal economic forces would be distorted by the size and speed of pipeline construction; it could cause undesirable consequences in other sectors of the economy. Interest rates and prices would be increased, and the exchange rate of the

Canadian dollar would rise, negatively affecting the manufacturing sector and exports in general. If there were no appreciable slack in the economy, these negative effects could be extremely serious. It was debatable if the impetus given to Canadian business, particularly the steel industry, would offset them.

2. The greater the Canadian content and control of the project, the greater would be the undesirable economic consequences. At the same time, public opinion and the August 1970 Guidelines appeared to demand Canadian equity control and participation.

3. Net benefits, either in job-creation or revenues, appeared too small to justify the massive effort required. Total revenues would be far lower than those accruing to Alaska, "minimal" according to the Report under the existing regulatory framework — about $85 million, as opposed to $300 million for Alaska. Changes in this framework to increase revenues on the transportation of Alaskan natural gas would invite American retaliation at a certain point, and therefore could not be pushed too far. A through-put tax would raise income, so long as the United States did not also apply one to the extensive Canadian pipeline system that traversed American territory. Under Canada's permissible corporate tax deferrals, government revenues might be even lower. An annual income of $85 million could only with difficulty justify the costs involved. In effect, the financial benefits to Canada from the export of frontier fuels were virtually nil.

Employment prospects were also bleak. Two hundred permanent jobs might be created after the construction period. Temporary construction jobs were also of doubtful benefit to Canada, even if native people would have employment possibilities for a few years, balanced as they would have to be, against the social and environmental costs of the destruction of native communities by a massive influx of men and equipment from the south.

All in all, it was a "mixed blessing" even if the most propitious circumstances, particularly a slack economy, converged at the initiation of the construction period. The outlook here was cloudy — not only James Bay, but other massive capital projects such as the

Pickering Airport were near decision points. Even without a Mackenzie Valley pipeline, pressure on the Canadian economy was going to be heavy.[1]

The Preliminary Report had little immediate impact on the Task Force for Northern Oil Development preparations for the construction of the proposed Mackenzie natural gas pipeline: the reaction of the Chairman was to bury it as an Appendix to the July 1972 *Progress Report* to Cabinet. The Deputy Minister of Energy, Mines and Resources apparently did not share the doubts of some colleagues about the prevailing state of Canadian-American relation. In addition, he was perhaps convinced that Canada was so far committed, so deeply in already regarding northern pipeline construction, that Government-business relations would be too badly damaged if Ottawa now backed off from earlier commitments. Bureaucratic momentum within the Task Force was too strong to be affected by a Preliminary Report. It could not dampen the optimism of the July *Memorandum* to Cabinet, nor had it any appreciable effect on Government-industry planning prior to the October election.°

The September 6, 1972 Task Force meeting illustrates this harmony. The general consensus was that planning was on schedule, with relevant committees phasing their work well with the schedules of Canadian Arctic Gas. Remaining tasks as outlined in the July Cabinet *Memo* were being systematically tackled. The Interdepartmental Committee on Industrial Supply to be headed by Industry, Trade and Commerce was in the process of formation. Indeed, matters were now well-enough in hand to consider a transportation network for hydrocarbons in the Arctic Islands.

Only in one respect can one detect a feeling of uncertainty among senior Task Force officials that might be related to the bombshell being finalized by the Economic Impact Committee; the Chairman of the Task Force expressed his concern about partial reports by individual Departments, as well as outright leaks. They would lead to "misrepresentation and inaccurate publicity" potentially damaging to the Liberal Party in the election. Strict control of information and interdepartmental clearance of all reports by individual departments were recommended.

° Only one pro-forma sentence of the *Cabinet* memorandum spoke directly to the Finance brief: "The important policy decision must be based on the total

The discussion of the Finance brief at the December 4 and 14, meetings respectively of the Environmental-Social Committee chaired by Hunt of Indian Affairs, and the full Task Force, chaired by Austin (and superbly attended) produced, in contrast, a dramatic impact. For the Chairman of the Task Force the timing could hardly have been more unfortunate. He had now finalized and was ready to announce the creation of the new Committee on Industrial Supply to determine the capability of Canadian industry to participate in the supply of goods, services and labour in the Mackenzie project, and to recommend the nature and degree of federal Government assistance to serve the Canadian interest. With the other committees working well with industry, and preparing for a Canadian Gas Arctic application in 1973, the Economic Impact Report introduced a jarring note.

In an extraordinary coincidence, a much publicized debate in Toronto between Eric Kierans and W.P. Wilder, Chairman of the Canadian Arctic Gas consortium, a week before had witnessed Kierans emphasizing precisely the negative effects outlined in the Finance brief. The effect was not lost on Task Force members. They noted that Energy, Mines and Resources, in response to queries from colleagues about the Economic Impact Report, repeated Wilder's argument — that the Mackenzie gas pipeline was necessary for *Canadian*, not merely American, markets. Frontier gas would be required by the end of the decade. The project should go forward on schedule. Indian Affairs and Northern Development agreed, and added that environmental considerations would not delay it more than one year at most. The National Energy Board also saw no difficulty, indicating that long-term benefits would far outweigh short-term costs. Its chief worry was more specific — determining the procedures to be used by Indian Affairs and Northern Development in handling Canadian Arctic Gas' application for a pipeline right-of-way on the one hand and the Boards's procedures for a construction permit on the other.

But these specific points could not dispel a sense of foreboding. Senior officials hurried back to their Ministers to explain the Finance brief. A special meeting of the Inter-Departmental

economic picture. Decisions would have to be different if the assumption about economic activity is wrong." The *Memorandum* then rambled on to discuss the "best alternatives" to assure long-term benefits "of a considerable magnitude" to Canada.

Committee on Oil was set up to discuss its implications for Canada's energy sector. The solidarity of the Task Force was now broken.

The breakthrough achieved in the Finance Report was the redefinition of the problem involved in the construction of a Mackenzie natural gas pipeline. Until the fall of 1972, Task Force officials were successful in obscuring the crucial problem: the long-term impact of Arctic resource exploitation on the Canadian economy as a whole. Instead, the discussions were limited to narrow and short-term issues associated specifically with the Mackenzie pipeline corridor itself. Even in these areas — environmental impact of pipeline construction and effects on native people — Task Force officials had been unsympathetic. But by 1972 they were reconciled to some social-environmental input, if not yet a land settlement with the natives. The Report of the Economic Impact Committee was not meant originally to focus in on broader economic concerns. It too, was to remain specific to the project in question. In this way its recommendation could not be linked to frontier economic development as a whole. For the framework of northern resource exploitation was extremely vulnerable as soon as the central problem was defined to be the role of the North in the long-term development of the Canadian economy.

Should northern resources be conserved for Canadian consumers? Did Canada's inventory of known fuels both South and North of 60 justify the export of any oil or natural gas? Did the prevailing ownership pattern and regulatory structure of northern resources render benefits to Canadians from exports negligible in any case? Would increased exports of Canadian oil and natural gas to the United States damage Canada's manufacturing sector? How, in these circumstances, should Canada time the development of northern resources as opposed to the harnessing of the Athabasca tar sands potential? These questions transformed the debate about the merits of a Mackenzie Corridor into a full-scale re-evaluation of northern development itself. The national interest in the Arctic would *have* to be defined.

The Finance brief forced Task Force officials to face these broader implications squarely. For most Canadians the role of bilateral relations with the United States in northern development, although predominant since 1968, had never been defined or articulated. Intelligent public debate could now begin on the *assumptions* underlying resource extraction in the Arctic. A virtual revolution had occurred in four years, 1968-1972.

2. THE OIL SHORTAGE

It was not coincidental that the Economic Impact Report failed to register until December 1972. Until the October 31, 1972 general election ended four years of majority Government, Trudeau was firmly in control. Retrospectively, his second Government, propped up by an apparently revived New Democratic Party, was a period of learning for Trudeau, and a prelude to a great personal victory less than two years later in July 1974. The immediate result, however, was weakness. He was in trouble.

The New Democratic Party had opposed the construction of the proposed Mackenzie natural gas pipeline during the October 1972 election campaign. It had been a minor issue in the election, and, apart from the Northwest Territories, where Wally Firth gained a seat for the New Democrats, David Lewis gained few votes from his opposition. But with Wally Firth in the House of Commons, and in a minority situation, Trudeau and the Task Force faced new dangers in the North.

Other political developments in Canada also suggested important changes in public opinion that indirectly at least affected the framework of northern development. The "corporate welfare bum" slogan had caught on well for the New Democratic Party. In British Columbia their stunning victory under David Barrett opened a period of social democracy in the far west. He was faced with the consequences of the ill-considered Columbia River project, and might want to assess the long-term costs of similar massive capital projects proposed by American interests. Moreover, British Columbia had a direct interest in the movement of Alaskan and Arctic supplies to southern markets.

These major political setbacks coincided with another development with even more striking implications for the Task Force on Northern Oil Development. The American energy shortage in the fall of 1972 and the realization that Alberta oil reserves were very limited and could no longer meet American long-term decisively undermined the prestige of the National Energy Board and the

Task Force. The Board in particular, was exposed to public scrutiny, and the bankruptcy of its policies mercilessly exposed.

The public had lived in a fool's paradise since the opening of the Leduc oil fields in 1947, and the Government made no attempt to educate it. The Board's refusal in November 1971 to grant further export permits of natural gas reversed a decade's tradition, and illustrated Canada's very modest proven and accessible reserves of gas. It had little impact.[2]

Warnings by distinguished Canadian scientists that Canada's oil and natural gas were not extensive relative to the long-term needs of a cold and large nation, similarly fell on deaf ears. Professor J. Tuzo Wilson for example, a month before the October 31, 1972 general election, pointed out that Canada should reassess the apparent willingness of the National Energy Board to transport oil to American markets without regard for Canada's own needs. This was particularly the case respecting the Arctic, now that reserves in western Canada were nearing depletion. Even the United States was exercising foresight by setting aside Petroleum Reserve Zones for future needs. In Aslaska, No. 4 Petroleum Reserve was well-known to be extremely rich in oil and natural gas.

> It seems clear that the Arctic holds Canada's main reserve of fuel which is also the main reserve for North America. Another reserve lies off the Atlantic provinces under the sea but even less is known about it. The United States Navy was sufficiently provident to set aside No. 4 Petroleum Reserve on the Alaska coast. If the Americans hold petroleum in reserve should not Canadians do likewise?[3]

Not until the American energy crisis in late 1972 forced a realization that Canada had better think carefully about its own energy supplies did public interest mount. A gradual pessimism began to seep into the press. The public learned that Alberta's conventional crude oil reserves were declining. For the fourth year in a row, more oil was being pumped out of Alberta than was being discovered, in spite of a record level of exploration. According to the Alberta Energy Resources Conservation Board, that left less than ten years supply at current rates of Canadian and export demand. Industry sources warned that "practically all of Canada's cheap fuels have been located".[4]

These unanticipated developments led the National Energy Board to an about-face in February 27, 1973 with its recommendation to impose the first Canadian quota on oil exports to the U.S. in order to ensure adequate supplies in this country. Further restrictions on gasoline and heating fuels imposed in June 1973 brought practically all petroleum industry trade between Canada and the United States under direct federal surveillance and control.

The position of the National Energy Board Chairman now became untenable, particularly after MacDonald's admission on February 15, 1973, that Cabinet was not informed that Canadian gas was under-priced in the U.S. He resigned in June 1973, replaced by a Trudeau pragmatist less obviously identified with the pre-1972 policy framework of Canadian energy production, distribution and trade, which now had to be dismantled without delay.[5] Mr. Austin, as Chairman of the Task Force (TFNOD) and Deputy Minister of EMR similarly began to look around for other employment. The Task Force as a whole lost its effectiveness.

Events moved rapidly. The end of the National Oil Policy with its division of Canada into two markets was announced; further restrictions on oil exports to the United States were introduced; and a two-price system for domestic and foreign (i.e., American) users was implemented with an oil export tax. The Mid-East war of October 1973 with the accompanying Arab production cut-back and supply problems further exacerbated the general confusion in the energy sector.

Taken together, these drastic policy changes rejected the continental approach to oil and gas development pursued since 1961 in favour of a genuine Canadian market. Relations between Government and industry deteriorated as Ottawa now pressed for a greater share of profits and announced its intention of establishing a publicly owned oil company, Petrocan. The producing provinces and Ottawa fought over marketing authority and royalty splits.

By mid-1973 the famous "political culture" of Canadian-American relations had eroded. As one observer pointed out, a week before the Liberal minority Government presented its Foreign Ownership Review Bill to the House of Commons in April 1973:

It has been clear for some time from Washington's point of view the special relationship no longer exists. But Ottawa has been slow to acknowledge the change, just as Britain slowly and reluctantly gave up its claim to special status in the period after the Second World War.[6]

The changed circumstances meant that Canada now had no alternative but to act, defining its own needs, rather than having American and other foreign-owned industry telling senior officials in Ottawa what to do. The proposed Mackenzie Valley gas pipeline, a major development project more than comparable to the TransCanada Pipeline and the St. Lawrence Seaway, begged the question of whose interests it was designed to serve. When American rather than Canadian users were identified as the prime beneficiaries, the Task Force on Northern Oil Development was in trouble. It appeared as if that well-known Canadian instinct for survival was now in evidence.

3. THE RETREAT — ARCTIC RAILWAYS

The first direct problem for the Task Force resulting from the changed environment was a sudden public interest in alternative methods of moving Arctic gas to southern markets. In particular, Ottawa came under a variety of pressures to examine an Arctic railway as an alternative to the proposed Mackenzie gas pipeline. Other alternatives such as the Boeing RC-1 resource-carrying aircraft also received greater attention. But an Arctic railway rekindled the national passion for railroads.

Confronted by public pressure, the Task Force now found that it would have to show it had done serious research on the railway option. At its December 14, 1972 meeting, it briefed the Transport Committee Chairman on possible strategies to contain this interest. The reply noted that no "further" study had been planned, but that in all probability the Task Force would have to reopen the issue to be able to answer questions at the forthcoming National Energy Board hearings on the Canadian Arctic Gas Study Limited application. The Chairman was vexed in retrospect by the Ministry of Transport press release of June 8, 1972 which, by indicating that studies on the rail option were progressing, might have given the wrong impression that it was a serious alternative. Perhaps the Task Force itself had contributed to the mess. Anyway there was now nothing to do about that — the Government simply could not find itself in the embarrassing position of having to admit that it was favouring the pipeline companies. An "environmental intervenor" could cause a furore if this became apparent, and the credibility of Canadian Arctic Gas Study Limited would also be undermined.

Actually the public pressure for an accelerated study of the railway option drew its strength from the simultaneous interest of quite distinct political constituencies in Canada. The most determined proponent, Professor C. Law of Queen's University, had sounded a war-cry against the proposed Mackenzie gas pipeline in his June 1972 Report* stressing the social, environmental, and broad economic advantages of the railway option.

First, the railway would be multi-purpose as opposed to a pipeline which would be geared to one commodity only. It would assist northern community development over the long-term and provide an opportunity for balanced development. In terms of permanent employment, the railway concept had obvious advantages over a pipeline.

Second, Law insisted that a railway could be less damaging to the environment and wild life. Although widely disputed, many observers, including native northerners, were convinced. As Wally Firth, M.P. from the Northwest Territories, pointed out on June 12, 1973, "After much study and investigation, I would say the best method of moving gas and oil would be by railway."[7]

The third argument, however, was the most powerful and brought the railway option to the attention of many otherwise disinterested Canadians in the south. An Arctic railway would not be foreign-controlled; and it would permit frontier supplies to be used for Canadian needs as they develop. In a word, it would not tie northern supplies once and for all to the American pipeline grid:

Do we need this oil and gas from the Arctic in Canada yet? We don't. But the Americans do. . . . The oil companies want one thing: they want to come in, and build and get out.[8]

* *Railway to the Arctic*, June 1972 (Kingston: Queen's University, Canadian Institute of Guided Ground Transport).

The Canadian public would no longer tolerate the comfortable assumption that the oil companies and the National Energy Board were acting in the public interest. It wanted evidence that all options had been explored. Despite repeated warnings from Canadian Arctic Gas Study Limited that a pipeline was less expensive than a railway, and that environmental and social costs of pipeline construction and operation would be minimal, it wanted evidence that the option had been explored as promised. Canadian National Railways and the Brotherhood of Locomotive Engineers put pressure on the Departments of Energy, Mines and Resources and Indian Affairs and Northern Development for follow-up studies to Queen's University's Canadian Institute of Guided Ground Transport's *Railway to the Arctic*. On February 22, 1973, Terminus Ltd. of Toronto suggested similar work. Two weeks later, on March 13, 1973, Premier Barrett of British Columbia endorsed a British Columbia-Yukon railway as an alternative route for the transportation of Alaskan oil and gas to southern United States markets. Now there were two rail routes proposed for the Canadian Arctic, neither initiated by the federal Government. Yet senior officials agreed that it was likely that the rail concept was operationally feasible.

By March 1973, the Task Force agreed that "in the light of the pressures being brought to bear . . . this must be considered one of the most critical issues to be handled at present." As a result, the Transport Committee was given responsibility for preparing "a more thorough examination" of the railway option in the context of a broader study of all non-pipeline works. The issue was one of re-establishing credibility: even on-site testing was considered to attain a degree of acceptability comparable to the pipeline companies. Moreover, the appraisal would have to be given out to an "independent consulting body with the stature and standing to command respect."

It was a difficult matter. Canadian National was pushing hard within the Government for the rail option. There was the clear possibility of a charge from industry that Ottawa was favouring its own Crown Corporation. The task therefore was to reassure the Canadian public that the Task Force was sincere about evaluating the rail option, while at the same time "avoiding or reducing the possibility of a Government supported railway proposal seeking to compete with an industry sponsored pipeline proposal." Canadian Arctic Gas Study Limited should be made to see that the study was in its best interests; and government participation should be minimized. Although convinced that a pipeline had a cost advantage over an Arctic railroad, the Task Force urged an early announcement of a rail feasibility study "to avoid the "image' of giving in to pressure." Terms of reference were hurriedly assembled. $500,000 was allocated immediately, and the study, ultimately to cost $1.5 million, was announced in June 1973. Officials hoped the public fascination with Arctic railways would blow over quickly.

4. THE RETREAT BROADENS

The Arctic railway idea did not initially question the whole strategy of northern oil and gas development mapped out by Ottawa and industry in 1968-72. While challenging the wisdom of the proposed Mackenzie gas pipeline as a transportation mode, it did not offer a systematic critique of the model of development selected for the North. But the economic argument used to support the Arctic railway option provided a wedge for a fundamental re-appraisal of northern policy as it affected Canadian energy policy as a whole. By summer, the press had taken up the demand for new and more realistic guidelines in Canadian energy policy. The Toronto *Globe and Mail*, for example, pointed out that.

> Canada needs a national *energy* policy. Not just an oil policy, but a policy which will determine a national approach to all sources of energy processed and unprocessed, and regardless of the means by which they are moved.[9]

Moreover, the Government of Ontario, concerned about Alberta's intentions and entering into a prolonged period of dispute with that province, called for a National energy policy. The old stability was threatened by the new confidence in the West.

Nor were authorative critics impressed by the release of *An Energy Policy for Canada* by the Minister of Energy, Mines and Resources, Donald Macdonald, in June 1973.[10] It turned out to be a compendium of useful information but it gave little hint of the future policy direction long heralded; indeed, awaited since April 1972, it was the usual federal product in energy matters — a bitter disappointment. As a guide to northern resource and pipeline planning, Macdonald's *Energy Policy* failed altogether.

In contrast, Canadian economists of international reputation initiated serious studies of the proposed Mackenzie natural gas pipeline, developing the approach used in the Task Force's Economic Impact Report. Canadian Arctic Resources Committee, in encouraging these studies, and integrating them into on-going research in other areas, now achieved depth and respectability. Economists of the stature of John Deutsch and John Helliwell, both well-connected in Ottawa and universally respected as professionals with integrity, impressed senior officials rather more than the swelling opposition of environmentalists and native groups.

Their conclusions were devastating. Canadian Arctic Gas Study Limited supporters had maintained that early approval of the proposed Mackenzie gas pipeline was imperative to avoid further shortages of natural gas supplies for Canadian consumers and to take advantage of the movement of Alaskan gas in order to minimize the cost of Canada's northern gas. In one form or another these two arguments formed the basis of Canadian Arctic Gas' argument against delay.[11]

In contrast Helliwell maintained that:

1. Canada would not require Arctic gas before the late 1980s, at which time it would require the full capacity of the line. Given its own needs, there would be no justification for an early construction date, as proposed by Canadian Arctic Gas to supply American users.

2. The construction of a Mackenzie gas pipeline system did not meet minimal priorities of a national industrial strategy. Revenues from the delivery system and export sales would in no way offset the costs imposed on Canada by inflationary pressures during the construction period, as well as the costs to native people, the northern environment, and the huge public expenditures that would be required for roads, airports, and river dredging on the Mackenzie.

3. Canada must carefully conserve and allocate remaining oil and gas supplies in southern Canada, and use northern reserves for domestic rather than American needs. The pace of development in the Arctic would have to be slower, but

geared to national priorities. That is what the natives and environmentalists were saying all along: not wholesale opposition to northern development, but rather a strategy of development that was purposeful and supportive rather than destructive of the North and Canada. In other words, the 1970 decision to shift the exploration focus in Canada to frontier areas north of the 60th parallel, in exchange for selling off cheaper Alberta and western Canadian oil and natural gas, demanded immediate re-evaluation.

4. The Canada Oil and Gas Land Regulations of 1961 required drastic revision in any case. As a framework for the exploration of scarce hydrocarbon resources, they were hopelessly inadequate. Ottawa must increase royalty rates at once and develop more appropriate leasing procedures and conditions. Existing permit holders would have to be affected in order for Canada to benefit at all from oil and gas production in the North.

5. The July 1972 *Progress Report* to Cabinet on the proposed Mackenzie natural gas pipeline included the assumption that Delta proved reserves totalled at least 15 trillion cubic feet, or over half the required threshold figure for pipeline construction. Task Force officials among themselves thought that natural gas discoveries being reported in industry circles would confirm a threshold level in the near future. They were completely unprepared for the solemn news a year later that Mackenzie Delta proved reserves were very modest — 7 t.c.f., of which perhaps 4 t.c.f. were recoverable.

The rules of the game between industry and Government needed change. Ottawa could not afford to be helpless in face of an industry monopoly over permits, leases and information. As for the National Energy Board, a full assessment of oil and gas reserves in all areas of the country, as well as data on supply and demand was urgently required.[12]

Groping for guidance, the Canadian public finally found informed advice.

5. THE LAND ISSUE

From Canadian Arctic Gas Study Limited's point of view it was imperative that further obstacles not delay a Mackenzie pipeline in the event of its approval by the National Energy Board. But the native people had been denied a land settlement. After October 1972, with a weakened Government, and in the changed context of northern resource development as a whole, Canadian Arctic Gas and the Task Force experienced another reverse: natives obtained the possibility at least of equitable treatment of claims prior to pipeline construction. First, public hearings under the Territorial Lands Act dealing with Canadian Arctic Gas' application to the Department of Indian Affairs and Northern Development for a pipeline right-of-way were wrung from a reluctant Task Force. Second, the courts came to the assistance of the native people regarding land claims in areas under Treaties 8 and 11.

Public hearings were of vital significance. They offered a method for uncovering information relevant to the pipeline and would be more dignified than selective leaks to the press or the occupation of Government offices. In addition, they would compensate for the Canadian Arctic Resources Committee's and Pollution Probe's limited budgets. Unlike hearings before the National Energy Board for a pipeline construction permit, these hearings would focus in on native land claims, the Arctic environment and, by implication, the whole pattern of northern development. The native people could present their case in an appropriate forum and educate a Canadian public interested in hearing their side of the story. The Government and industry as participants in pipeline planning would have to defend their plans shorn of the privilege of secrecy.

In the aftermath of the October 1972 general election and widespread criticism of the Government's policy respecting pipeline planning and a land settlement, the Task Force increasingly felt that hearings, however unpalatable, were essential to restore confidence, to show that Ottawa was genuinely concerned about native people. As with the Arctic railway study, it staged a calculated retreat.

Scarcely more than six months after Cabinet acceptance of the Expanded Northern Pipeline Guidelines, Donald Macdonald, Minister of Energy, Mines and Resources, announced in January 1973, that the Department of Indian Affairs and Northern Development would, in fact, hold a second set of hearings on the right-of-way question. It took three months more for the latter Department to confirm this breakthrough officially but eventually it came on March 1, 1973. The event, a major landmark in northern economic planning in general, demonstrated the striking changes related to pipeline construction that had occurred since the July 1972 Task Force Report to Cabinet. Moreover, the choice of Mr. Justice T. Berger ensured fair hearings. Again, the weakness of Trudeau's second Government, and his dependence on the New Democrats, brought a policy decision of great significance to the North. The Berger Commission, appointed March 21, 1974, would be "one of the most important inquiries ever held in this country" and would be conducted with the tenacity and integrity characteristic of Berger's distinguished career.[13]

Court action in support of native land claims was equally dramatic. In a stunning decision, the Supreme Court of the Northwest Territories, in April 1973, issued a restraining order freezing development of 400,000 square miles of land in response to a petition from representatives of the Territories' 7,000 Treaty Indians. A month later, the Indian Brotherhood of the Northwest Territories won the right to argue its claim to ownership of western Arctic lands.

Opposition from the federal Government's Justice Department was intense. Mr. Ivan Whitehall, acting for the federal Government, maintained that Mr. Justice William Morrow of the Northwest Territories Supreme Court had no jurisdiction to decide matters involving Crown Land held by the federal Government. He argued that the colonial status of the North gave the Northwest Territories Supreme Court no authority over northern Crown Land. Morrow retorted that he would hear the case regardless of the position of Ottawa and that Ottawa's claim was an unheard of affront to the integrity of Canadian courts. After hearing evidence concerning Trudeau's claim of unfulfilled treaty obligations, and obtaining testimony regarding the signing and history of Treaties 8 and 11, Morrow ruled that the Indians could file a *caveat* against title to the lands encompassed by the Treaties, but only after all appeals by the federal Government had been exhausted.[14]

For the Indians, Morrow's decision represented an important psychological victory. It was the first opportunity granted them to argue a case of crucial importance before the Courts and in an atmosphere where there appeared a real possibility of fair treatment. By July 1973, Indian Affairs and Northern Development and the federal Government had come around somewhat to the new reality. In that month, negotiations began between the federal Government and the Council for Yukon Indians representing both Treaty and non-Treaty Indians. On August 8, the Government officially recognized "that Indians should be compensated for the loss of their traditional interest in land" and for the first time Ottawa also expressed its willingness to negotiate Inuit (Eskimo) land claims. By January 1974, Indian Affairs and Northern Development announced the formation of a committee to provide the groundwork for a comprehensive claims settlment in the Northwest Territories.

But Indian Affairs and Northern Development still held back on the promise of a land settlement *prior* to pipeline construction. Remaining defences against Justice Morrow were mobilized. In December 1973, a federal appeal of the September decision in Yellowknife was initiated on the grounds that the *Land Titles Act* did not permit a *caveat* to be raised against unregistered Crown Lands. The reflex remained. According to Indian Affairs Minister Chretien, speaking in early 1974:

> This government, after weighing all the factors involved very carefully, has come to the conclusion that a gas pipeline down the Mackenzie Valley is in the national interest. We will safeguard the rights of the people and we will protect the environment, but we will build the pipeline.[15]

Canadian Arctic Gas Study Limited executives were not so sure. The Alaskan situation seemed ominously similar, except that in Canada the process was just beginning. "We are not going to be so reckless here" (in ordering pipe before Government approval).[16] Privately, Task Force officials also foresaw the prospect of perhaps several years of legal battles concerning aboriginal rights and the registration of a land settlement.

A meeting of the Task Force's Social-Environment Committee, called for May 22, 1973 to discuss Justice Morrow's decision, concluded that it was likely to delay construction for some time. According to Indian Affairs and Northern Development, the *caveat* had cast a cloud over the title to the lands along the proposed pipeline route, a fact which could prevent the financing of the enterprise. Indian Affairs and Northern Development

194

expected the April 1973 freeze to be lifted; and, indeed, Morrow's September opinion permitted the filing of a *caveat* only *after* federal appeals had been disposed of. Pre-pipeline activity could therefore proceed while such appeals were being prepared. Nevertheless, according to Task Force officials in May 1973, "the fact of its having been issued may well signal an extended court action concerning Treaty and aboriginal rights."

6. THE WEAKENING OF CANADIAN ARCTIC GAS POSITION

The emergence of opposition within Canada to the construction of a Mackenzie pipeline system necessarily affected the momentum that had developed during Government-industry planning in 1970-72. While denying that "politics" had any bearing on its decision, a Canadian Arctic Gas spokesman announced as early as November 20, 1972 that the filing of an application for a construction permit before the National Energy Board would be delayed until the next summer. Despite a strong promotional effort in February and March 1973 by its chief executives, V.l. Horte and W. Wilder, President and Chairman respectively, further indications of delays emerged.[17] A company statement to the Ad Hoc Committee on American-Canadian Supply of the National Association of Regulatory Utility Commissioners forecast a late summer 1973 application and National Energy Board approval in early 1975. By mid-1977 Mackenzie Delta gas could be moved and the pipeline extended to Alaska in the winter of 1977-78. Canadian Arctic Gas was optimistic that ALYESKA would be given a prompt go-ahead by the American Congress; and that Canadian environmental sensitivities would be satisfied in its application.

Meanwhile the Task Force urged Canadian Arctic Gas not to be alarmed over public opinion in Canada. As far as Canadian Artic Gas was concerned, the Chairman of the Social-Environmental Committee argued in June 1973, no major changes in the Expanded Pipeline Guidelines (June 28 1972) need be anticipated. But among themselves, they were more cautious. Criticism by the Canadian Arctic Resources Committee of the Expanded Pipeline Guidelines, including a recommendation for public hearings, received a careful reply, "temperate and respectful . . . to . . . minimize any follow-on debate."[18] Digby Hunt, Assistant — Deputy Minister of Indian Affairs and Northern Development went so far as to indicate to Austin that "it may be desirable to consider some revisions concerning Indians and Eskimos and their 'land claims'." The July 1972 *Memo* had anticipated one more document prior to action before the National Energy Board. Now, in the changed circumstances, it was impossible to draft and the process was stalled. Canadian Artic Gas would have to go forward without the earlier optimism and consensus, faced with a mixed reception and powerful opposition. The Canadian Arctic Resources Committee had formed a special Northern Assessment Group to study Canadian Arctic Gas' application in detail. The Berger Commission added another obstacle. Eventually a partial application was filed in March 1974, with a further submission in November 1974. The anticipated controversy raged immediately.

Moreover, serious rivals had now appeared, eroding Canadian Arctic Gas' apparent monopoly of official attention regarding northern pipelines, and casting increased gloom over the proposed pipeline system. Three challenges had emerged by 1974.

1. *El Paso*: If one immediate consequence of the American oil shortage was official pressure to get the trans-Alaska pipeline moving over the objections of environmentalists, another was the recognition that American security required less reliance on energy imports and foreign delivery systems. The security of supply argument had been pressed home during AYLESKA's rivalry with the Canadian alternative. It now surfaced again regarding an all-American pipeline and liquefied natural gas tanker route to transport Alaska's proved gas reserves of 26 t.c.f. El Paso Natural Gas Co. of Houston, Texas indicated its intention to pursue the scheme as an alternative to the Mackenzie pipeline system proposed by Canadian Arctic Gas.

The project was immediately popular in Alaska, and perceived as a major threat to Canadian Arctic Gas. While Canadian Arctic Gas had not been able to obtain firm commitments from Alaskan producers, Atlantic Richfield Co. of Los Angeles agreed to fund the rival El Paso Project. Given Atlantic Richfield's position as a major North Slope producer, its support for the proposal to move Alaskan oil through a pipeline parallel to the trans-Alaska line, and to tranship the fuel in a liquefied form by tanker to the American west coast, represented a major setback. Horte, President of Canadian Arctic Gas, indicated that the loss of Alaskan natural gas to the pipeline system would result in delays until the necessary reserves of natural gas in the Arctic (15-20 t.c.f.) were located. The decision lay in the hands of American authorities: Canadian Arctic Gas' chief rationale had been the attractive economies of scale to be achieved by the transportation of both Alaskan and Canadian reserves.[19]

2. *Foothills Proposal*: With internal morale already low as a result of El Paso's proposed project, Canadian Arctic Gas was further weakened by an alternative proposal for an all-Canadian Mackenzie pipeline put forward by Alberta Gas Trunk in July 1974. According to Blair, "we take issue with the argument that, if we do not take Alaskan gas (in a Mackenzie Valley pipeline system) Delta gas will be lost."[20] The so-called Maple Leaf line would be smaller, 42″ rather than 48″, and less expensive — an estimated $3.7 billion rather than Canadian Arctic Gas' projected outlays of $7 b.

Alberta Gas Trunk's withdrawl from Canadian Arctic Gas (as El Paso was filing its application before the American Department of the Interior and the Federal Power Commission for a trans-Alaskan alternative) appeared to strengthen objections expressed by economists regarding further exports to the United States when Canada's remaining dwindling natural gas supplies should be held in reserve. Alberta Gas Trunk had played such a key role in the formation of Canadian Arctic Gas that the split appeared serious indeed. Although Wilder of Canadian Arctic Gas maintained it would be "wasteful and folly" to build two pipeline systems from the same corner of the Continent, separate American and Canadian natural gas pipelines, each for their own domestic needs and each under national control, seemed very possible by November 1974.[21] Canadian Arctic Gas' November 1974 presentation of the second pact of its application in Ottawa had little of the earlier conviction.

3. *Other Priorities*: The rapid change in the Canadian energy landscape after the fall of 1972, alongside increased public

concern for secure and moderately priced supplies, generated interest in alternatives that threatened to postpone for sometime the delivery of Mackenzie Delta natural gas. With El Paso's project gaining ground on Canadian Gas Arctic, promoters took a hard look at Delta oil, coal gasification, and natural gas delivery from the Arctic islands.

First, in October 1974, Imperial Oil Ltd. announced that five companies, Imperial, Gulf Oil Canada Ltd., Shell Canada Ltd., Interprovincial Pipe Line Ltd., and Trans Mountain Pipe Line Co. Ltd., had formed a group to study the feasibility of an oil pipeline from the Mackenzie Delta-Beaufort Sea area to link up with the existing crude pipeline network in Alberta. The so-called Delta Oil Project would, in effect, take up the work of the Mackenzie Valley Pipeline Research Company which had terminated research activities after the trans-Alaska pipeline had been approved. Since that time significant oil discoveries had been located in the Delta and offshore in the Beaufort Sea, although their full extent remained to be determined.[22]

Second, TransCanada Pipelines of Toronto proposed a feasibility study of a coal gasification plant to produce synthetic fuel at commercially feasible rates. According to one observer:

While officially TransCanada maintains the coal gasification proposal is parallel to the proposal to build a Mackenzie River Valley pipeline, to bring Canadian and Alaskan gas south to markets, industry experts are already suggesting the coal gasification scheme, if it proves feasible, could represent yet another reason for postponing, possibly cancelling the Canadian Arctic Gas pipeline proposal.[23]

Despite the environmental costs associated with coal gasification technology and strip mining, there appeared to be advantages worth pursuing in a major research programme. With natural gas deficits expected to appear in western Canada, the plants could be built with existing technology, they would be near the existing natural gas fields and pipelines for distribution across the country, and they could be added one at a time as gas shortfalls increased. The last point underlined again the problems associated with the enormous cost of northern pipeline construction:

Capital intensive projects such as the Mackenzie Valley pipeline, in order to be financially viable and to minimize per unit energy costs, must operate with a maximum throughput which exceeds Canadian demand and must be absorbed by a single, North American market.[24]

Third, interest in the delivery of natural gas from the Arctic islands would likely pick up if the focus of interest shifted away from the Mackenzie Valley. Panarctic Oils Ltd. had made significant discoveries in the area, totalling 12 t.c.f. as of November 1974 (as well as undetermined crude oil finds). The islands gas resource base, therefore, seemed more secure than in the Mackenzie Delta-Beaufort Sea area; and unlike Canadian Arctic Gas, Polargas, composed of Panarctic, TransCanada Pipelines, Canadian Pacific Investments and Tenneco, did not rely on Alaskan reserves.

As early as December 1972, the President of Panarctic Oils, Mr. C. Hetherington, had predicted:

Because of current publicity most people seem to take it for a foregone conclusion that the Delta gas pipeline will proceed before one can be built for the Arctic islands. I am not at all sure of that. As a matter of fact, I think the odds are that an Arctic islands pipeline network might well precede a Delta pipeline.[25]

Panarctic and its partners in Polargas might well take heart at Canadian Arctic Gas' increasing problems after 1972. Task Force officials, in the spring of 1973, immediately articulated the possibility of this shift in industry focus. Nevertheless, formidable engineering and logistical problems confronted the Polargas project. Despite Panarctic's confidence that gas deliveries to Canadian and American markets could begin in the fall of 1980, it was far from certain if these problems could be resolved before the mid-1980's at the earliest, if at all.

In short nothing was clear; everything seemed uncertain. There appeared a real possibility that the proposed Mackenzie pipeline system would be stalled for some time — permitting the Canadian Government an adequate breathing space to develop a coherent energy policy.

7. CANADIAN ARCTIC GAS REGAINS THE INITIATIVE

Among the various arguments raised against the early construction of a Mackenzie gas pipeline in the period 1972-74 Dr. John

Helliwell's analysis of the financial implications of the project was the most persuasive. Helliwell's contention that a Mackenzie gas pipeline could be delayed into the late 1980s rested on the premise that increased natural gas deliveries from existing western Canadian sources could supply domestic market and export commitments. Canada would suffer heavy financial costs by *premature action* in the Mackenzie project.

Eventually frontier fuels would have to be brought to southern markets. But the attractiveness of an extended period of grace could readily be appreciated: time to learn more about the North; time to plan adequately for a northern pipeline system; an opportunity for the native people to adjust to a new way of life, and to overcome their fears of economic development. For Canadian energy policy as a whole, however, the delay would be even more important. It would provide a genuine opportunity for a fundamental overhaul of energy policy in Canada not merely in the natural gas field but in all areas of the sector: oil, nuclear power, hydro electric energy. Options in fields, delivery systems and sources could be geared to a national industrial strategy.

Fortune seemed to have smiled again on Canada. On the very edge of proceeding under false assumptions with an extremely costly project, events had hauled the Government back from the precipice. The export rationale for the Mackenzie pipeline system had collapsed, probably for good. There was no surplus to export and the reserves in the Mackenzie Delta were slow in firming up. If the pipeline system proposed by Canadian Arctic Gas were to be used primarily by the United States, then it was obvious that the project was not worth the heavy environmental and political costs that Canada would face. A golden opportunity now appeared for Canada to do its homework in the energy field, to replace the defunct National Oil Policy with one appropriate to a new period.

Nevertheless by the summer of 1975, Canadian Arctic Gas had regained the initiative in promoting the early construction of a Mackenzie Valley gas pipeline and Ottawa was no nearer a coherent energy policy. So rapid a re-emergence of Canadian Arctic Gas after its 1972-74 doldrums represented a formidable accomplishment. Two developments are worth underlining to provide some understanding of this event.

a. *The National Energy Board Natural Gas Hearing, November, 1974, Februray, 1975:* If the export rationale for a Mackenzie pipeline were dead, Canadian Arctic Gas had an alternative argument — that *Canadian* markets urgently required the early construction of the system. Natural gas supplies in western Canada were so critically low, it was argued, that commitments to consumers would be jeopardized by any delay in the delivery of frontier fuels.

This line of attack had been introduced by Canadian Arctic Gas already in late 1972 at the outset of the so called energy crisis. As indicated above, the Task Force on Northern Oil Development had taken it up immediately and echoed the sentiments of W. Wilder, Chairman of Canadian Arctic Gas Study Limited.[23] But Helliwell and other critics rejected this contention, as had various Government sources in 1973. For example, in March 1973 Vice-Chairman of the National Energy Board, Mr. D. M. Fraser, indicated that proven reserves in the western producing area were "ample to cover Canadian deliverability requirements until the end of the 80s or into the early 90s." The same sentiment was revealed in June 1973 in the federal Government's energy policy Green Paper. This document, which was widely heralded to mark the development of an integrated energy policy for Canada, stated that "the present volume of reserves is sufficient to meet export commitments and growing Canadian demands in the areas now served through the 1980s."[27]

A clear division of opinion emerged therefore after 1973. Critics of the early construction of a Mackenzie pipeline both within and outside the Government held that available Canadian sources were sufficient to meet Canadian needs to the late 1980s and that therefore the delivery of frontier fuels could be delayed to that time. On the other hand, Canadian Arctic Gas and its allies in the federal Government argued that the supply system was now so critical that no extensive delay could be tolerated.

It was an interesting situation indeed. Only two years before, industry and Government had never tired of extolling the ample reserves that were possessed by Canada for both export and domestic use. As late as July 1971, the Minister of Energy, Mines and Resources had replied to criticisms from Bruce Wilson, President of Union Gas, regarding federal optimism concerning Canadian reserves of natural gas. According to Mr. Greene, "I would hasten to assure you that the figures which I quoted are considered reasonable not only by the National Energy Board but by the industry as well. . . . The current problem of supply, as I see it, is one primarily of existing pipeline capacity limitations and of a contractual surplus, rather than one of insufficient proven gas reserves to meet Canadian requirements."[28]

In 1973, it was still too early for a complete aboutface. The embarrassment in Ottawa was still too great. But as the months passed, as 1975 approached, as senior officials reflected on the earlier commitments made to Canadian Arctic Gas, the consortium began to win back the waverers within the federal Government. Imperceptibly at first, then aggressively, Canadian Arctic Gas took the offensive. By the summer of 1975, the momentum of the 1970-72 period was all but regained. An intimation of inevitability again surrounded the proposed Mackenzie Valley pipeline.

What happened essentially was that the consortium was able to convince the National Energy Board that further delays could not be tolerated, that Canadian domestic requirements now necessitated the earliest possible delivery of frontier fuels. This was the crucial variable. Without this conviction, Helliwell's argument was obviously more attractive. The National Energy Board Hearing held across Canada in late 1974 and early 1975, "to make an appraisal of the supply and deliverability of natural gas in relation to reasonably foreseeable requirements," played a central role in buttressing Canadian Arctic Gas argument.

The National Energy Board Hearing fulfilled an important political function: intended as a means of gathering information on natural gas supply and demand, they helped calm public scepticism about the industry's claim of impending shortages. In addition, they provided symbolic reassurance to somewhat doubtful Canadians; through the active involvement of public interest groups, the Board gave an impression of an open decision-making process. Of course it was not possible in all cases to allay suspicions that the National Energy Board was once again simply following the tune of industry. The abrupt reversal in the industry's presentation of a natural gas situation prompted the British Columbia Energy Commission, for example, to indicate in its final arguments that:

The Board must explain in a convincing fashion why estimates of natural gas reserves have reversed direction so dramatically in the past two years, for otherwise it will not be clear that the forecast shortage is not as distorted today as was the forecast surplus in 1970.[29]

All the evidence available, however, suggested that the National Energy Board had again prejudged the situation. First, the Board's April Report, released in July, 1975, was based on information provided by the gas industry during the Hearing and therefore reflected industry's assumptions in data collection. More important, the outcome was predetermined by the frame of reference established from the Board.[30]

Although the hearings were to address themselves to a twenty-year time frame, it quickly became apparent that the Board's concern was with the short-term situation. As a result, recommendations were based increasingly on a very narrow set of considerations. By requesting interveners to present supply and demand projections to 1995, varying only pricing assumptions, the Board received estimates which fell within a relatively narrow range from each other as they were based on similar premises. Thus, past policies were used as a guide for future developments. Innovative, conservationist and alternative energy strategies were therefore ruled out. It also meant that industry-favoured policies would again likely be advocated as a solution to present and future problems. The hearings were heavily weighted in favour of the *status quo*.

Moreover, the presence at the hearings of the two competing consortia vying to build a Mackenzie gas pipeline, Canadian Arctic Gas and Foothills, transformed the proceedings not only into a preliminary investigation of the merits of the pipeline itself but also of the comparative advantages of each project proposed. Detailed studies into policy options, including the merits of a lengthy postponement of the pipeline, did not emerge. Natural gas was studied in isolation from the energy sector as a whole, preventing the debate of alternatives, including coal gasification.

In this regard, it is interesting to note that one of the three National Energy Board members sitting on the gas panel, Mr. G. C. Edge, outlined his position to the Chairman of the Board on December 18, 1974, midway through the hearings and therefore before he had had a chance to study the findings. Nevertheless, Commissioner Edge accepted the view that there was no solution to the present shortage of natural gas except the early availability of frontier gas. On December 18, he volunteered that "surely the Hearing has brought into focus the urgent need for frontier gas at as early a date as is practicable."[31]

But had it? Appearing before the House of Commons' Sanding Committee on National Resources and Public Works after the Calgary hearings, Prof. Helliwell disagreed:

"The broad conclusion of our studies about the best timing for the development of Arctic gas, still indicates that it is in the latter rather than the early 1980's, because before that time it will be cheaper for us to develop non-frontier sources than to tie on Arctic gas... I am arguing that the haste that is being advocated must be resisted, that the need for hurry does not exist and that the demands for more adequate research are justifiable."[32]

Industry had made it clear during the Hearing that it favoured the early construction of a Mackenzie Valley pipeline. Helliwell feared that the National Energy Board, despite its incomplete research on Canadian energy supply and demand — frontier and non-frontier; oil as well as synthetic and natural gas production — would uphold the view of industry.[33]

The April, 1975 *Report* of the National Energy Board, *Natural Gas: Supply and Requirements*, did just that: frontier natural gas was required as soon as possible to offset impending shortfalls. East of Alberta the situation was alarming:

"Based on the Board's forecast of supply and demand, a deficiency will occur almost immediately and will continue to grow throughout the forecast period. The 1976/77 level of supply could be maintained until 1987 but the forecast supply will be unable to meet growing Canadian requirements beyond 1978"[34]

Nor would the elimination of exports to the United States offer much relief in the opinion of the Board. Such action would invite retaliation, decrease incentives for industry, and postpone the projected shortfall by only a few years.

The Board's *Report* revealed a determination not to repeat what it perceived as its chief error of the past — the exaggeration of available natural gas supplies in Canada. It would not, it now explained, accept without question the old forecasting formula that had led it astray in earlier years. It was a chastened group, the *Report* stressed.[35]

However, having pointed out previous miscalculations and the necessity for careful analysis, the *Report* inexplicably reverted to dogmatic conclusions on both the supply and demand side which were inappropriate given the incomplete research on the Board's staff in these areas. The data provided may have satisfied Canadians a few years earlier; wiser with experience, they now wanted adequate documentation. The design of a rational energy policy for Canada cannot proceed on a satisfactory basis if natural gas and northern pipelines are considered in isolation. But comprehensive and integrated studies of the energy sector as a whole have not been completed. In short, it appeared that the Board had panicked.

The April *Report* of the National Energy Board cleared the way for a Hearing on the respective merits of the Canadian Arctic Gas and Foothills pipeline proposals along the Mackenzie valley, schedualed for October, 1975. Yet much of the spadework required to ensure that a northern pipeline system was in the national interest remained incomplete.

First, research lagged.

Second, matters relating to the native people of the North and the northern environment remained unsettled. It would in particular be short-sighted and potentially disastrous for the Government to remain opposed to legitimate native land claims and refuse a settlement prior to pipeline construction. By mid-1975 Robert Blair of Foothills had come around to the importance of this issue.

Third, there would be heavy economic risks, discussed at length above, in prematurely initiating so vast an undertaking as a northern pipeline system unless it was demonstrated to be essential for Canada. The ragile secondary manufacturing sector could be severely affected by an inappropriate construction timetable dictated by immediate political pressures rather than the national interest.

Fourth, it remained imperative that the implications of northern pipeline planning for Canadian American relations be explored and debated. In 1970 this had been a crucial component of decision making in Ottawa. What tradeoffs, if any, were likely five years later? What are American interests and capabilities in the Islands and waters of the Canadian Arctic Archipelago? How does the sovereignty issue mesh with pipeline and resource development and foreign ownership?

    b.   *Crisis in the Drilling Industry*: Assuming that the postponement of the proposed Mackenzie Valley pipeline was in the national interest, the expansion of exploration and development remained essential in stepping up the deliverability of conventional gas fields to meet Canadian consumer needs into the late 1980s.

In fact, one variable which imposed an important immediate restriction on a substantial increase in western Canadian gas deliverability was the scarcity of drilling equipment. It has been therefore of the utmost importance to keep the drilling industry active in the most promising areas of western Canada, particularly the Foothills region. Canadian drillers were respected in industry circles for their expertise and competence and the drilling industry had the rare virtue of being Canadian-owned. Most of all, however, stepped up exploration south of the 60th parallel was the key to a postponement of a Mackenzie gas pipeline, and therefore to the generation of policy options.

Yet since the beginning of 1974 the outflow of drilling rigs primarily to the United States has been alarming. Between December 1973 and January 1974, 10 per cent of the total or 35 rigs left Canada and the exodus is accelerating. In April 1975, there were only 284 rigs remaining in Canada. Within a year and a half the Canadian drilling industry will have lost 30 per cent of its inventory.[36]

Of particular concern is that a significant portion of this outflow has been composed of deep capacity rigs capable of drilling 12,000 feet or more which are required to explore and develop the Alberta Foothills region. Since 75 per cent of rig manufacturers have moved into off-shore equipment and since Canada has no manufacturing capacity in this sector, the loss of these rigs may have a permanent effect on the Canadian drilling industry. Moreover, many of the rigs being moved to more profitable regions in the United States and elsewhere are being sold rather than leased to contractors. Since there is no significant construction of land rigs anywhere in the world, it will be difficult to replace the lost inventory even on a long-term basis.[37]

This development, which Ottawa has permitted to occur, has severely affected the level of exploration and development in the western sedimentary basin.° Unless the continuing crisis in the drilling industry is immediately resolved, a self-fulfilling prophecy may be emerging in which the earliest delivery of frontier fuels will be essential to cover shortfalls of natural gas.[38] Rapid action is required to prevent the narrowing of options in the North and Canadian energy policy.

Assessing the overall situation, it is evident that Ottawa has failed to provide incentives for maintaining an active drilling industry in a period of uncertainty. Despite the tensions between Ottawa and the provinces and between industry and Ottawa, it was imperative to ensure a continued high level drilling programme in western Canada as well as the frontier areas. Petrocan, or a special agency created for this purpose, would have fulfilled an important national purpose. It was partially reassuring, however, that the exodus of drilling rigs and expertise seemed to be easing off by 1975.[39]

8. CONCLUSION: FOOTHILLS VERSUS CANADIAN ARCTIC GAS

If Canadian Arctic Gas had succeeded in persuading the National Energy Board that the early construction of a Mackenzie gas pipeline was in the national interest, there remained the potentially thorny problem of dealing with the Foothills consortium's proposal to build an all-Canadian pipeline. Two applications would be before the National Energy Board rather than a single industry submission. Foothills Pipe Lines Ltd. had the advantage of offering a far less expensive construction project as well as a system that appealed to critics of further gas exports to the United States. The smaller 42-inch diameter line would be more appropriately geared, it was argued, to domestic rather than export requirements. It also claimed the delivery of fuel at lower cost than the 48-inch diameter joint Canadian-American line planned by Canadian Arctic Gas Pipelines Ltd.

At the same time, Foothills confronted the awkward problem of

° Why has Ottawa allowed this to happen? The answer is complex. Many operators charge that the federal-provincial confrontation over revenues has undercut the incentive to explore and develop for oil and natural gas in Canada relative to the United States and other areas. Second, it is alleged the

gas reserves in the Mackenzie Delta and the Beaufort sea. Disappointingly low (The Canadian Petroleum Association gave estimates of 4.0 trillion cubic feet proved, and 4.8 probable reserves at the 1974/75 National Energy Board Hearing), the reserve situation meant that the Foothills would have to convince the Board that the prospects for additional discoveries required to support the all-Canadian route were good enough to warrant construction.[40] Some 11.5 trillion cubic feet of threshold reserves were required to cover debt payments on the pipeline over 15 years; nearly 16 trillion cubic feet for a twenty year term.

In contrast, Canadian Arctic Gas could argue that the disappointing results in the Beaufort-Mackenzie basin underlined the wisdom of its proposal — Alaskan gas would make it possible to bring down frontier supplies as a reasonable price. Canada's best hope was to piggyback proved reserves in the Delta on Alaskan natural gas passing through a joint U.S. Canadian pipeline.[41]

But what were the facts on Beaufort-Mackenzie basin reserves? The chief producers in the area, Imperial Oil and Shell were committed to Canadian Arctic Gas and therefore had an interest in down-playing proved reserves available for production. Should these reserves approach threshold levels the position of Foothills

---

curtailment of Canadian oil exports since 1973 has lowered the need for additional drilling equipment and reduced industry cash flow and thus the revenues available for investment. Third, given the growing unavailability of American funds which have traditionally played a significant role in financing gas drilling activity in Canada, independent operators may have had difficulty in raising capital. For example, with the approval of the Federal Power Commission American pipeline companies extended advance payments amounting to $367 million between 1970 and 1973. After 1973, the Commission clamped down on this funding given the unlikelihood of significant Canadian gas exports in the wake of a re-evaluation of its supply situation. Fourth, it has been argued that "the current tight situation in equipment and supplies could force drilling contractors out of business faster than the politicians. The industry is suffering from the building of foreign off-shore drilling rigs at a record rate. These rigs are literally buying manpower and tabular goods at a rate with which we cannot compete." In other words, the intense international competition for drilling supplies in the wake of OPEC actions in 1973 may have led to equipment shortages in Canada. Finally, the utilization rate of rigs in Canada has averaged historically only half that of the United States and this has constituted a powerful incentive to move rigs south to achieve a higher rate of return. The implementation of policies in the United States aimed at increasing American self-sufficiency has intensified the strength of this inducement. (National Energy Board Hearings, Calgary, page 26.)

would be greatly strengthened. Shell and Imperial had also committed considerable funds for a gathering system in the area.

However 4 trillion cubic feet of proved reserves represented a very low figure indeed after seven years of exploration, low enough to cause serious doubts about the wisdom of proceeding at all.[42] Were the producing companies again manipulating the data?

Ottawa didn't know one way or the other.

Canadian Arctic Gas campaigned aggressively to block support for Foothills Pipe Lines Ltd. by lining up supporters in both Canada and the United States. By mid-1975, Foothills had failed to attract outside financial support beyond the original consortium. In contrast, Union Gas Ltd. of Chatham, Consumers' Gas Co. and TransCanada Pipe Lines Ltd., both of Toronto had endorsed Canadian Arctic Gas. The Canada Development Corporation also backed the joint project. TransCanada went further by purchasing four trillion cubic feet of Imperial Oil's reserves in the Mackenzie Delta, freed up when Imperial, in an important shift of policy, opted to repay exploration funds from American utilities in exchange for advance sales of Delta natural gas.

On the American side, Exxon's sale of Prudhoe Bay gas to American midwest pipeline companies confirmed industry interest in the Mackenzie route. El Paso was attempting to persuade the American Federal Power Commission of Canada's unreliability as a land bridge between Alaska and the United States mainland and therefore the advisability of an all-American route, but there were rumours that a Canadian-American pipeline treaty was nearing a final draft, a development that would considerably dissipate the force of El Paso's argument. By February 1975, Washington felt sure enough about Ottawa's preference for Canadian Arctic Gas to threaten the curtailment of the project in retaliation for cancelling natural gas export agreements with the United States. But as Canadian Arctic Gas jockeyed back into a favoured position, it appeared that Ottawa officials remained blind to the social, political and economic dangers of its proposal.

NOTES

1. *Canadian Forum*, June-July 1973, pp. 15-21.
2. *Oilweek*, November 29, 1971.
3. Toronto *Globe and Mail*, September 21, 1972.
4. Toronto *Globe and Mail*, March 12, 1973. This now became a standard theme among oilmen.
5. Sykes, *Sellout*, *op. cit.*, p. 94.
6. Toronto *Globe and Mail*, April 5, 1973.
7. *Toronto Star*, June 15, 1973.
8. Quoted in the *Toronto Star*, above.
9. Toronto *Globe and Mail*, June 15, 1973.
10. Government of Canada, Department of Energy, Mines and Resources, *An Energy Policy for Canada*, (Information Canada, Ottawa: 1973).
11. Earle Gray, "Why Canada Needs the Arctic Gas Pipeline," in P. Pearse, *The Mackenzie Pipeline*, *op. cit.*, pp. 33-47.
12. John Helliwell, "More on the National Economic Effects of Arctic Energy Developments", *House of Commons Standing Committee on Natural Resources and Public Works*, June 5, 1973, pp. 22 ff; *Appendix* pp. 41-80. Other research findings can be found elsewhere, for example in P. Pearse, *op. cit.* pp. 143-183; and Canadian Arctic Resources Committee, *Gas From the Mackenzie Delta: Now or Later?*, May 23-24 Conference, 1974, pp. 1-15.
13. Geoffrey Stevens in the *Globe and Mail*, November 2, 1974. Berger had litigated on behalf of the Nishga Indians in British Columbia.
14. Reported in Toronto *Globe and Mail*, April 30, 1973.
15. For perspective on the Government's policy in respect of resource and pipeline development, see Peter Cummings, *op. cit.* and *Arctic Alternatives*, *op. cit.*, pp. 70-160.
16. Toronto *Globe and Mail*, June 30, 1973
17. For example, V.L. Horte, "Statement to Canadian Pipeline Contractors Association," Vancouver, B.C., April 12, 1973.
18. Canadian Arctic Resources Committee, *Statement on Guidelines for Northern Pipelines*, October 18, 1972.
19. *Toronto Star*, November 16, 1974. Toronto *Globe and Mail*, October 12, 1974, "El Paso appears in front by a pipeline mile in Anchorage confrontation over Arctic Gas."

20. *Toronto Star*, November 16, 1974; Toronto *Globe and Mail*, July 30, 1974; July 31, 1974; August 11, 1974.

21. *Toronto Star*, November 16, 1974.

22. Toronto *Globe and Mail*, November 2, 1974; *Daily Oil Bulletin*, November 4, 1974, p. 3.

23. F. Bregha et al. *A Case for Delaying the Mackenzie Natural Gas Pipeline*, York University, pp. 35 ff; Toronto *Globe and Mail*, August 15, 1974.

24. Toronto *Globe and Mail*, August 15, 1974.

25. Quoted in Rohmer, *op. cit.*, p. 150-51; Toronto *Globe and Mail*, November 19, 1974.

26. Toronto *Globe and Mail*, March 13, 1973.

27. *An Energy Policy For Canada, op. cit.*, Vol I, p. 47.

28. *Correspondence*, J.J. Greene and Bruce Wilson, July 8 and 29, 1971

29. National Energy Board, A *Public Hearing in the Supply, Demand and Deliverability of Canadian Natural Gas*, Calgary, Final Argument, p. 2.

30. Mr. Francois Bregha, Faculty of Environmental Sudies, York University, has very kindly assisted me in this section. Note also the "Presentation To the National Energy Board," Workgroup on Canadian Energy Policy, York University, Calgary, December, 1974.

31. Confidential Memorandum, C.E. Edge to Marshall Crowe, Chairman of the National Energy Board, December 18, 1974.

32. Government of Canda, House of Commons, *Minutes of Processing and Evidence of the Standing Committee on National Resources and Public Workèrs*, First Session, Thirtieth Parliament, May 8, 1975, 22:7

33. *Ibid*, 22:7

34. National Energy Board, *Canadian Natural Gas: Supply and Requirements*, Ottawa, April, 1975, p. 72.

35. *Ibid*, Preface FF.

36. *Correspondence*, R. W. Woronuk, Vice-President, Computer Research Associates, to York University, Workgroup on Canadian Energy Policy, April 14, 1975.

37. *Ibid*.

38. Toronto *Globe and Mail*, June 6, 1975.

39. NEB Report, op. cit., p. 35. The NEB in its report defined "proved reserves" as "those reserves considered to exist with a high degree of certainty." Probable reserves are reserves also considered to exist with a high degree of certainty, but the basic reservoir data used in their calculation are less well defined. p. xii.

41. Toronto *Globe and Mail*, August 21, 1975.

42. Note that Shell Canada Ltd., at the 1974-5 Hearing, estimated Beaufort/Mackenzie reserves at 7.3 t.c.f. *NEB Report, op. cit.*, p. 42.

CHAPTER ELEVEN
Conclusion: The Cost of Muddling Through

Ottawa's true religion is *drift*: a lack of innovation; a failure of comprehensive planning; an unwillingness to define the national interest. Thinking only in the short-term, senior officials found themselves outflanked again and again in a rapidly changing northern policy environment. Crisis succeeded crisis in the period 1968-75; improvised solution succeeded improvised solution. Senior officials and the Cabinet lacked any notion of creativity or distinctiveness. Rather than an opportunity for a unique experiment in resource and environmental management, the North after 1968 was perceived as an added burden on an already over-taxed bureaucracy.

Defined as a problem rather than as an opportunity, it is not difficult to understand why the North and its people after 1968 were subordinated to the demands of business and Canadian-American relations. At no time did Ottawa's inner circle consider the interests of the native people as a central component of northern development: their participation in planning remained marginal; their rights were grudgingly accepted only under pressure. Rather, the Government reacted on an *ad hoc* basis to broader imperatives. For example, when Canadian-American energy relations after 1968 suggested the desirability of a continental approach, northern planning was geared to facilitate this objective. Caution was thrown to the wind; Ottawa begged Washington to take Canadian oil and enticed the integrated companies into the North. Then, to its surprise, the Government discovered in later 1972 that its approach was wrongly premised: Alberta was running out of oil. The Mackenzie pipeline system, which would weld the North (and northern supplies) to the United States, no longer seemed as attractive. Further persuasion by industry after the summer of 1974, however, brought the Government back onto the pipeline bandwagon.

In all this, the preferences of northerners were ignored. They were neither consulted nor informed.

Yet a very few policy-makers aside, the top elite worked with relative dedication and loyalty to "develop" the North. One cannot fault many individuals on personal grounds for failures in the North. Pipeline planning appeared attractive, at least superficially, and the Task Force on Northern Oil Development adapted it to northern development. The problem was method, rather than talent. A secret policy process, in which the "legitimate" interests were business, and in which business and Government collaborated in economic development, necessarily yielded the framework that emerged in the North after 1968. Shoring up North American capitalism has its price.

Yet it is precisely the fact that the individuals involved were not evil or wicked that is distressing. It would then be easier to isolate and discipline them, after which, presumably, policy-making in Canada would be cleansed. Instead this book reveals fundamental obstacles to an open system in which the Northerners, environmentalists, public interest groups, or even Parliament, can assist creatively in the formulation of national objectives. It also reveals the heavy costs incurred by the North and Canada.

1. UNEQUAL DEVELOPMENT

The development of the North since 1968 illustrates in an unusually acute form both the problem confronting public policy in Canada and the urgent requirement for change. The problem lies in what John Kenneth Galbraith has termed the "technostructure" or the planning system in advanced industrial states such as Canada.[1] The great corporate entities in the pipeline and resource field and the enormous public bureaucracies dealing with the North developed a symbiotic relationship, sharing goals, information and planning. Competition has been eleminated in the name of efficiency. Canadian Arctic Gas, for example, nurtured by

Ottawa, solved the problem of competition by including all potential rivals.[2] Both senior officials and corporate executives aimed for industrial stability in a partnership.

The result in the North has been an extreme form of unequal development. On one side, the bureaucracies both public and private have planned billion-dollar pipeline and resource projects. On the other, stand the people and the environment of the North, both excluded from these deliberations. All the money and power lie with Government and business. Neither is accountable to the public; neither is interested in, or must submit to, detailed criticism from Members of Parliament who are also excluded from the policy process. In northern development, whatever the stated goals and priorities of the Government and the commitment in theory to comprehensive planning, the reality of economic and political life is the interpenetration of public and business elites. It is also powerfully defended.

Senior officials, for example, agree that comprehensive planning in the North did not exist for the period 1968-75. They realize that the native people were left out of the policy process, but still defend pragmatism or "muddling through" as the most workable approach to northern development. It is safe: going slow and reacting to policy initiatives from the private sector and abroad limited risks. It is "accountable:" the Government remained in close touch with the *dominant* interests affecting the North. It is flexible: a reactive rather than innovative posture prevented Ottawa from an exclusive commitment to any one course of action or ideology. Options could be left open; Ottawa could bend more easily with the prevailing winds from the South. What appears as drift was in fact a method. Pragmatism suited the chief reality of policy-making in the North and in Canada as a whole: the complex and often conflicting pressures affecting the work of the narrow official cartel directing policy in Ottawa.

The "national interest," according to senior officials, does not lie in some abstract scholarly definition, but rather in what legitimate groups are demanding at any one moment. The Government's task is to accommodate and balance conflicting demands, not to impose a pattern of development from above. It therefore follows that the national interest in the North cannot be predicted because the interests concerned may alter their demands from time to time. "Tailoring to possible demand" sums up the incremental approach from 1968 to 1975: a piecemeal advance as business claimed the North.

In no other area has the problem of unequal development been as acute as in the Government's handling of the native role in the North. Ottawa's pragmatism accepted demands from what the Government considered legitimate interests; the native people were not among them. Denied access to information and without a significant electoral base, Northerners have been forced to exert pressure *against* Indian Affairs and Northern Development, the very Department that was designed to assist them.

For example, a paramount decision now facing the North concerns the land settlement long desired by the native people but unpopular with Indian Affairs and Northern Development in the past. Without an imaginative resolution of this issue, the destruction of native culture cannot be prevented. According to the President of the Indian Brotherhood of the Northwest Territories:

> A land settlement is seen as the only means to self-protection and survival in the face of the enormous changes being programmed for the N.W.T. A solid land base is essential for survival as a cultural entity and protection from the devastation which promises to be part of the proposed plan of development for the N.W.T. Such devastation has happened consistently in the past and there is no reason to assume it will not happen here — unless it can (and it must) be avoided in the context of a land settlement.[3]

Unlike the United States where the Alaskan native people found early allies in their struggle for a land settlement, Canadian Northerners are almost completely isolated. Ottawa officials appear blind to a gathering confrontation with an aroused native community with ominous implications for native-white relations throughout Canada.

2. THE DIRECTION OF REFORM

The gap between the *formal* structure of Government in Canada described in textbooks and the *informal* but effective political rules of the game is very great. Some general comments are worth stressing:

a. The National Energy Board, a captive of industry, must once and for all be dismissed as an "impartial" body as regards the North. In view of the record, in which the Board solicited, supported and helped prepare the proposals from industry, in which it eased the competing consortia into one group, the Board has destroyed its legitimacy.

b. It is an unhappy reflection on the decline of political life in Canada that the policy process as currently structured leaves little hope for effective Parliamentary debate or insightful press coverage of Government operations. Parliamentarians in the period since 1968 have been most unimpressive in matters relating to the issues discussed in this volume — but opposition Members no more so than *Liberal* backbenchers. They have no research staffs worth mentioning and they have no access to the continuing *internal* debate within the top elite in Ottawa. Attempts to reform the House of Commons Standing Committees, to equip them for meaningful investigation and debate, have not been successful.

For its part, the press in Canada lacks the maturity and contacts inside the relevant bureaucracies to interpret critically on-going developments in the North which are of great importance to all Canadians. It is, for example, of grave concern that none of the major newspapers dug out the facts surrounding the sovereignty debate of 1968-70. At the same time, however, the overarching reach of the Official Secrets Act and the official vigilance against selective leaks leave journalists at an initial disadvantage. Nevertheless, the Canadian press lacks the necessary investigative talent to watch the Ottawa bureaucracy.

c. There is little likelihood of political reforms that could strengthen public accountability in the North. At first glance, public hearings, such as those conducted by the Berger Commission, offer some hope for the future. But seen in perspective, the Berger Commission is an accident, an anomaly, which no future Liberal Government will entertain again. Born of a minority Government, with Prime Minister Trudeau on the defensive, it was the product of unique circumstances.

Similarly, it is difficult to imagine any Liberal or Conservative Government permitting Parliament greater control over policy formation. The rebirth of the Legislature offers the most attractive means of protecting the public against the public and private bureaucracies. But in Canada, apart from periods of minority Government, there is no incentive to move in this direction.

The reality of our national life is policy control by a narrow elite in Ottawa. No one Prime Minister is to blame for that. Rather, the system has emerged and solidified as successive Governments have found it in their interest to control that fundamental flow of information upon which power, and therefore their political fortunes, depend. In the process of restricting that flow, the life of Parliament is increasingly weakened.

d. The role of public interest groups in the North after 1968 has been most impressive. Given sufficient funding, groups such as the Canadian Arctic Resources Committee might offer an independent source of constructive criticism and policy proposals of considerable value to both the Government and the public. However, with minimal funding, and subject to continual sniping from Departments such as Indian Affairs and Northern Development, public interest groups live dangerously.

e. Canadian universities have failed to develop scholars and students in sufficient numbers and with appropriate skills to offer an independent analysis of northern development. Rich in research talent on practically all other regions and countries of the world except Canada, university faculties have apparently considered the Canadian North, 40 per cent of the country's land mass, of marginal importance.

It is a telling commentary on recruitment and scholarly priorities in our publicly funded universities. Bodies such as the York University Workgroup on Canadian Energy Policy have initiated significant work. Important as they are, they are only a beginning and urgent action is required to produce interdisciplinary research capability on northern problems. Faced, however, by severe budgetary cutbacks, universities will be hard pressed to attract and train faculty and students for this task.

f. The politicization of northern development, or even one aspect of the North such as the Mackenzie Valley pipeline along the lines of the great pipeline debate of 1956, could produce sufficient tension in Parliament and within the Government to induce a greater sensitivity, at least for a while. The 1956 debate helped defeat a Government; a parallel challenge on the Mackenzie project might force a fundamental reappraisal of the whole question. Even if it compromised the Trudeau Government seriously enough so that it would commit itself to a land settlement prior to pipeline construction, much would be achieved. This would not get around to comprehensive planning but it would at least start chipping away at the most vicious aspects of the proposed timing of construction. Second, increased public interest might acquaint more people, particularly Parliamentarians, to look again at the implications for Canadian American relations of the Canadian Arctic Gas proposal.

Canada does not need another National Energy Board hearing; it needs a debate on the policy implications of a Mackenzie Valley gas pipeline. With a solid majority in Parliament, and with a lesson learned in 1956, the Trudeau Government will make every attempt to stifle the first intimations of dissent.

3. UNPLEASANT REALITIES

If, as the argument has suggested above, there is little reason to believe that significant changes in Ottawa's style or approach to the North are likely to occur — if we seem fated to watch helplessly as Ottawa "muddles through" some more — what can Canadians grasp as yardsticks of damage that it inflicts on the country?

The future of the native people is the first obvious touchstone, a land settlement prior to pipeline construction forming the unconditional basis for satisfactory long-term development of the North.

Why cannot the federal Government understand the importance to *all* Canadians of committing itself to a land settlement? The Americans, with a much more certain sense of power, immediately comprehended the value of such an approach to all parties concerned in Alaska. It is of the greatest importance to initiate a new era in relations with Canada's native people and to set a precedent for future behaviour.

Beyond a land settlement, the broader issue of the purposes of resource development in the North remains. Will Northerners and environmentalists gain access to the policy process; or will business and Government maintain their monopoly of political and economic resources? Therefore, a second benchmark is the willingness of Government to assist public interest groups active in monitoring Government policy in areas such as the environment. The support of groups such as the Canadian Arctic Resources Committee would, for example, underline to all Canadians Ottawa's determination to implement the stated Government objective of protecting the northern environment as a priority above that of resource development.

To the extent that the discretion of senior officials and regulatory boards is replaced by precise legislation, such as the National Environmental Protection Act (1970) in the United States, Parliament will regain some control over events in the North. Similarly, the public will benefit from well-directed and more intelligent debate in the House of Commons on the so-called "northern problem."

Northern issues form part of an immensely complicated pattern of Canadian-American relations. The sovereignty question remains very sensitive; pipeline and resource developments affecting the North are similarly significant in bilateral energy and trade relations. But outstanding points of friction between the two countries are now so numerous that the contribution of the North to the growing complexity of Canadian-American relations cannot easily be isolated and weighed. In 1970, the sharpness of the clash over Arctic sovereignty, together with the coincidence of a decision point on American oil import quotas, permitted Washington to link the two issues. Ottawa responded in kind to ease the strain. While it will not be forgotten in Washington that Trudeau felt himself too weak in 1970 to inform the Canadian public of the American challenge, the rich potential for leverage in bilateral relations which the sovereignty issue provides the United States may well be more difficult to exercise in the future.

In two respects, however, Ottawa's approach to northern development 1968-75 has hurt Canadian-American relations:

a. The effective conduct of foreign affairs depends on maintaining a minimal consistency in policy. Breaking traditions suddenly and without warning can be expected to cause resentment and may also encourage retaliation. It is for this reason that advance planning is essential in the conduct of relations with other states.

Insofar as the integration of the Arctic into North American energy supply and demand encouraged the careless pursuit of

Canadian oil and natural gas exports to the United States, and nutured expectations of secure supplies without regard for the fact of limited Canadian reserves; and insofar as approval-in-principle of a Mackenzie natural gas pipeline encouraged American midwest consumers to rely on Ottawa, Canada can rightly be criticized for inconsistent about-turns in bilateral relations. The point is not that Canadians are mistreating the United States; they are not. It is rather that a major power such as Canada should have learned long ago to stop acting like a child in Canadian-American relations. Its current dilemma is of its own making, not Washington's.

b. Canadians must educate themselves more adequately in the realities of power politics. The Mackenzie natural gas pipeline system proposed by Canadian Arctic Gas contains two hidden foreign policy dangers which so far have not been adequately debated. First, the transhipment of Alaskan supplies across Canada inevitably raises U.S. national security interests in the United States. With an American presence in Canada that is overwhelming in any case, this added invitation to interference appears gratuitous.

Second, once a Mackenzie natural gas pipeline is in place, the pressure on Canada to approve fuels for export will increase exponentially, particularly if industry can convince the National Energy Board that huge surpluses exist. In view of the most recent reversal of position by the National Energy Board, one cannot rule out another sudden flip-flop.

Here lies the attractiveness of the Foothills proposal for a Mackenzie gas pipeline over that of Canadian Arctic Gas. A smaller 42″ pipeline specifically oriented to Canadian markets and requirements would check from the outset the throbbing export imperative in industry circles and in Canadian-American trade relations. Deliverable frontier fuels in the Arctic must be safeguarded for Canadian markets.

In relations with the integrated oil companies as well, Ottawa has encouraged a northern policy which later had to be altered, in some cases retroactively. "Unfairness" to the majors and their subsidiaries is not the issue — they have been more than well-served. The real question is why Ottawa gave them such far-reaching commitments and concessions in the North in any case.

Comparable oil-producing countries, Norway for example, have been much more careful in their dealings with the oil industry. A cautious approach permitted greater flexibility in meeting unexpected contingencies and it promoted a more forthright relationship with industry. Companies knew what they could expect and planned accordingly.

In the North, on the other hand, there is now uncertainty after the golden years of 1968-72. The exact terms and impact of Ottawa's new policy on land tenure, land distribution, working terms and royalties North of 60 remain unclear. Moreover, the sudden change in the National Energy Board's export orientation altered the rules of the game as originally established between Government and business. Although a welcome move in its own right, Canadian consumers will pay heavily for Ottawa's headlong stampede into commitments that only a few years later had to be revoked.

They will pay because Canada has no alternative, within the current political system, short of a major restructuring of the industry, to reliance on the integrated oil companies for the delivery of frontier fuels. Ottawa is not questioning the purposes of development; it is merely wanting a portion of the profits. But, at the same time, the companies have enormous potential for squeezing Ottawa and the economy by curtailing expenditures and projects. The failure of planning in the North has contributed to the lamentable situation that has emerged.

A striking failure of the Government in relations with business, however, involves less the integrated oil companies than the small but decisive Canadian drilling industry. Permitting the decline of this irreplacable component of national energy capabilities is a heavy blow to the country. The loss of oil and gas drilling rigs to the United States and elsewhere after 1973, when difficulties emerged in Government-industry relations, could have been prevented by energetic action in Ottawa. In any case, it is imperative that further losses be halted.

Finally, the responsible development of the North and the Arctic basin offers a unique opportunity for Canada in the international community. Yet there has been neither the insight nor the will to face a responsibility that geography and history have allocated to this country. A great deal of concern has centred on the jurisdictional issue; almost no intelligent action has been taken to link that issue with the pattern of resource development to be encouraged in the North. The exploitation of zinc-lead reserves at Strathcona Sound on Baffin Island by Nanisivik Mines Ltd., for example, raises fundamental questions about Arctic resource management, but the official rationale for supporting this project (at great cost to the Canadian taxpayer) fails to address them.

But who will face these many interrelated problems? The Department of Indian Affairs and Northern Development is not interested; the Advisory Committee on Northern Development and the Task Force on Northern Oil Development are moribund; the Departments of External Affairs and National Defence are grinding other axes. Other units concerned with the North, such as the Ministry of Transport and the Department of the Environment, are also busy fighting fires elsewhere; the Ministry of State for Science and Technology may not even be muddling through.

4. CONCLUSION: THE NEW TEAM

The 1968-75 period was dominated by pipeline planning, and forthcoming decisions in Ottawa concerning the construction of Northern pipelines, whether from the Mackenzie Delta or the Arctic islands, will remain the bell—weather of northern development in the near future. But pipelines are only part of a broader issue: The objective of balanced growth North of 60 in which the people and environment of the Arctic are not subordinated to profit maximization.

The breakthrough in the North coincided with Trudeau's emergence as Liberal leader and Prime Minister of Canada. His near defeat in October 1972 helped to precipitate far-reaching changes in the context of northern planning and energy developments. With his triumphant return in July 1974 to head another majority Government, new possibilities and dangers awaited the North. If the years 1968-75 form an identifiable phase in the emergence of the Arctic, a second uncertain stage has now opened.

The most important factor shaping the future of the North will remain the top elite around Trudeau, the character of the inner circle that advises him. Most members of the 1968-74 mandarinate dispersed, rather suddenly, after the election and new faces have appeared: Pitfield for Robertson; Shoyama for Riesman via Energy, Mines and Resources; NcNab for Austin; Crowe for

Rowland. Austin landed on his feet in the Prime Minister's Office before early retirement in the Senate; and Johnson left Treasury Board.

But would they stop the drift? Not likely. The crushing inertia of the system was not broken by 1975. Imagination, leadership, and skill could yet control the system; but who would fight for the North? In the end, the Northerners remain alone.

NOTES

1. John Kenneth Galbraith, *The New Industrial State* (New York: Houghton Mifflin, 1967).
2. That is, until Blair's Alberta Trunk left the consortium in 1974 to head up a rival group.
3. James J. Wah-shee, "A Land Settlement — What Does It Mean?", Paper presented to a Conference, *Delta Gas: Now or Later?* Canadian Arctic Resources Committee, Holiday Inn, Ottawa, May 24, 1974.